Father Figures and Gender Identities in Scandinavian and Comparative Literature

Studies in Honor of Ross Shideler

THE WILDCAT CANYON ADVANCED SEMINARS

Publication Series
Occasional Monograph Series
Cultural Studies
Folklore
Mythology
Nordic Studies
Classic Studies Reprints

OCCASIONAL MONOGRAPH SERIES
Volume 3

Father Figures and Gender Identities in Scandinavian and Comparative Literature

Studies in Honor of Ross Shideler

Edited by

Kathleen L. Komar

NORTH PINEHURST PRESS
BERKELEY • LOS ANGELES

Publisher's Cataloging-in-Publication data

Names: Komar, Kathleen L., editor.
Title: Father figures and gender identities in Scandinavian and comparative literature : studies in honor of Ross Shideler / edited by Kathleen L. Komar.
Series: Wildcat Canyon Advanced Seminars Occasional Monographs, 3.
Description: Includes index and bibliographical references. | Los
        Angeles and Berkeley, California: North Pinehurst Press, 2016.
Identifiers: ISBN 978-0-692-64234-4 | LCCN 2016902562.
Subjects: LCSH Patriarchy in Literature. | Comparative literature. | Fathers in literature. | Fatherhood in literature. | Gender identity in literature. | BISAC LITERARY CRITICISM / European / Scandinavian | LITERARY CRITICISM / Subjects & Themes / General.
Classification: LCC PS228.F38 F38 2016 | DDC 810.9/3520431--dc23

COVER PHOTOGRAPHY BY TIMOTHY R. TANGHERLINI AND KATHLEEN L. KOMAR
COVER DESIGN BY TIMOTHY R. TANGHERLINI

North Pinehurst Press
Berkeley and Los Angeles

Printed on acid-free paper

ISBN: 9780692642344
LCCN: 2016902562

Ross Shideler

Tabula Gratulatoria

Tabula Gratulatoria

JAN REIFF
KENNETH REINHARD
AMELIA RIBBENS
NANCY & JOHN RICHARDSON
CHIP ROBINSON
DAVID RODES
KAREN ROWE
LINDA HAVERTY RUGG
MARK SANDBERG
KARIN SANDERS
C. P. HAUN SAUSSY
SCANDINAVIAN DEPARTMENT, UC BERKELEY
SCANDINAVIAN SECTION, UCLA
DAVID SCHABERG
JENNIE SCHOLICK
VIVEK SHETTY
VALERIE SHIDELER & THOMAS SHIDELER-FUENTES
SHU-MEI SHIH
BARBARA SMELTZER & MARK MILLER
JORDAN A. YAMAJI SMITH
RICARDO DA SILVEIRA LOBO STERNBERG
TIMOTHY R. TANGHERLINI
DOUG THOMPSON
M. BELINDA TUCKER
CAROLE VIERS
DAVID WELZ
PHILADELPHIA SHIDELER WELZ
STEPHEN YENSER
MARGE AND DANIEL ZEREBNY

Contents

Part III—Gender Identities

Epilog

Acknowledgements

I would like to thank the Chair of Comparative Literature, Efrain Kristal, and the Head of the Scandinavian Section, Tim Tangherlini, as well as the Dean of Humanities at UCLA, David Schaberg, for their support of the initial conference in honor of Ross Shideler from which these essays were largely drawn. Thanks also to Olivia Diaz and Michelle Anderson and the staff of the Humanities Administrative Group who worked tirelessly to make the conference a success. Thanks also go to the graduate and undergraduate students of the Scandinavian Section and the Department of Comparative Literature, who generously donated their time, energy and enthusiasm. Chip Robinson's help was invaluable in work on the Bibliography, and Tim Tangherlini benevolently donated his time and expertise in formatting the volume and preparing it for publication. I would also like to thank the editorial board of the Wildcat Canyon Advanced Seminars for their thorough review of the volume. And finally, special thanks go to Amelia Ribbens, student and colleague, without whose editing skills and relentless generosity of spirit and time I could not have brought this volume to fruition.

Kathleen L. Komar

Introduction

Kathleen L. Komar

The essays in this volume grew out of a conference celebrating the work of Ross Shideler. A Professor of Scandinavian and Comparative Literature for over 40 years, Ross Shideler has published on an array of topics ranging from 19th century literature and drama to 20th century poetry and 21st century detective fiction. He is an accomplished poet and translator as well as researcher. Among the recurring themes in his creative and research work are: issues of gender equality and stereotyping, family dynamics, phenomenological approaches to poetry, the life of the mind and imagination, the appreciation of beauty and wonder in everyday life, power struggles in relationships, and the historical and political contexts of contemporary Scandinavian fiction. The contributors to this volume took their inspiration from this extensive and diverse body of work, and particularly from Professor Shideler's recent volume, *Questioning the Father: From Darwin to Zola, Ibsen, Strindberg, and Hardy* (Stanford University Press, 1999). The essays in this collection deal with father figures—biological, literary, intellectual, and cultural—as well as the gender challenges that they invoke and the gender identities that they help to shape. These essays are meant both to question father figures of all kinds and to honor the father figure that Ross Shideler has come to represent to generations of his students and colleagues.

In their contributions, the scholars represented in this volume interpret father figures in a number of different ways. In the opening section, the essays examine "fathers" in both their biological and literary aspects. In "Male Reproductive Rights: Mark Twain, August Strindberg, and Literary Paternity," Linda Haverty Rugg looks at Mark Twain and August Strindberg both as literal fathers attempting to support their biological offspring and as literary fathers who had to fight for their reproductive rights in terms of the piracy of their intellectual property. Rugg finds striking parallels in the paternal struggles of these two contemporaries. In his essay, "Erasing the Father," James Massengale takes another approach to the intersection of biological and literary fathers and offspring. He analyzes the troubled relationship between Carl Michael Bellman and his biological father, who becomes the offspring of his own son as the father is transformed in Bellman's literary work. In "Minor Characters: Fathers in Hans Christian Andersen's Novels," Karin Sanders examines the curiously minor role that fathers play in the novels of Hans Christian Andersen; she suggests that Shideler's demonstration of the radical loss of power suffered by patriarchal figures in Scandinavia's "Modern Breakthrough" can be glimpsed already in Andersen's work. And Susan C. Brantly, in "Murdering the Father: Hjalmar Söderberg's *Doktor Glas*," traces the early 20th century shift away from an optimistic embrace of science as a new authority to a more pessimistic view revealed in the murder of a father figure by a physician in Söderberg's novel.

In the second section of the volume, father figures move from the biological to the cultural and metaphorical. In "Cavafy, Debt, Translation," Stathis Gourgouris takes us from the countries of the far North to Greece and into a comparative context as he examines the untranslatability of Cavafy's work, which nonetheless curiously exerts extensive influence on poets internationally. Gourgouris uses instances of mistranslation to delve more deeply into both Cavafy's own work and poetic language more generally. In his essay "A Promise Concealed, Revealed, and to be Fulfilled: On Some Affinities between Figural and Political Interpretation," Efrain Kristal explores an intellectual paternal relationship between Fredric Jameson and his Yale mentor Erich Auerbach, who might have served as Jameson's *Doktorvater* if he had lived a bit longer. Kristal analyzes Auerbach's use of figural interpretation and Jameson's Marxist approach to find striking and suggestive similarities between the two and to reveal Auerbach's influence on Jameson's work. Ricardo da Silveira Lobo Sternberg takes the concept of fatherhood into the cultural and national arena as he examines a German tutor experiencing the culture shock of Latin America. In

"Ach Grete! A German Tutor in 19th century Brazil," Sternberg uses the fictionalized letters of one of the earliest female travel writers on Brazil in the 19th century to reveal the clash of expectations regarding behavior and propriety engendered by a German *Vaterland* and the Brazilian sensibility of the New World.

In the third section of this collection, authors come to focus more specifically on gender identities and diversity in families and cultures. Joanna Niżyńska, takes the reader again into new geographical territory in her essay "Gender is the Real Queer: Gender Wars in Contemporary Poland." Niżyńska investigates the Polish bishops' use of the term "gender ideologies" to imply a foreign and malevolent influence on the Polish family and morality. She also delves into the significance of the concepts of queer and gay in the context of Polish religion, culture, and politics. In "Champagne Seduction and Sewer Putrefaction: Homosexuality and August Strindberg," Brian Martin brings the discussion back to the Scandinavian context as he scrutinizes Strindberg's complicated, sometimes homophobic and sometimes sympathetic views of homosexuality. But amidst Strindberg's alternating disdainful and compassionate attitudes, Martin finds in Strindberg's conclusion to "The Perverse," a radically progressive vision of queer sexuality, family, complexity, and diversity. Finally, Kathleen Komar moves beyond geography itself into cyberspace in order to probe the complexities of the culture-defining family conflict embodied in the House of Atreus but transposed onto the worldwide web in "The Ultimate Father and Daughter: Agamemnon, Electra and their Legacy." Beginning with characters from classical Greek tragedy, Komar explores changes in paternal and gender relationships by examining websites named for Agamemnon and Electra. This move to the Internet produces both familiar and newly defined gender identities as well as power structures in the 21st century.

And finally, in the Epilog, Mary Kay Norseng turns to the work of Ross Shideler himself in "The Longing of the Seasoned Man (A Shaggy Dog Story aka A Tribute to Ross)." In this piece, Norseng examines several of the published poems and some of the unpublished narratives that mark moments in Ross Shideler's life. She helps readers understand the poet Ross Shideler, who watches the world and records its gestures in his work. And Norseng connects Shideler the poet with other writers—the Norwegian Sigbjørn Obstfelder, the British author C.S. Lewis, the Swedish poets Gunnar Ekelöf and Tomas Tranströmer, and the Brazilian-American-Canadian poet Ricardo Sternberg—to reveal a kinship born of feeling as well as intellect. Hers is a fitting tribute to the creative as well as the scholarly Ross Shideler, who is part of both earlier poetic tradition and that which follows him.

Vita

Ross Shideler's professional career is marked by his dedication to teaching as well as to research. He won UCLA's Distinguished Teaching Award in 1985, and several of his students are among the contributors to this volume. Having earned a bachelor's degree in English and Creative Writing from San Francisco State University, Ross went on to study French at the Sorbonne and received his master's degree in Comparative Literature with an emphasis on *Nordisk Litteraturhistoria* from the University of Stockholm, eventually earning his doctorate in Comparative Literature at the University of California at Berkeley with areas of specialization in Swedish, French, and American Literature.

Professor Shideler began his professorial career at Hunter College in New York and moved to the University of California at Los Angeles in 1969. At UCLA, Ross, along with Arnold Band, founded the Interdepartmental Program in Comparative Literature, which eventually grew into the current Department of Comparative Literature. Generations of students and colleagues in Comparative Literature, Scandinavian, and many other departments have been mentored by Ross. They attest that he is a wise and caring father figure himself. Ross Shideler was elected president of his national scholarly organization, the Society for the Advancement of Scandinavian Study (1998-2000), and was elected to the board of the International Comparative Literature Association (2004-2010). He was a Senior Fellow at the Freiburg Institute for Advanced Studies in 2012.

Ross Shideler has published over 75 articles, poems and reviews in a wide variety of journals, and his books include: *Questioning the Father: From Darwin to Zola, Ibsen, Strindberg, and Hardy* (1999), *Per Olov Enquist—A Critical Study* (1984), *Voices under the Ground: Themes and Images in the Early Poetry of Gunnar Ekelöf* (1973), and *Lyrical Symbols and Narrative Transformations: Essays in Honor of Ralph Freedman* (1998), co-edited with Kathleen L. Komar. Ross's translations include a number of poems by Swedish poets as well as the plays *The Night of the Tribades* (1977) and *The Hour of the Lynx* (1990) by Swedish author Per Olov Enquist. Professor Shideler was equally accomplished as an administrator and served as Head of the Scandinavian Section and Chair of the Department of Comparative Literature as well as Associate Dean of the Graduate Division at UCLA (2003-11).

The colleagues who have contributed essays to this volume hope to honor the career and life of Professor, Mentor and Father Ross Shideler.

Part I
Fathers: Biological and Literary

Male Reproductive Rights:
Mark Twain, August Strindberg, and
Literary Paternity

Linda Haverty Rugg

In "What Is an Author?" – a seminal essay on the history and problematic status of authorship in the West – Michel Foucault meditates on the relationship between the author as biological and historical entity and the author as construct and effect, something Foucault calls the "author function."[1] Though Foucault ultimately proposes a divorce between the author's corpse and his corpus (he ends by asking "What matter who's speaking?"),[2] there is, not surprisingly, a strong tradition among authors and readers of binding the author's literary production to his writing body, and even attempts to force that connection to continue beyond the grave. I use the masculine pronoun for the author advisedly in this context, as I want to pay particular attention to the way in which two male authors move, through metaphor and specific social and legal actions, to make a patrimony of their writing. I am inspired to pay attention to this father complex in part by the work of Ross Shideler, whose book *Questioning the Father: From Darwin to Zola, Ibsen, Strindberg, and Hardy* examines literary representations of fatherhood and patriarchy. In this essay I will pick up on an aspect of Shideler's reading of August Strindberg's play *The Father* of 1887. He observes that the play proposes a "turn to language and texts as a potential replacement for the lost sense of structure and stability" implied by the demise of the patriarchy.[3] "Books and writing," he further notes, "perform essential functions in this play as symbols of identity and male dominance."[4] I want to continue along this line of thinking, combining the notions of biological and literary paternity, considering these in the light of technologies of

3

reproduction, and adding another author to the mix: Samuel
Clemens, better known as Mark Twain.

Placing these two contemporaries side-by-side allows us to
think about yet one more aspect of literary paternity: Mark Twain
and August Strindberg might be considered (and have been named
as) the literary fathers of entire national traditions. American
novelist William Dean Howells, in his panegyric memoir *My Mark
Twain*, famously dubs his recently deceased friend "the Lincoln of
our literature," and while critics have taken issue with that
assessment ever since, the tribute reflects broad popular American
sentiment regarding Mark Twain's authorship. [5] Like Father
Abraham, who is given credit by his admirers for the reforging of
the nation, Clemens rises to the status of progenitor of an
essentially American culture. A statement by Ernest "Papa"
Hemingway is often provided as evidence of this: "All modern
American literature comes from one book by Mark Twain called
Huckleberry Finn."[6] August Strindberg's reception in Sweden does
not quite match the enthusiastic American embrace of Mark Twain.
Strindberg cultivated a provocative persona that tends to discourage
hagiography in his readers and critics, but even those who express
hesitation about Strindberg's misogyny or cite the unevenness of his
(sprawling) corpus find themselves unable to deny Strindberg's
preeminence on the Swedish national scene. His contemporary,
Oscar Levertin, even while writing a dismissive review of one of
Strindberg's late works, has to acknowledge Strindberg as "Sveriges
främste nu lefvande [författare]" ["Sweden's foremost living
author"], recalling the "litterära revolution [Strindberg]
åstadkommit" ["the literary revolution Strindberg brought about"].[7]
That revolution has been regarded as the founding of a new
literature, not only in national terms, but internationally, as Thomas
Mann notes:

> Als Dichter, Denker, Prophet, Träger neuen
> Weltgefühls stieß Strindberg so weit vor, als daß
> heute sein Werk im geringsten ermattet anmuten

könnte. Außerhalb der Schulen und Strömungen und über ihnen stehend, vereinigte er sie alle. Naturalist so gut wie Neuromantiker, nimmt er den Expressionismus vorweg, [...] und ist auch zugleich noch der erste Surrealist—der erste in jedem Sinn.[8]

[As a poet, thinker, prophet, and herald of a new vision of the world, Strindberg was so far advanced that his work is not in the least dated, even today. Outside any schools or movements and standing above them, he unites them all. As much Naturalist as Neo-Romantic, he anticipates Expressionism, ... and is at the same time the first Surrealist – the first in every sense.]

Thus the drumbeat of reception for Mark Twain and August Strindberg emphasizes the seminal character of their works, the way in which their innovations (whether in the use of American voices and dialects in Mark Twain's case or the radical overthrow of traditional generic forms in Strindberg's) spawn new literary movements. In the twenty-first century, the notion "literary father" calls up associations with psychoanalytic theories that equate the phallus with the pen and language with the patriarchal order, both in a negative sense. The authorial phallus easily transforms into the literary canon, to enlarge upon a Freudian image. Here I will not engage Freudian theory explicitly, but the reader can sense its shadow in the background of my argument, and sometimes my authors make over-determined Freudian statements of their own. August Strindberg offers rather remarkable examples of the biological/literary complex, for example, with his fondness for sexual metaphor; in writing in a letter about his own influence on Ibsen, for instance, he famously declares: "Do you now see that my seed has fallen into

Ibsen's brain-pan – and fertilized! Now he carries my seed
and is my uterus!"[9]

     The works and lives of Clemens and Strindberg reflect the
anxiety provoked by becoming literary fathers at this historical
crossroads. Both of them devise an authorship that strives to
preserve the links between text, author as living human being, and
Foucault's "author function." They forge the link between corpse
and corpus through consistent focus on autobiography, tight
control of the dissemination of their works and their public images,
and by assuming, even during their lifetimes, the stature of literary
icons. They do all of this in part because they are fathers, and
writing is the bread they use to feed their families, support that has
to stretch beyond the corpse's grave. I would like to examine here
the notion of literary paternity and its relationship to the
reproductive technologies involved in copyright and the creation of
a celebrity image – in other words, technologies designed to keep
the authorial body linked to its writing. I will then look briefly at a
work by each author in light of the anxiety I feel the works express
about literary and biological paternity.

     August Strindberg and Samuel Clemens battled to support
their families through literary production, and, in order to make a
living, they had to assert their control as literary fathers. A broader
international market for literature had begun to develop in the latter
half of the nineteenth century due to innovations in printing and
book manufacture and distribution, increased ease of travel and
communication, and more extensive systems of public education.
American literature, which had not excited much attention in
Europe before the Civil War (with the notable exceptions of the
Transcendentalists and Poe), achieved a breakthrough with the
introduction of what was taken to be a typical American genre:
humor. Evidence for this exists in the publication in Sweden of
collections of humorous sketches by Mark Twain and others, one
volume of which lists A[ugust] S[trindberg] as translator.[10] A look at
the publication history of these volumes of American comic

sketches reveals the downside of literary popularity; some of the sketches were simply lifted from the *Minnesota Stats-Tidning*, an immigrant newspaper published in Minneapolis.

Strindberg too would later feel the sting of piracy when his autobiographical novel, *A Madman's Defense*, which he had written in French for French publication, was translated into Swedish and published in Sweden without his permission. The reason he had written the book in French in the first place became abundantly clear when Swedish readers responded with outrage to the slanderous representation of Strindberg's first wife. Blows to Strindberg's image could have had an impact on both his biological and literary paternity, destroying his relationship with his publisher and his chances of retaining some custodial care of his children, which was a significant legal struggle for him at the time. In a letter to the editors of the journal *Budkaflen*, which had published a portion of the pirated translation, Strindberg makes his position clear:

> Jag vill erinra Er att jag ännu är Svensk medborgare, att litteratur är egendom, och att tillgrepp af egendom straffas. Min bok, som Ni tillgripit, var aldrig ämnad att utgifvas på Svenska Språket, ochjag har redan ombesörjt att Er publikation blir förhindrad. Boken är skrifven på Franska och vi ha konvention med Frankrike![11]

> [I would like to remind you that I am still a Swedish citizen, that literature is property, and that property theft is actionable. My book, which you have appropriated, was never intended for publication in the Swedish language, and I have already taken measures to block your publication. The book is written in French, and we have a publication agreement with France!]

He did pursue legal action, to no avail.

Samuel Clemens' popular books often fell victim to publishing piracy. The first major theft occurred when a Canadian publisher produced an edition of *The Adventures of Tom Sawyer* and flooded the American market, undercutting sales by Clemens' publisher. Canadian law demanded that an author apply for copyright at the Department of Agriculture, a provision that seemed to demean and ridicule the author and his work. Like Strindberg, Clemens was inspired by such property theft to keep tight rein on his publisher and his financial returns. He worked out a highly calculated plan, for instance, to boost the sales of *Huckleberry Finn*, engineering the timing and placement of reviews, and disseminating bits and pieces of the book in journals and a speaking tour. His strategy for publishing his autobiography was to withhold certain portions for up to 100 years after his death, citing the need to spare the feelings and reputations of the people he depicts. But another motivation was the prolongation of income for his heirs; if he and his publisher, Harper's, could extend the public interest in his authorship beyond his death, this would benefit Clemens' daughters.[12]

Later in life, Clemens became an active crusader for international copyright. Much of Europe (Scandinavia was one exception) and the colonies and possessions of Great Britain and Spain had all signed onto the Berne Copyright Union in 1887. The United States was party to discussions at the formation of the Union, but refused to sign, in part because there was a concern about the welfare of publishers, paper manufacturers, printers, binders – in short, those responsible for the reproduction and distribution of books as material objects. The author's role as owner of intellectual property could not, in the view of the government, take precedence over the rights of material property owners. Thus in Samuel Clemens' testimonies before Congress over copyright, he strove to accentuate the material nature of the author and his ideas. He quips that he hoped "a day would come when, in the eyes of the law, literary property will be as sacred as whiskey, or any other of the necessities of life." He testifies before Congress in 1906, dressed entirely in white with a little cape, the Copyright Crusader, appearing as the star witness among a group of artists that included the composer John Philip Sousa. Declaring that publishing piracy "takes my children's bread," he added, "my daughters [...] can't get along as well as I can because I have raised them as young ladies, who don't know anything and can't do anything. I hope Congress will extend to them the charity which they have failed to get from me."[13] His ironic evocation of the paternal role demonstrates how authorship, authority, patriarchy, and economics are thoroughly entwined as a complex of metaphor and reality.

Another important reproductive technology of the period was photography, which, like printing, could reproduce a representation of the author, but unlike printing, referred directly to the author's body. The crafting and management of photographic images becomes a key element in producing a public persona for both Strindberg and Clemens, in an era when international journalism and the proliferation of images could produce worldwide recognition and celebrity (or in Strindberg's case, infamy). Samuel Clemens was perhaps one of the most consummate self-image-makers in nineteenth-century America. There are 470 images of Mark Twain filed in the archives of the Mark Twain Papers at the University of California, Berkeley, most of them by far of the author alone, two-thirds of them taken after his sixty-fifth birthday. It is during the later years of his life that his concern about his patrimony and the struggle to secure copyright for his writing becomes most intense, and this period sees his greatest focus on the crafting of his self-image as well as his legacy, both in photographic and autobiographical forms. In 1906 he employed the former studio photographer Albert Bigelow Paine to work with him on his autobiography, and at the same time record Twain's life in photographs. And like the marketing of Mark Twain's books, the overriding issue governing these photographs is authorial control, which takes several forms. The first is in the costume and posing of images – the majority of the images, taken of Clemens as an older man, emphasize white hair and white clothes, which became his trademarks. The white costume, replete with cape, pointed toward his identity as Crusader, as mentioned above.

Clemens liked to pose as if caught by surprise, in the midst of giving an interview or writing, offering the viewer of the photograph a sense of intimacy. This intimacy can be read as an invitation into the family circle, allowing readers to see the author not only as a public, but as a private person, a friend and pater familias as well as a writer. An early stereoscopic image shows Clemens in his study, supposedly hard at work on a manuscript (at the time, the manuscript would have been *Huckleberry Finn*). In fact, this image comes from a period when it would not have been technologically possible to take a photograph without posing the subject, but it was a custom of Clemens' in posing for photographs to pretend candor – that is, to pretend that the image is taken while he is unaware and in an entirely "natural" pose, thus sustaining the aura of intimacy. A favorite motif in the posed photographs by his biographer, Bigelow, is of the author in bed, supposedly hard at work on a manuscript, pen in hand. Clemens repeatedly invited journalists into his bedroom for a photo session, something the journalists experienced with some discomfort, but which could be read at one level as Clemens inviting them in as "family." Despite the "natural" and informal aspect of his photographic poses, Clemens exercised firm authoritarian control over the reproduction and distribution of photographic images. He got into disputes with photographers on several occasions, arguing that he, as the photographed subject, should control reproduction of his image. Ironically, this position undermined the copyright of photographers, who considered the images their own artistic property. As one of them complained to Clemens: "I could no more afford to give you these pictures than you could afford to write books for free."[14] Clemens, on the other hand, felt that since it was his body and face that were depicted, he ought to have dominion over the images. In his mind, authorship, body, and control were inseparable, and linked to his ability to earn a living for his family.

Strindberg, too, acquired an early interest in photographic technology. Rather than relying on a hired photographer, he actually preferred to take his own pictures of himself, saying that the reason he worked with photography was that all the photographs that others had taken of him were poor. "I don't care a thing for my appearance," he said, "but I want people to be able to see my soul, and that comes out better in my own photographs than in others."[15] An early example of self-photography is a suite of photographs taken in Gersau, Switzerland in 1886, during the period when Strindberg was writing the first volumes of his autobiography. Like Clemens, Strindberg sets out to create images in this suite that seem to invite the viewer into the private spaces of his life. He posed and took the images himself, using a self-timer. One of the photographs shows him with his two little girls in a garden, an image of pastoral and familial tranquility. Another depicts him playing cards with his wife, Siri von Essen. Since Strindberg had already achieved a reputation in Sweden as a misogynist and a radical, he seeks to establish a counter-image as the head of a happy family, a good father and husband. And like Clemens, he stages a portrait of himself, pen in hand, looking as if he has been captured in the act of writing. Strindberg sent the suite of images to his publisher, Albert Bonnier, asking that they be published in photo-gravure with his autobiography, in time for the Christmas trade in 1886. Bonnier rejected the idea as too costly; at the time there was no way to print photographs as part of the text of a book. Instead, individual photographic images had to be glued into the book by hand, something occasionally done in very small specialty runs, but it was hardly suitable for a larger public. Thus Strindberg failed in this attempt to uphold his image as a loving patriarch.

As Ross's work in *Questioning the Father* makes clear, the anxiety surrounding patriarchal control finds expression in the literary works of the period, two of which I will briefly explore here: Strindberg's play *The Father* and *Pudd'nhead Wilson* by Mark Twain. Both of these texts combine a concern about questionable biological paternity with representations of threats to the patriarchy, and both deal with questions of political power, revolving around gender in Strindberg, and race in Twain.

In Strindberg's *The Father*, the Darwinian theory of "pangenesis" underlies the play's anxiety. Darwin was troubled by the apparent influence of environment and the appearance of "throwbacks" in the process of natural selection. Why, he asks, does reversion occur, in which "the child resembles its grandparents or more remote progenitors?"[16] He comes up with the notion of what he calls "gemmules," "minute granules of atoms which circulate throughout the body."[17] Thus not only the sperm or egg are involved in intercourse and heredity, but all of the cells of the body, and these gemmules remained in the bloodstream to be passed on to the offspring of new partners. That Strindberg is fascinated (and horrified) by the idea of pangenesis becomes evident in a conversation between the Captain/Father and the Doctor, in which the Captain inquires whether it is true that a zebra crossed with a horse will produce striped foals, and then if the mare is later mated with a stallion, she will continue to produce striped foals. The Doctor, man of science, agrees soberly that this is true, causing the Captain to proclaim: "Det vill säga: faderskapet kan icke bevisas" [That is to say, it cannot be proved who is a child's father.][18]

The father's anxiety about paternity finds similar expression in Strindberg's worries about his own family. When he met his first wife, Siri von Essen, she was married to another man and had had a child with him. The notion that her first husband's features appeared in the bodies, faces, and gestures of the children she later had with Strindberg haunted him as regularly as his fears that she was unfaithful to him. And as Shideler points out in his analysis of the play, the woman's power to disrupt male reproduction has a literary parallel in the female disruption of the father's authorship. She blocks his mail, undermines his research, and in general tries to make it impossible for him to write.[19]

Samuel Clemens wrote *Pudd'nhead Wilson* in the early 1890s, when backlash against Reconstruction politics led to a brutal outbreak of white supremacy in the American South, where Clemens had grown up. The novella is set in ante-bellum Missouri, and it is a rather bizarre tale of switching babies, not unlike Twain's children's novel, *The Prince and the Pauper* (1882). We hear that "two boy babes were born in [the house of a leading White family of the town]: one to [the slaveowner], the other to one of his slave girls, Roxana by name"[20] (Twain 919). The lack of parallelism in this sentence attracts my interest. It is telling that the white child is born of a father, while the black child is born of a mother, father unnamed. This is in keeping with Hortense Spiller's article, entitled "Mama's Baby, Papa's Maybe," which points out that a slave mother determined the status of her child as black and slave absolutely, whether the father was black or no.[21] Roxy is herself only one-sixteenth African, and her child, as the narrator slyly tells us, is one thirty-second black. Here Clemens draws attention to the peculiarity of the "one drop" rule that governed Jim Crow legislation. He writes, "To all intents and purposes Roxy was as white as anybody, the one sixteenth of her which was black outvoted the other fifteen parts and made her a negro."[22]

Roxy experiences a flash of insight in looking at the babies, realizing that her master, who has threatened to sell his slaves down the river, will not notice if she switches the two physically identical children, saving her child from that fate and giving him the advantage of the father's name and race. That he will also acquire all the disadvantages of the father's culture – namely, an arrogant disregard for the humanity of people marked as black, including his own mother – only becomes clear later.

Roxy's transgression remains undiscovered for more than twenty years, until Roxy's biological son commits a murder. The identity of the criminal is discovered by Pudd'nhead Wilson, a Yankee lawyer who has developed the hobby of fingerprinting by taking the prints of everyone in the town, from babies to the oldest. In the book's climactic murder trial, the fingerprints not only identify the murderer, but also uncover the dark "secret" of the young man: he is really black. While blood, heredity, and the attendant notions of race prove to be fluid and unstable (social categories), fingerprints provide a stable referent for identity, inscribed on the individual's body by "Nature."

In this racist society, paternity deserves to be questioned, as the novella richly illustrates. But then the patriarchal authority comes roaring back, in the form of writing and also in the form of legal "justice." At the conclusion of the narrative, science finds out the truth about crime and female transgression. Once the "actually black" criminal has been identified, law and commerce enter the scene:

> [the creditors of Percy Driscoll's estate] rightly claimed that 'Tom' was lawfully their property and had been so for eight years; [...] that if he had been delivered up to them in the first place, he would have sold him and he could not have murdered Judge Driscoll; therefore it was not he that had really committed the murder, the guilt lay with the erroneous inventory. Everybody saw the reason in this. Everybody granted that if 'Tom' were white and free it would be unquestionably right to punish him – it would be no loss to anybody; but to shut up a valuable slave for life – that was quite another matter. As soon as the Governor understood the case, he pardoned Tom at once, and the creditors sold him down the river.[23]

The devastating irony of this ending brings forward once again the connection between paternity, property, and law, though in this case, the context of slavery blackens the connection between these things, a connection that Clemens, in other contexts, hopes to use to his own advantage. Here the problematic nature of paternity finds a voice, albeit an ironized one.

In my account of August Strindberg and Mark Twain at the turn of the last century, I hoped to illuminate the way in which scientific and cultural theories of reproduction and paternity, along with technological and economic developments, led to a threat of traditional notions of fatherhood and authority. I also wanted to show how the writing and actions of the two authors both represent and respond to that threat. Despite the complexity and perplexity surrounding the idea of a literary canon generated by literary "fathers," there is ample evidence that these national icons were, themselves, aware of the tenuous nature of their positions at the apex of the patriarchy. In a way, their survival as literary fathers, enforced by their focused response to attacks on paternity, is evidence of the strength of their anxiety.

Notes

[1] Michel Foucault, "What Is an Author?" in *Language, Counter-Memory, Practice,*113-138.

[2] Foucault, "What Is an Author?", 138.

[3] Ross Shideler, *Questioning the Father: From Darwin to Zola, Ibsen, Strindberg, and Hardy,* 106.

[4] Shideler, *Questioning the Father,* 110.

[5] William Dean Howells, *My Mark Twain: Reminiscences and Criticisms,* 101.

[6] Ernest Hemingway, *Green Hills of Africa,* 23.

[7] Oscar Levertin, *Strindberg,* 58, my translation.

8 Thomas Mann, "August Strindberg," *Reden und Aufsätze 2*, 371, my translation.

9 August Strindberg, *Letters: Volume I*, 438.

10 *Amerikanska humorister: ny följd.*

11 August Strindberg, *Samlade verk 25. En dåres försvarstal*, 567.

12 See Alan Gribben, "Autobiography as Property: Mark Twain and His Legend," in *The Mythologizing of Mark Twain*, 39-55.

13 Mark Twain, *Mark Twain's Speeches*, 326.

14 Unpublished letter by Joseph G. Gessford, 8 August 1904, Mark Twain Papers, Bancroft Library, University of California, Berkeley.

15 August Strindberg, *Mannaår och ålderdom*, 182.

16 Cited in Ashley Taggart, "'A Provisional Hypothesis: Paternity or Pangenesis?'", *The Modern Language Review*, 4.

17 Cited in Taggart, "A Provisional Hypothesis," 5.

18 August Strindberg, *Samlade Verk 27. Fadren. Fröken Julie. Fordringsägare*, 60. Translation mine.

19 Shideler, *Questioning the Father*, 103.

20 Mark Twain, *The Tragedy of Pudd'nhead Wilson and the Comedy Those Extraordinary Twins*, 22-3.

21 Hortense Spillers, "Mama's Baby, Papa's Maybe: An American Grammar Book," in *African-American Literary Theory: A Reader*, 257-279.

22 Twain, *Pudd'nhead Wilson*, 32-3.

23 Twain, *Pudd'nhead Wilson*, 303.

Erasing the Father

James Massengale

Writing from his cell in debtor's prison, Sweden's greatest musical poet set to work on a humorous retrospective sketch of his early life. His story begins:

> Kongl. Slottet den 8 Maj, 1794. Som jag almänt är känd så på den Moraliska som Physiska sidan, det wil säga till hiertat, min wandel, ock min constitution, så är jag En herre af mycken liten djupsinnighet, ock frågar eij efter om solen går eller jorden axlar sig...

> [Royal Palace, 8th of May 1794. As I am generally known, regarding my moral as well as physical side – that is to say – my heart, my conduct, and my fundamental makeup, I am a gentleman of very little intellectual depth, and ask not whether the sun goes around the earth or the earth turns itself on an axis...] [1]

The fragmentary autobiography by Carl Michael Bellman (1740-95) has been valued by Swedish scholars, since despite a number of inaccuracies and lapses of memory, it contains the best, most intimate account of the least well documented years in that poet's life. Like a number of other quotable reflections by talented authors, it inadvertently discloses a shadow of civilization well beyond what Bellman might have intended or known. The sea change of patriarchy in Sweden had already begun. Today we might trace it retrospectively, starting with a mysterious bullet taking down a warrior king in 1718 and still reverberating, when a modest heir to

17

the throne weds her personal trainer in 2010. But it is too vast and glacial a change to contain much meaning at any given moment. A bit like pondering whether the Ptolomaic or the Copernican model works better for us on a daily level, we still flounder ahead as Bellman did then, hoping against hope that our practical choices don't make us vulnerable to being crushed by some astronomical or Darwinian force. And yet, as they say, we are what our practical choices are.

One practical choice by Bellman was to erase his father. But to place his action in context, a certain amount of explanation is required. Let us take the poet concretely at his word.

> Huru mina föräldrar krånglade blef jag som sagt, född den 4 feb 1740 – min mor wacker som en dag, oändligen god, charmant i sin klädnad, god mot alla meniskor, delicat i omgänge – hade En förträffelig röst ock hade wänt sig att ligga i 21 Barnsängar – honij qvi mal y pense, men detta lekwärcket gjorde husets Ruin...

> [However my parents muddled things up, I was brought into the world on February 4, 1740 – my Mother beautiful as the day, infinitely good, charming in her dress, warm towards every human being, delicate in company – had a splendid voice and had accustomed herself to lie in 21 childbeds – honi [soit] qui mal y pense, but those little games brought the house to ruin...][2]

In the autobiography, Bellman continually returns to his mother's side – or her lap – for support and consolation.[3] And the reminiscences of the ailing 54-year-old poet may be corroborated by indicators dating from Bellman's earliest poetic apprenticeship. His debut at age 15, a translation of David von Schweinitz' *Hundert Evangelische Todes-Gedanken*, was prefaced by his "first original poem," "To my most gracious Mother, Mrs. Catharina Bellman...With All Filial Veneration, By Carl Michael Bellman." There is no mistaking the veneration:

Städ, hulda Mor! min fjäder måla
På denna duk en sådan drift.
Som intet smicker gjort till gift,
Som inga konster hjelpapråla,
Som aldrig af omskiften vet,
Som brinner större än den lyser,
Som mer i ord än hjerta fryser
Och heter vördsam tacksamhet...

[Let, dear Mother, my pen draw
Upon this cloth a desire
That no flattery turn'd to poison,
That no artifice helps to flaunt,
That alteration never knows,
That burns more brightly than it shines,
That freezes more in words than heart,
And is called – my reverent thanks...]

At the same time, balancing the German translation with a proof of his skills in modern French, he rendered a lengthy book by Philippe Sylvester Du Four: *Instruction Morale d'un Père à son Fils qui Part pour un long Voyage.*[4] The dedication prefacing this second publication is in prose, but is equally heartfelt:

I de fast yngre åren jag nu är stadder, är jämwäl tiden för mig mycket nära, at jag bör gå in i den stora werlden...Om en sådan resa mig är förelagd,...är en sak, som står i den alwetande Gudens händer. Skulle sådana omständigheter framdeles yppa sig, at min wälfärd äfwen utom mitt Fädernesland kunde...blifwa befrämjad, så wore jag för min del wäl dertil hågad...

> [Although still in my younger years, the time for
> me is very near in which to enter into the wide
> world...If such travel is arranged for me,...is a
> thing that lies in Almighty God's hands. But
> should such conditions in the future be actuated,
> that my well-being also beyond the borders of
> my fatherland could...be successful, I would for
> one be well inclined for it...]

However, notwithstanding the book's theme of fatherly love
and filial submission, the poet's *dedication* is not addressed to his
father, but to his uncle, Jacob Martin Bellman, the Swedish consul
in Cadiz. It is clearly a supplication letter by the teenager to be
allowed to get out of town – indeed, to leave Sweden entirely.[5] It is
not too far-fetched, *prima facie*, to interpret this early "erasure" of
the father as a kind of revolt against the immediate demands of the
patriarchy, as they presented themselves in Bellman's own family.
The point in Bellman's case – whether or not any real antipathy
between the father and son emerged so early – is that the conflict,
once it surfaced, appears never to have been resolved.

The 18th-Century Patriarch

So who was Bellman's father? Let us pick up the few known
traces of the father's side, which is to say, the career and socially
acceptable side of Bellman's existence. The kingdom of Sweden in
1750 had the appearance of a modern, Enlightenment model of a
benign, rational society.[6] That is, certain nominally democratic
aspects of government, narrowly defined, shared legal authority
with the king. Furthermore, the belief in "divine right" was no
longer commonly assumed.[7] Oddly enough, the Swedish
constitution was afforded this divine quality: since "it corresponded
with the law of nature, it took precedence over the wills both of the
four estates and of the king...In parliament, the constitution was
compared to the Lord's Prayer."[8] The national parliament or
"Riksdag" met for a period of some months at about three-year

intervals. Here the four estates – a division of family fathers into nobility, clergy, burghers and farmers – held debates, setting the course of the nation. By the 1730's, two ideological groups – "Hats" and "Caps" – emerged, lending the political debate an even more modern appearance. While they often behaved more like factions than political parties, the emphasis on differing views rather than estate solidarity contributed to the ultimate breakdown of the estate system a hundred years later.[9] But this too began as a small wave in the sea change; its ultimate effects would not have been foreseen in Bellman's time.

Stockholm, with slightly more than 70,000 people, contained the bulk of the wealth of the country, while most of the population (90%) were subsistence farmers. The four estates represented only a tiny fraction of the total number of people: 0.5% nobility, 1.0% clergy, 2.0% burghers.[10] But the modernization of government, starting back in the 17th century, acknowledged the need for a working bureaucracy (an early forerunner of the modern civil service). This in turn gradually led to a unique situation in Stockholm, where the bureaucracy was mostly housed. By 1750, a substantial number (somewhere around 2.0%, i.e., equivalent numbers to the traditional burghers) fell under a new category of "non-noble ranking persons," who had no "burskap," no direct representation in the Riksdag. The category applied to diverse groups: they were mostly civil servants, but also doctors, tutors and academics, inspectors and bookkeepers.[11]

It is to that new, ill-defined, non-noble ranking group that Bellman's family would be assigned. They lived in an unstable, but also opportunistic urban atmosphere. Individuals within the group could presumably attain high rank or ennoblement. The leading poet of the previous generation, Olof von Dalin (1708-63), had risen to nobility and the high position of Cabinet Minister, largely due to his talent at producing moralizing and comic prose and poetry. But for numerous others, a tedious, economically deprived life of office drudgery lay ahead.[12] Furthermore, the tax system was not well coordinated with the financial needs of the salaried bureaucracy, so the situation of the young civil servant was particularly exposed. He (it was always a he) might work for years, first as an "aspirant," then as an "extra ordinarius" (a non-salaried clerk). A job with a regular salary might have to be purchased from its previous owner, even if the clerk was deemed qualified for advancement. All this notwithstanding, the "non-noble ranking man" might be considered lucky. He had titular high status, and titles such as "secretary" were used (sometimes spuriously) to differentiate glorified clerks from those who lacked such rank. This complex and relatively numerous group ultimately contributed to the emergence of a "middle class" in Sweden (the concept was not known during Bellman's lifetime) and, once again, to the gradual undermining of the estate system.

The poet's father, Johan Arendt Bellman (1707-65), was the son of a brilliant university professor and Latin poet of the same name. [13] It is commonly assumed that Carl Michael Bellman inherited his grandfather's poetic bent as well as his cittrinchen. [14] Although orphaned at age two, Bellman's father was probably aided by his own wealthy maternal grandmother to a substantial education, including five years of foreign travel. But no sign of cosmopolitanism, poetic flair or even unusual acumen as a public official may be traced in the few bits of information left behind regarding Father Bellman. From the beginning at age 22, an adequate, but not particularly exciting career appears to have followed:

> 1729 – 31: "extra ordinarius" clerk in the
>   Chancellery College.

> 1731 – 34: clerk or copyist in the College office,
>   unsalaried.

> 1734 – 40: clerk, but now with a salary.

> 1740 – 46: registrar, a promotion within the
>   hierarchy.

1746 – 49: de facto "first chief notary"; but now
Bellman writes to the King, complaining of
being passed over for the position of Protocol
Secretary in the Ministry of Justice.

1749 – 63: titular Secretary in the Castle
Chancellery, but with only half the applicable
salary, the other half remaining with the
previous (retired) secretary.

1763: Secretary Bellman is granted retirement on
the grounds of "ill health and other
circumstances."

1764: Secretary Bellman is given the honorary
title of "lawman," after his retirement.

In a system based on the patriarchal web of society, Johan
Arendt Bellman (we shall refer to him, deferentially and loosely, as
"Lawman Bellman") was not unconnected.[15] He had remnants of
his own father's – Professor Bellman's – circle to support him, and
his marriage to Catharina Hermonia in 1738 brought her father's
powerful clergy group into the home.[16] Lawman Bellman's wealthy
grandmother, Catharina Daurer, was still alive in 1740. She owned
the estate on Södermalm (the island immediately south of
Stockholm's Old Town) until her death in 1743, when Lawman
Bellman managed to purchase a piece of it (the "little Daurer
house") for his family.

Lawman Bellman's eldest son was clearly the center of family
attention, especially because their home economy initially allowed it.
As the babies came and went, Carl Michael remained the hope for
the father's (and of course, the household's) future.[17] Carl Michael
was the focus of a throng of tutors, although his sisters might have
been allowed some rudimentary instruction.[18] There is no evidence
to reconstruct with complete certainty what plans Lawman Bellman
had for his eldest son. But musical poetry, it is safe to say, was no
part of it – not to mention bawdy drinking songs. Nonetheless,

Bellman "awoke" as a poet at about age 14. His awakening is
described in the autobiographical sketch:

> Äntlig opklarnade dagen, Mina Föräldrar, hade
> funnit då jag låg i feber, at jag under paroxismen,
> talade all ting på wers. ock sjöng för min Mor –
> så, at de föllo i förundran… Mig waldes till
> Jnformator Ett genie wid namn Clas Ludvic
> Ennes…där lärde jag att af honom hantera
> Apollos' lyra, under hans inseende har jag
> författat flere bref ock Poesier, ock bland dem
> 1755 Öfwersättningar af psalmer i Halliske
> psalmboken…Senare Arbeten känner man nog –

> [Finally the clouds cleared away. My parents had
> found, once when I lay in a fever, that in my
> paroxysm I spoke entirely in verse – and sang for
> my   Mother   –   such   that   they   all   were
> astonished…A tutor was chosen for me: a
> talented man by the name of Clas Ludvig
> Ennes…I learned from him to wield Apollo's lyre.
> Under his tutelage I composed numerous letters
> and poems, and among these were translations of
> psalms   from   the   Halle   Psalmbook   in
> 1755…Works after that are well enough
> known][19]

What is "Apollo's lyre"? The simple answer, and likely the
answer Bellman might have proffered, is that in order to do poetry
certain technical skills must be attained: how to count syllables, to
know what words may qualify as rhymes, how to fit thoughts into
strophic entities. Since Bellman would soon be a public performer,
skills on an instrument and singing would also come to mind. But
Apollo's lyre was, and is, much more than this, as the metaphor also
implies.

The hidden structures that support the social and economic system must be revealed, because they appear reworked into symbols appropriate to a poetic construct. The task of an 18th-century professional poet was to mythologize reality, to make the ordinary objects of the patriarchy (kings and nobles, commissioners and family members, pastors, farmers and commoners) into participants in a higher conceptual world of Greek, Roman, biblical and legendary parallels. This correspondence with immortal or historical models was the accepted way of showing continuity, if not eternity, in a stable socio-economic system. The study that Bellman engaged in was no quick or facile matter, for his nonchalant reference conceals about four years of arduous work, even though he was both supremely talented at it and highly motivated. Emphasizing Ennes' tutelage, Bellman continues with a long list of early student works, translations and original poems, his appointment as an "Ämnesven" [student intern] at the Royal Science Academy, and a possible contact with Olof von Dalin (1708-1763). [20] But the long passage conceals another erasure: omitted entirely from the story is that Bellman had begun a mind-numbing bureaucratic career at the National Bank of the Estates.

The omission is clearly connected to his father. However little the poet ever knew or cared about the universe, he would have understood as a teenager a good deal about the conditions regulating the life of the "non-noble ranking" civil servant at mid-18th century. No alternative to this life would have been proposed or even envisioned in the "little Daurer house." Two problems then presented themselves to the young poet. First, the civil service career was sustained not only by writing copy, but by mathematics and bookkeeping, subjects for which the he had neither inclination nor talent. Second, thirty years of conscientious labor in his father's case – with the aggravation that Carl Michael had certainly heard voiced at home – did not provide an enticing example for him to follow. On the other hand, the "profession" of poet did not exist, as an important study by Bo Bennich-Björkman has shown.[21]

References of several types indicate that Olof von Dalin at this time was the young Bellman's polestar, both in terms of literary production and as a career model. But Dalin had been an extraordinary exception to the rule. Dalin was the right person at the right time (1730's), with the right balance of moralizing and humorous works, to be recognized by the right patriarchs. So how was one to repeat this act? Bellman's own early publications of political and moralizing poetry ("Tankar om Flickors Ostadighet" [Thoughts on Young Ladies' Inconstancy], 1758) and ("Månan" [The Moon], 1760), arguably updated versions of Dalin's early literary satires, may reflect the young poet's ambition. But soon it would appear that his father directed him (arranged for him? ordered him?) to seek unpaid employment at the National Bank. For a while it would appear that a mild teenage revolt came to a screeching halt.

The Career in Banking

Using the network of family connections, the poet applied to the National Bank in December of 1757, and began as an unsalaried "extra ordinarius" in January of 1758. Carl Michael also acquired a book called *Institutiones arithmeticae* ("Men nu förökt med...tydelig vnderrättelse om wexel-räkningen och italienska bokhålleriet" [But now expanded with...clear instruction concerning monetary exchange and Italian bookkeeping"]).[22] There may have been no tutor at home now, so Bellman reportedly had private lessons in mathematics from a certain Peter Diurman in the Old Town.[23] For whatever reason, these lessons accomplished virtually nothing. The poet did not receive the standard minimal recommendation for "skickeligt snille" [skillful performance] from Diurman. After a few months of this clearly painful work and study, Bellman took leave from his job, and spent a short term at the Upsala Academi [Uppsala University].[24] Nothing is really known about this brief sojourn, but a later Bacchanalian song is an oblique indication that his reason for university training was not useful for the purpose of promotion at the bank:

Movitz skulle bli Student;
Han Upsala betrakta,
Börja mumla excellent
Grammatica contracta;
　　Dum och tjock,
　　Hic haec hoc
　　Han sig genast lärde,
Hyrde sig en svarter rock,
Kyronii öl förtärde.

Där satt han som misanthrop,
Men röder som en vallmo,
Vid sin stånka och sit stop,
Och conjugera Amo;
　　Hur han drack,
　　Ölet stack,
　　Kärlek hjärnan brydde;
Movitz tog sitt pick och pack,
Och lärdoms sätet flydde.

[Movitz was to be a student;
He came to observe Uppsala,
Began to mumble brilliantly
Grammatica contracta;
Dumb and fat –
Hic haec hoc
He immediately got right;
Rented a black gown,
Drank the local beer.

There he sat, a misanthopist,
But red as any poppy,
By his tankard and his glass,
Conjugating "Amo";
How he drank,
The beer all vanished,
His brain was plagued by love;
Movitz packed up all his stuff,
And fled from the seat of
learning][25]

The omissions in the autobiography preclude a reconstruction of the trip to Uppsala. As the purest guess: Bellman got himself out of Stockholm. He needed a break from the brain-dulling work and bookkeeping lessons, and found Uppsala an appropriate alternative. But he had no money of his own, and his father would never have supported the years of study it would have taken for a "magister" degree, leading to a change of career. Soon Bellman was back at the National Bank, now being examined in simple mathematics and bookkeeping (January 27, 1759). His examiners noticed some deficiencies in Bellman's understanding – among other things, he mixed up the definitions of the numerator and denominator of a fraction – but leniency prevailed, and they gave him the title of "extra ordinarius" on June 27, which was at least a step above that of "aspirant." On July 14, 1761, Bellman applied for a regular salary, pointing out that he, by that time, had worked for three years without one. He was turned down.

The Catastrophe

A grandiloquent poem in praise of the directors of the National
Bank on New Years' 1760 – for which he was also rewarded 150
dalers – was, in retrospect, the high water mark of his banking
career.[26] But Bellman had already begun to tread the primrose path
that would be his inspiration for decades to come. We may begin
this period where he does in the autobiography, noting again the
matriarchal twist:

> 1759 – war jag första gången öfwerlastad ock
> placat, såfwande i min Mors knä, sedan jag hos
> holländske Ministern Martewill på Södermalm, i
> granskapet af mina föräldrars hus tagit mig ett
> Pontaks-rus. // // jag kom hem så röd ock skön /
> eftermiddagen mot fyra, / då till dagens aftonbön
> / man såg folcket sig utstyra / Mina Systrar pjåkiga
> / med bindmössor syntes niga / men jag
> rosenblommig stiga, / till min Mor ock kjortlarna.
> // // :/: Min Carl Mickel, sade hon / hwar min
> Gåsse har du warit, / åh min Mor, jag har erfarit –
> / en mig något stor portion. / ja så, så så – Calle
> lilla, / luta du ditt hufwud ner, / lägg dig på mitt
> knä jag ber, / wet din Mor will dig eij illa.

> [1759 – for the first time, I was over-intoxicated
> and befuddled, sleeping on my Mother's knee,
> after having gotten me a bordeaux-soaking at the
> house of the Holland Ambassador Martewill on
> Södermalm, near my parent's house. /// I came
> home so red and fair / in the afternoon, about
> four/ when at the time for evening prayer /
> people were getting dressed; / my sisters, nervous
> types / were curtseying in their little caps, / but I
> come in, red-faced / to Mother and her skirts. //
> // :/: Now, Carl Michael - so she said / where, my

boy, have you been? / Oh, dear Mother, I've imbibed / a rather too large portion… / Well, so, so so, little Calle / let your head bend down / lie down on my knee, my boy, / you know, your Mother wishes you no harm.][27]

The aging poet's remembrance drifts from prose into verse, as he recalls staggering down the street on Södermalm from the van der Noot palace to the "little Daurer house," to collapse on his mother's lap. Once more, any involvement by the father is expunged. In fact, Johan Arendt Bellman had to have become centrally involved in the debauchments by the time the national economic convulsions, and Bellman's personal finances, reached a point of no return.

The political party of "Hats" had started a useless war in Pomerania in 1757, for which Sweden had inadequate resources. To pay for this adventure, they had printed paper money which quickly lost value, and people of all ranks found their fortunes ruined, while the national debt grew by a factor of ten in six years, 1757-62, and prices doubled. Ingmar Simonsson has noted the precarious situation, particularly with regard to the class of "non-noble ranking persons":

> Young men who had just begun their civil service careers went without salary as "extra ordinarius," but as sons of the ranking class, they were associated with finer circles. This demanded a certain style of dress, wigs and accessories, to maintain the appearance of wealth in good society. If one were in addition part of a hedonistic circle of younger civil servants, it is clear that money was thrown away, but it was money the value of which was unknown, and might decrease daily. Picnics were arranged and dances were visited; conversations were held in cafes and taverns; card

games and other sports were part of the entertainment. In the heat of the moment, it was easy enough to write I.O.U.'s for each other – to sign one's name and then have an extra glass in order to forget the consequences.[28]

By the summer of 1763, Bellman and some of his friends had fallen prey to loan sharks. Facing debtor's prison, the friends decided to flee the country, and sent Bellman to Norway to find accommodation for them all. The plan was apparently to meet in Trondheim, out of reach of the creditors. But Bellman stopped at Fredrikshald, just across the border, and negotiated (or was advised to negotiate) on his own behalf. His letter to King Adolf Fredrik, dated 14 September 1763, is a plea to allow him to return to Sweden without being imprisoned. The letter acknowledges his "youthful indiscretion," combined with distress over his lack of promotion within the National Bank. He notes that creditors holding notes had begun to "vigorously harass" him. Longing to satisfy these creditors as well as to "serve his country," he asks for leave to return home. This plea was brought up in a lower court in Stockholm. Certain principal usurers (Grim, Tharmouth) were called in, and voiced no objection to Bellman's settling his debts without being incarcerated.[29] Their indulgence may indicate that a deal had been struck, but how (or with whom) is not part of the record.

The documents noted here have been known about for a long time. They are often combined with the young poet's early verses, to demonstrate how – in the midst of the general misery – he had honed his considerable skill at depicting masquerades, carnivals, taverns and light-footed women, all in impeccable rhyme set to contradances and minuets, French vaudevilles and Swedish folk tunes. All this is completely true, and the few eyewitness reports of the sorts of activities outlined by Simonsson do confirm the idea that Bellman now played a central role in the wild activities of the "non-noble ranking" youth and their noble friends.

Johan Arendt Bellman was also greatly present at this juncture, however, and a few sparse records may help to fill the omissions left in the poet's own gapped autobiography. We will recall that Bellman noted that his mother, "beautiful as the day," had accustomed herself to lying in twenty-one childbeds – honi soit qui mal y pense (as the Order of the Garter puts it) – but that "those little games brought the house to ruin." In fact, it may be the case that it was Carl Michael himself who contributed in a decisive way to bringing "the [little Daurer] house to ruin."

By the early summer of 1763 he had accumulated 18,000 dalers in debts and I.O.U.'s. The "little Daurer house" had survived a terrible fire on Södermalm in 1759, so that it was still intact, valued at 43,800 dalers in 1761, although Lawman Bellman had an outstanding loan of 18,000 dalers. During the early 1760's – that terrible period of Swedish financial collapse – the poet's father had begun to dig further into the equity. On October 7, 1761, he borrowed 11,750 dalers. Then an additional loan of 5,000 dalers followed on November 4, 1762, and then 24,000 dalers more on January 15, 1763. It is very difficult to determine at this point in time what precipitated these loans, but Björkman's clarification: "The numerous flock of children forced all sorts of retrenchments" seems curiously out of line with the enormity of the father's pecuniary need. We will recall from above that from all the childbeds Catharina Bellman had been accustomed to (probably 15, not 21), only eight children remained in 1763 – six dependents, since Catharina Christina had married and moved away and Carl Michael was supposed to manage his own affairs. It was a large household, but not that of the old woman who lived in a shoe.

However, just as the poet's economy began to show signs of complete calamity, his father moved to sell the house. It went for 60,000 dalers on March 29, 1763. Three months later, on June 14, Johan Arendt Bellman wrote to King Adolf Fredrik, requesting permission to retire from the Palace Chancellery. The request was granted forthwith, "in consideration of his weak health as well as several circumstances which were put forward." [30] No extra "circumstances" were specified in his resignation letter; so the acceptance document would appear to refer to a verbal appeal that preceded or accompanied Johan Arendt's official request.

The ailing father moved his family down to Årsta, south of Södermalm, apparently waiting for the opportunity to acquire a permanent retirement residence. It is thus reasonable to assume (since the poet had no resources at all) that the Bellman family was well aware of Carl Michael's downward spiral at least some months prior to his flight to Norway. The question may be posed whether Lawman Bellman was initially privy to the escape plan to keep his son and his son's friends out of debtor's prison. When Carl Michael was granted leave to return home from Norway, it is at least certain that the angry father began to lay down the law, rather than to fight for his son's continuation at the National Bank. Apparently it was Lawman Bellman who asked for the termination.[31] Carl Michael then wrote a formal letter in this regard, hoping that "better promotion might be achieved elsewhere." His letter was dated from Årsta, 26 November 1763. The resignation was accepted on 1 Dec. 1763.[32]

There would be additional repercussions, however. Since other young civil servants were also embroiled in creditors' webs, a protocol by the bank directors in early April 1764 includes the harsh statement that "the extra ordinarius Bellman, who had fled because of his debts and been allowed to return, to the extent he had been the one who had led several other civil servants into such dereliction…and had not been heard from since his return, should be banned from the bank, since he was no ordinarius but only a civil servant on trial there." A response to this in the protocol notes that he had already, on behest of his father, requested dismissal. It is unknown whether Bellman's father was privy to the possibly actionable condemnation that his son had been the instigator of others' dereliction. It is possible that the protocol remained secret, but equally possible that some of the language leaked out, if indeed it was not Lawman Bellman's opinion already.

We are now in a position to understand to some degree why the poet might, in retrospect, wish to erase certain matters from his autobiography. The relationship between the father and son between the last months of 1763 and the summer of 1764 may reasonably be described as a kind of black hole in the poet's life.[33] If Lawman Bellman paid or satisfied his son's creditors in some provisional manner, as has been speculated, it would not be far-fetched to posit an atmosphere of rigid disaffection, if not worse, in the household. But as noted above, traces of dissociation are already found, some ten years back, in the poet's actions. We must also keep in mind that Carl Michael had become an accomplished and recognized poet and performer during his "years of debauchment." He was now well-known to families of the nobility as well as within his own civil-servant group.[34] An overview of his early production also shows his increasing independence from his father's hearth. There is a marked shift in poetic form as well as subject concealed in the statistic below of his poems:[35]

Year:	Religious:	Political:	Occasional:	Bacchanalian:
1757	3	0	1	0
1758	2	1	0	0
1759	1	0	1	0
1760	2	1	2	0
1761	1	0	0	0
1762	0	0	0	0
1763	1	0	2	2
1764	0	0	1	17
1765	0	3	1	29

This development (quite disregarding a continual improvement in the quality of the material) also corresponds to the increase in the poet's notoriety in Stockholm. The ambiguity in that term may be allowed to stand. Neither the fame nor its reverse side would have been looked upon kindly by Lawman Bellman. The early flowering of religious poetry, clearly encouraged in the home, had wilted away by 1764, and the subject of piety would not be versified again for the next twenty years. In contrast, Bellman's bacchanalian songs (difficult to date, but numbering in the hundreds by the late 1760's) were soon known all over Sweden. There was now no mitigating element in the poet's production or general behavior that could have served as a source of reconciliation with his father. The sober and cautious Björkman sums up the father's situation in 1764-5:

> Lawman Bellman was, at the height of his career, a dutiful and zealous official, who conscientiously fulfilled his duties. But the feeling of having been passed over by persons who in no way were better qualified embittered his life. And when to this was added both economic troubles and sorrow caused by the debauchery of his eldest son, his strength was broken. The consciousness of being unable to control his own finances drove him to his grave.[36]

If this is the case, paternal anger may not have been shared, or shared fully, by Bellman's mother; but she may have been too ill to intercede, weakened by the consumption that would end her life in 1765. As a long standing civil servant, Lawman Bellman was apparently allowed by the chancellery to take over an older tax-free farm owned by the government, if he committed himself to maintaining or improving the property. It is this final perquisite that permitted the Bellman family to move to the Wisbohammar estate, south of Södertälje, in late 1764, after their yearlong residence at Årsta.

During the last unpleasant months at home, Carl Michael applied to another bureaucracy, the Manufacturing Office. His letter of 16 August 1764 appealed to the directors to allow him the position (once again) of "extra ordinarius" "in the secretariat or some office." His wait – for three months – for a reply may well have seemed like a lifetime of misery.

A Wedding and Five Funerals

A key component in the handling of Apollo's lyre was that of constructing eulogies. As in the case of other manifestations of the elite in a class-conscious, ostentatious society, such as proper attire and mastery of the steps of a minuet, any upwardly striving "non-noble ranking civil servant" needed to spend long hours in acquiring proper decorum that would be considered appropriate in the public forum and at the royal court. But for the young poet, the stakes included other aspects that were immeasurably higher. Not only did his poems have to make it past the Scylla of the censor or the consistory, they could founder, once published, at the Charybdis of self-appointed poetic gatekeepers.[37] While young Bellman was transitioning between his student efforts at religious psalms and his natural bent for bacchanalian songs, he tested these exclusive rhetorical waters, eulogizing King Adolf Fredrik in a published poem in 1759, and (as noted above) flattering his employers at the National Bank in 1760. These manifestations of support for the patriarchy were regarded as a natural element of the Enlightenment poet's métier – it was what public poets did, it was what they were expected to do.

But no eulogy was more important than a funeral elegy, the permanent verbal capstone of a life lived well and successfully, mourned by many, not only "humanity" or "the Nation" itself but, as the poet would say, even by anthropomorphic abstractions like "Virtue" or "Death." At the same time, a fervent concluding passage would depict the happiness the deceased experienced on being welcomed into the afterlife.[38] It is an extraordinary leap from the type of musical poetry that Bellman delighted his friends with, but one which he dutifully pursued, unabashedly and competently, to the end of his life. Funerals and weddings played a central symbolic role in the hierarchy of the four estates. The discussions surrounding these ceremonies might seem surprising to our more secular view, but, as Kurt Johannesson has clarified in an important article:

> Funerals in 17th- and 18th-century Sweden were, to a great degree, an expression of tensions within the hierarchical estate-society, used in the struggle for social rank and its political-economic

advantages. Within all the four estates, families
expended, by our standards, enormous resources
on burials, epitaphs, crypts, etc....For the
government, this was an economic problem,
when such a large portion of the country's
resources were frittered away on this
ostentatiousness...So the regime and the church
together produced a number of ordinances
closely regulating bell-ringing...the number of
persons and wagons in a funeral procession, the
amount of refreshments in the receptions, the
types of clothing allowed and the material used in
the winding sheets, etc. They attempted to make
funerals into a ceremonial language, in which
every act, object, gesture and phrase would
express specific ideas...a language in which the
interests of the church, the state and the different
classes would approach an artistic synthesis and
apparent harmony.[39]

There are six ceremonies during the poet's early life that have
bearing on the present argument. All but one of these have been
discussed in the literature, because of Bellman's prominent status as
a poet.[40] Here each of Bellman's ceremonial poems from 1760 to
1765 will be noted, in terms of the relationship (or what is known
of the relationship) of the young poet to the eulogized persons.

1. Bengt Rudenskiöld: a published elegy, 1760. [41]
Rudenskiöld (1702-60) was a noble, the son of a
famous bishop and poet, Thorsten Rudeen; his
brothers Carl and Ulrik were also very well known as
poets. It is unknown why Bellman wrote this elegy, but
at age 20, he may have been testing the waters as a
professional, public eulogist, rather than as an actual
friend of the deceased.

2. Claes Arrhén von Kapfelman and Catharina
Christina Bellman: a published wedding poem, 1763.[42]

The wedding of Bellman's closest sister and the nobleman Claes von Kapfelman was celebrated on February 11, 1763 at the Nybohof estate, Brännkyrka Parish, near Årsta, where the Bellmans were living. The ceremony appears to have been attended by Carl Michael, who graced the couple with his elegant wedding verses appropriate to their station.

3. Anders Adolph von Heynne: a published elegy, 1763.[43] Von Heynne (1732-63) was a young second lieutenant in the cavalry, and a nobleman who had been a page at King Adolf Fredrik's court. At the time of his early death, he was living out in the country near the estate of Arrhén von Kapfelman (n:o 2 above). It is speculated that Bellman had met von Heynne through his brother-in-law, so the eulogy was an act of friendship to preserve and glorify his memory.

4. Hedvig Eleonora Hallman: a published elegy, 1764.[44] The elegy, is titled "Tankar vid fru H. E. H.:s graf, den 7 Maj 1764" [Thoughts at the graveside of H. E. H....], which would indicate that Bellman recited his poem at the interment ceremony of his neighbor, who left her husband, the parish priest, with two small children. As Ekman has noted, a gracious act of poetic memory was performed by a sorrowing neighbor and parishioner, tailoring his rhetoric to the feminine gender.

5. Catharina Bellman: a published elegy, 1765, revised and reprinted in 1777.[45] Bellman's most important elegy, titled "Tankar vid min hulda Moders...graf, den 17 Martii 1765" [Thoughts by my gracious Mother's...grave], is the most personal and intimate of his funeral poems. By the time his mother died, Bellman had left the paternal home to begin a new bureaucratic career at the Manufacturing Office. Catharina Bellman had died on March 8 of tuberculosis. The burial occurred at Wårdinge

Church.[46] Bellman must have known that his mother's health had been failing for some time, probably as early as 1760 or 1761. The elegy was republished in the Göteborg newspaper Hwad Nytt? Hwad Nytt? – twice (July 7 and 29, 1777) the second time with an additional three strophes and other alterations, attributed by Stefan Ekman to the poet himself: "The revised version is...no longer a funeral elegy, but rather a [new] memorial by a son sorrowing over the death of his mother twelve years before."[47]

But to the five early documents showing the poet's professional skill and personal engagement in ceremonial poetry for acquaintances and relatives, we must add the following fact:

> 6. Johan Arendt Bellman. Bellman's father died on December 27, 1765, only surviving Catharina Bellman by about nine months. He was buried, like his wife, at Wårdinge Churchyard. There is no funeral elegy preserved. Bellman apparently never wrote one, either at his death, for graveside recitation, for publication, or retrospectively.[48]

The end of Lawman Bellman's story may be quickly told. The father had taken over the estate of Wisbohammar in November 1764. Pressed by creditors who demanded that the property be subject to their claims, he had submitted his request for bankruptcy to the local (Öknebo County) court on October 21, 1765, asking at the same time for a delay in the proceedings. He had been granted the delay, but died before the court could declare him bankrupt. The inventory proceedings for the bankrupt estate were handled later that winter by Carl Michael's brother-in-law, Claes Arrhén von Kapfelman. No inheritance remained, when the creditors were finished. Von Kapfelman and Catharina Christina became the guardians of the poet's orphaned brothers and sisters. Bellman did maintain contact with the Arrhén family: he wrote a eulogy over their child, Claes Gustaf, who died as an infant in 1773. He even remembered their poultry-keeper, old Anna Berg, who died that same year; she had formerly been a nanny at the "little Daurer house" for the Bellman children. So the lack of a funeral elegy for Lawman Bellman, not only in the face of all the other eulogies, but also for formal reasons, is all the more remarkable. Was there no filial remorse that might have brought the mild-mannered, gentle poet back to his father's grave? Was there no acknowledgement of the father's authority? Was there not an implicit formal requirement to eulogize the patriarch? Was there no realization that the family finances would restrict the ostentation of the funeral proceedings (see the Johannesson quotation above), so that the only way for the family to assert its rank was a eulogy designed for publication in Stockholm? Were there no qualms in the mind of the young poet, that the lack of such a eulogy would be noticed?

Epilog: or How to Erase an Erasure

The filial silence, here traced from Bellman's middle teens to his literary breakthrough and beyond, was undoubtedly intensely personal, not structural in terms of Swedish society. In the extremity of his despondency in the summer of 1764, we recall that the poet applied for a new position, placing his fate in the hands of a new patriarch. But Commissioner Anders Lissander (1705-86) knew very well whom – and what – he wanted to bring to Stockholm. His words have survived in the protocol of the Manufacturing Office on August 16, 1764:

> Commissioner Lissander declared that not only did he have intimate knowledge of Bellman's behavior, but was fully capable of commending him for his capability and decent life-style, in addition to possessing a highly developed sense of humor…so that in that case [of the acceptance of his application] the commissioner declared himself willing to take him under his personal supervision and advise him…so that he in time might become a useful member of society.[49]

It is safe to assume that both Lissander and his fellow officials in the Manufacturing Office knew exactly who Bellman was – or at least who he was known to be. The "personal supervision" effected by the Commissioner had, however, little to do with the implication of the protocol. Lissander turned his home on Södermalm into a semi-public poetic salon. Here Bellman appeared regularly as the principal entertainer, and was joined by other prominent poets and men about town. The hungry young poet was also offered a seat at the Lissander supper table for the better part of a decade, and there was proximity to the Commissioner's daughter, Ingrid Margareta. There are numerous poems in praise of her – especially regarding her cooking.[50] But most importantly from our standpoint: the bacchanalian legacy was preserved for posterity, in four large volumes of carefully copied musical poetry, in Lissander's own hand.[51]

Clearly the poet became a "useful member of society," if an anachronistic definition may be applied. Even taking into account the portions of Lissander's manuscripts that were subsequently lost, a sequence in the poet's development may easily be traced from the extant remainder. Out of the chaos of the early drinking songs and satires on biblical figures, cycles of songs and dramatic scenes gradually appeared, culminating in the series of Fredman's Epistles, starting in May, 1770. These poems quickly added a new dimension to Bellman's fame, and ultimately were congealed into Sweden's most famous song book.

Part of the genius of Fredman's Epistles lies in its consistency as a "world view." But Apollo's lyre has been radically restrung. Bellman casts his poetic glance back on the 1760's with apolitical amusement and amoral nostalgia, and distills its adventures into a systematic "gospel."[52] Reality and myth, concrete details and absurd situations are blended together in an alternative world that has its own rules. Money is seldom encountered, but chalk marks on a tavern tablet are rife; rank is equalized, but hats and buckled shoes, lace sleeves and fripperies are necessary; inebriation is the typical goal, but the gutter or Charon's ferry is waiting to catch the tippler. The Swedish patriarchy – if we exclude the specter of Charon himself – has been reduced to a few nasty, willful representatives of the "decency police," outsiders who raid the taverns, looking for girls to take to the Spinning House.[53] But these are peripheral characters in the context, despised and largely ignored. The central taverns and picnic grounds, by contrast, are mythologized as the domains of Bacchus and Venus. Their smoking altars are tended by matrons immortalized in the songs: the old lady at Thermopolium Boreale, Mother at "The Brown Door," Boman's Widow, Beckman's wife, and Mother at "The Cock." Not to overlook all their girls: Ulla Winblad, Sister Lisa, Anna Greta, the girls at "The Snake," the sisters at "The Lynx," and all. The fantasy world of Fredman's Epistles is then distinctly – matriarchal. And Fredman himself? Bellman explains:

> Här ser du en Skugga af en Bacchi Hjälte, en matt rök efter en utblåst krogdanck. Hvem är det menar du, jo det är Urmakaren Fredman, han som i sin lifstid varit äfven så allmänt kjänd för dess skickelighet att dela tidens lopp uti Timmar och Minuter, som för dess behändighet, att gjöra tiden till intet uti ett litet grönt Timglas med Finckel...

> [Here you see the shadow of a hero of Bacchus, a wisp of smoke from an old tavern candle that had been blown out. Who is that, you say? Well, it is the watchmaker Fredman, he who during his lifetime was just as reknowned for his skill at dividing up time into hours and minutes, as he was for his deftness in eradicating time completely, with the help of a small green hourglass full of cheap brandy...][54]

Fredman, the principal player, voyeur and promoter of the underworld lifestyle, should not be confused with his creator, the poet-ironist. But precisely this distinction allows Bellman the luxury of conjuring up his father in a poetic scene that was apparently impossible to realize in real life. The poet evokes a fantasized specter of Fredman's father in Epistle 23, one of the most famous of all the songs. Epistel 23, "Ack du min moder" [Ah, tell me, Mother] is Fredman's rueful soliloquy, as he lies in the gutter one night near the steps leading down into a locked-up cellar tavern, right across the square from – the National Bank building[!]. Experiencing that his plight is similar to that of Job, Fredman curses both mother and father for the sex act that brought him into the world. But as the dawn comes and the cellar tavern door is opened, he stumbles down the stairs to get his morning drink, and the transformation of the habitual alcoholic is soon begun:

> Nu är jag modig,
> Tapper och frodig,
> Och jag fruktar ej.
> Ännu en sup ell' par.
> Tack min mor och far…

> [Now I'm courageous
> Valiant and thriving,
> Afraid of nothing at all.
> Let's have a dram or two.
> Thanks! to Mom and Dad…]

Fredman's hyperbole increases as the liquor takes hold. He concludes:

> Tack för din låga,
> För din förmåga,
> Du min gamla Far:
> Kunde vi råkas,
> Skulle vi språkas,

Supa några dar;
Min bror du blifva skull,
Och som jag så full…

[Thanks! for your fire,
Your propensity!
You, my good old Dad:
If we could meet up,
Just have a chat,
Tipple for a few days;
We'd be like brothers!
And like me, so stewed…]

In this twice-removed image: removed from Fredman's reality as an alcoholic fantasy, just as Fredman is removed from the poet's reality as an ironic creation, the father and son link arms and wander off, ready to erase themselves together. Which part of this fantasy – whether the filial curse or the subsequent invitation for brotherhood – would have been more appalling to Lawman Bellman is hard to imagine. He was lucky to have been spared either humiliation. But for Fredman and his poet, the scene is that of a world declawed, of an underworld free of estates and of striving for rank, and of a reckoning permanently deferred. It can even allow the impossible miracle of the father as brother, sharing in an animalistic paradise of peace, in a foggy but sexually contented dipsomania. Bellman's complex irony – his best of all possible worlds – would later be lamented by the 19th-century Romantic poets (with a wry smile) as a world Sweden had lost forever.

Notes

[1] Or "shoulders itself"; it is a play on words (Bellman 1947, 1st sheet). The reference to the "Royal Palace" is also ironic: the detention center for citizens of standing was located in an attic wing of the Palace; but it was

drafty and unhealthy, and Bellman was already marked by the sickness that ended his life less than a year later.

[2] Bellman 1947, 1st sheet.

[3] Cf. Bellman StU VIII, p. 1ff. Olof Byström's commentary [ibid., 12] signals the inclination that I find: "It is clear that the skald was and felt himself to be strongly related in his essence to his mother...He gives us, by contrast, no portrait of his father in the autobiography."

[4] As Torkel Stålmarck has pointed out, the German translation and its French companion were completed in 1755, and submitted to censorship that year (Stålmarck 2000, 26). The two translations appeared in print in 1757. See also the discussion in Thorén 1986, 31-65.

[5] Jacob Martin Bellman (1706-86) traveled out to Cadiz in 1732 as a merchant. He became consul there in 1744. After some complaints and apparently shady transactions, an "assistant" was assigned to his duties in 1763, but Consul Bellman kept his title and also married a rich widow in 1768, which allowed him to continue a rather lavish lifestyle.

[6] It was at least considered so by Voltaire and Rousseau (Sennefelt 2006, 20).

[7] Adolf Fredrik of Holstein-Gottorp had been voted in by the four estates as a compromise monarch, when the previous king and queen produced no heir to the throne.

[8] Sennefelt 2006, 22.

[9] Sennefelt 2006, p. 41.

[10] Carlsson 1949/1973, 22-33. Simonsson 1995, 15f.

[11] This list is derived from Carlsson 1949/1973, 21. The traditional way of classifying burghers in Sweden was by "burskap," a centuries-old right or privilege to carry on business, connected to the guilds.

[12] Carlsson also points out that Sweden had a very small noble class (9,208 nobles in 1751), and that after an upswing in new ennoblements at the start of the 1700's, the number of noble families had hardly grown after 1730. The poet Dalin was then one of only about 60 ennoblements during the period 1730-50 (Carlsson 1949/1973, 22).

[13] Johan Arndt Bellman (1664 –1710) became an early a member of the Royal Musicians; after extensive study at Upsala Akademi (Uppsala University) he became Professor Eloquentiae in 1699.

[14] Or "Hamburger Zittrinchen"; a small 6-course, lute-like instrument.

[15] "Lawman" was a very high title (once even restricted to the noble class). It is important to note, however, that in J. A. Bellman's case it was strictly honorary; he never worked as a "lawman," nor did he draw the salary of that position.

[16] Michael Hermonius (1680-1749) was pastor of Maria Magdalena Church, near the Bellman residence, and a prominent representative of the clergy estate.

[17] Catharina, born 1741, married well to C. A. von Kapfelman. Johan (jr.), born 1743, died early. Johan Henric, born 1744, died early. Lovisa, born 1745, never married. Fredrika Elisabeth, born 1746, died early. Jacob, born 1747, died early. Fredrika Charlotta, born 1749, died early. Johan Arndt (2nd jr.), born 1750, became a businessman; his education is unknown. Fredrika Eleonora, born 1751, married well. Maria, born 1753, married well. Adolph, born 1755, died early. Hedvig, born 1756, died early. Gustaf, born 1758, and Adolph, born 1760, did live to adulthood, but their education is unknown.

[18] The poet is careful to record the full list of tutors in his autobiographical sketch: Rutström, Norman, Swaliung, Höckert (whose

teaching of geometry felt "worse than Golgatha" for the child), and finally the poet Ennes, under whose tutelage the early poetry and translations were completed.

[19] Bellman refers here obliquely to the bacchanalian songs. He addresses his thoughts to his friend, Doctor Blad, who knew Fredman's Epistles well.

[20] See Massengale 2014, passim, and Ingemar Carlsson's introduction, 9-21, in which the connection between Bellman and Dalin is discussed.

[21] Bennich-Björkman 1970, 15-91.

[22] Agrelius 1655/1738. Axel Gauffin suggests the use of a newer edition, published by Salvius in 1754. See Gauffin 1930, 37ff. Gauffin has also recorded the information regarding Bellman's study and the examination at the National Bank.

[23] The records do not show when Ennes left the Bellman family (Bellman 1947, 18f.), but he is known to have joined the Tessin household in September 1758.

[24] He apparently registered as a student on October 3, 1758, but was definitely back in Stockholm by mid-January 1759 (Björkman 1892, note on 56, and Gauffin 1930, 36).

[25] From *Fredmans sånger*, Bellman StU II, no: 28. In later years, "Movitz" was one of Bellman's jocular pseudonyms.

[26] "Daler kopparmynt" [dalers in copper coin], referred to in this article simply as "dalers," were only one of a number of currency designations at the time of this complicated economic period. My references are only for comparison, and fluctuations in value are not noted.

[27] Bellman 1947, sheet 3-4, cf. Bellman StU XII, 19f.

[28] Simonsson 1995, 34.

[29] Björkman 1892, 87. My use of "usurer" as a translation of "procentare" implies an illegality that I am not sure was actually true at that time. Simonsson speaks of the creditor Grim as being "of ill repute" for his high rates; but I have not seen record of his being prosecuted for them (Simonsson 1995, 42).

[30] Björkman 1892, 39f.

[31] So says Björkman 1892, 87: "The father requested that the directors allow his son to be released from service to the bank."

[32] Björkman 1892, 88.

[33] Simonsson 1995, 40, has emphasized this aspect as well: "Carl Michael's life style was probably a source of confrontation with his father, who had paid not only for a good education, but also for publications, to help his son into a career of civil service. And it is likely that Lawman Bellman was forced as well to borrow on his equity in the "little Daurer house," in order to hold the most importunate of his son's creditors away."

[34] Byström 1944; the young count, Carl Bonde, has left us a characteristic eyewitness account from 1762.

[35] From Gunnar Hillbom's *Register*, Bellman StU XX. Dating is extremely difficult in some cases, as Hillbom notes (164ff.). The drinking songs in particular were often written some time before their first appearance in a dated manuscript (the *terminus ante quem* procedure used in the *Register*).

[36] Björkman 1892, 32.

[37] Censorship was lifted, however, in 1766. But a consistory in Lund reacted to one of his early bacchanalian songs, "Old Man Noah" (probably from an unauthorized broadside) in 1768 (see Bellman StU II, commentary on 153ff.); and both amateur and professional gatekeepers were a threat to his reputation (Weibull 1895). Public discussion of the

quality and moral standards of poetic works was common in 18th-century Swedish newsprint.

[38] Ekman 2004, 31-92. Ekman distinguishes between *laus* (praise), *luctus* (sorrow) and *consolatio* (condolence for the survivors). He also notes differences in the requirements for elegies regarding dead friends, family members and children.

[39] Johannesson 1972, 102f. Cf. Sven Baelter 1762, cited by Johannesson.

[40] Bellman StU VIII, nos: 3, 4, 5, 6 and 11; see Ekman 2004, especially 36-92 and 135-9. A number of early songs are included in StU VIII as "occasional poetry" (see for example nos: 7, 8, 9 and 10). They are bacchanalian pieces, however, not eulogies.

[41] The nobleman died on 22 April 1760, and Bellman's first elegy appeared as an undated freestanding publication (Stockholm: Nyström & Stolpe, n.d. [1760]).

[42] Separate publication (Stockholm: Nyström & Stolpe, n.d. [1763]).

[43] Separate publication (Stockholm: Hesselberg, 1763). See Ekman 2004, 55.

[44] Separate publication (Stockholm: Nyström & Stolpe: n.d. [1764]). See Ekman 2004, 47f.

[45] Separate publication (Stockholm: Kongl. Tryckeriet, n.d. [1765]). Two later printings (with some additional material) were made in Hwad Nytt? Hwad Nytt? (Göteborg: 5 and 29 July, 1777).

[46] Wårdinge parish Church Records: Provincial Record Office, Uppsala.

[47] Ekman 2004, 136-142.

[48] Olof Byström has clearly reacted to the omission as well: "No portrait of the father has he given us in the autobiographical sketch, and no poem to his father has been preserved, not even in that so commonly occurring elegy at graveside." See Bellman StU VIII, Commentary, p. 12.

[49] Björkman 1892, 90.

[50] Stålmarck 2000, 46: "If you look closely at the many poems Carl Michael addressed to Inga Lissander, you find that it is often a mother's care which he praises in her, rather than the attraction of a beloved woman."

[51] Only two volumes of the set have been recovered: KB Vs 104b:I and Vs 104b:III. From Lissander's careful numbering system, the following is known: vol. 1 contains 204 songs, 107 by Bellman; the lost vol. 2 had 314 songs (the number by Bellman is unknown); vol. 3 has 140 songs, 88 by Bellman; the lost vol. 4 cannot be quantified. See Hillbom 1991, 8ff.

[52] The idea, however, that "Saint" Fredman, like St. Paul, addresses his epistles to a congregation, was largely laid aside after the first twenty-five poems.

[53] The technical term is "separationsvakt" [separation police]; they were charged with finding "loose women" in taverns and taking them to a prison for periods of six months or more, where they became a source of cheap labor, spinning wool for clothing manufacturers (Bellman StU I, commentary on CXXVIIIf.)

[54] Jean Fredman (1712/13-1767), Royal Watchmaker in 1745, had become a helpless alcoholic by the end of his life. In Bellman's songs, known people like Fredman were placed into situations – both quasi-realistic and mythologized – that were the products of the poet's imagination (Bellman StU I, commentary on XVf.)

Minor Characters: Fathers in Hans Christian Andersen's Novels

Karin Sanders

In his book *Questioning the Father* published in 1999, Ross Shideler argues that the patriarchal father figure suffered a radical loss of power during the so-called Modern Breakthrough in Scandinavia. Shideler demonstrates how the "questioning" of the name of the father implicitly shifted the balance in bourgeois family structures and that this shift in turn became ascertainable in literary form. In Émile Zola, as Shideler shows, the result is human depravation, family tragedy, and murder; in I.P. Jacobsen, social downfall matched with (masochistic) sexual gratification; in Henrik Ibsen, rebelliousness coupled with confining patriarchal legacies; in August Strindberg, menacing gender anxieties and battles; in Thomas Hardy, death and self-denial. The questioning of the "father name," he concludes, did not create a straightforward or uncomplicated foundation for new gender roles, far from it. But the family and gender conflicts that resonated from the paradigm shift bore fruit, nevertheless, in the form of brilliant, if somber, authorships.

But what of fathers in the works preceding the generation discussed in Shideler's monograph? What kind of crisis of authority and identity can we find here? The conventional assumption in Scandinavian literature is that this is the time of "Faderhuset" [House of the Father] as *Nordisk kvindelitteraturhistorie* [The History of Nordic Women's Literature] aptly named its second volume; and that the mid-nineteenth century struggled through various phases in which "æstetiske udtryk" [aesthetic expression] in an age of "den patriarkalske selvforståelse" [patriarchal self-perception] had to reconcile with the idea of "jeg'ets ret til fuld udfoldelse" [the individual's right to full self-realization].[1] We can find a cohort of burdened authors during this period wrestling with prescribed authorities embodied in fathers.

Yet in the novels of one of Denmark's foremost nineteenth century authors, Hans Christian Andersen (1805-75), fathers serve but as minor characters, if at all. In his novels, six in all, fathers are often missing entirely. In *Improvisatoren* [*The Improvisatore*] from 1835, Andersen's first novel, the main protagonist's father is never mentioned. In his last, *Lykke-Peer* [*Lucky-Peer*] from 1870, the main character becomes fatherless on page two. In his second novel *O.T.* [*O.T.*] from 1836, Otto, the main character, never knows his father, a weak and spineless son of power and wealth, who seduces and impregnates a servant girl. He (the father) then persuades her to take the blame for a theft that he has committed and leaves her to die in childbirth in a penitentiary, whose name Odense Tugthus [Odense Prison] is tattooed by initials on the shoulder of the son, ironically mimicking his proper name Otto Thulstrup. The trauma of the prison heritage is formative for young Otto, yet the deed of the father remains curiously unimportant, partly because Otto remains unaware of his paternal heritage until the very end of the novel. Instead, the scar from the prison tattoo is linked to his mother's presumed shame. It is this shame, rather than the father's absence, that is formative for Otto. In his fifth novel with the Shakespearean title *"At være eller ikke være"* [*"To Be or Not to Be"*] from 1857, the already motherless protagonist Niels Bryde loses his father, again just a couple of pages into the novel, in a swift and almost comical way, when, after the narrator's extended deliberations on the nature of serendipity and choice (in this case whether to turn left or right when exiting a house) the father turns left only to have a window fall out of a servant's hand from the third floor, onto his head, killing him. Thus Niels's father is erased not only from the novel but also from any real impact on his son's further life story. Had he turned to the right, we are left to imagine, this Andersen novel might have had a father!

Nonexistent or missing fathers often yield great power by their very absence. Yet this is not the case in Andersen's novels, neither on the level of plot nor as a factor in character formations. Instead we find a curious absence of this absence. His novel characters hardly ever seem to absorb or wrestle with patriarchal laws; rather, they are repeatedly constructed with ambiguous and eccentric characteristics, often the victims of patriarchal circumstance, yet unable or unwilling to completely internalize the patriarchal laws—remaining strangely unaffected and unaware of the forces of paternal agency. This may explain why the internal turmoil of Andersen's characters was often seen by his contemporary Danish critics as a result of weakness and softness, not as a way to question, challenge, or arm-wrestle with authoritarian and dogmatic fathers.

Most famously, Søren Kierkegaard (1813-55) produced a caustic and patronizing review of Andersen's third novel *Kun en Spillemand* [*Only a Fiddler*] from 1837, in his *Af en Endnu Levendes Papirer* [*From the Papers of One Still Living*] published a year later in 1838. In a chapter called "Andersen som Romandigter" ["Andersen as a Novelist"], Kierkegaard argues that a novelist must be an omnipotent creator in charge of his characters: He notes:

> ... den egentlig talentfulde Roman-Digter formaaer det, midt i Fortællingens Løb ved en eneste oblique Yttring ligesom at erindre Læseren saa stærk om en eller anden Person i Romanen, at denne nu pludselig staaer paany lyslevende for ham og maaskee tydeligere end nogensinde før, kort sagt, af et eneste Ribbeen at skabe os hele Individet, kan Andersen ikke sikkre sig for ...

> [The really talented novelist is able by one single oblique remark in the course of the narrative to remind the reader, as it were, so strongly of some character in the novel that he now suddenly appears once again as large as life before him and perhaps more clearly than at any time before—in

short, from a single rib he is able to create the
whole individual for us. Andersen is far from
doing this].[2]

Andersen, Kierkegaard suggests, is unable to craft his characters
with authority because he folds himself into his characters (in this
case the protagonist Christian) and renders them characterless,
anemic and pathetic like the author himself. The novel presents
Christian as a misunderstood genius, but as Kierkegaard famously
notes in a parenthesis, "(...Geniet er ikke en Praas, der gaaer ud for
en Vind, men en Ildebrand, som Stormen blot udæsker)" [(...
genius is not a rush candle that goes out in a puff of air but a
conflagration that the storm only incites)].[3] Andersen consequently
"taber sin poetiske Ligevægt, og herved sine poetiske Figurer" [loses
his poetic balance and thereby drops his poetic character][4] for as
Kierkegaard concludes "Noget af det, der mest pleier at udmærke
Geniet og give det sin Overvægt over Verden, er Stolthed, som
pleier at blive stærkere i Modgang, som derfor ogsaa formaer at
holde Individet opreist. Hos Christian er derimod Alt
Forfængelighed." [One of the things that usually characterize the
genius and give him his ascendancy over the world is pride, which
usually becomes stronger in adversity and is therefore also often
able to hold the individual's head erect. With Christian, however, all
is vanity].[5] Kierkegaard rightly notes that Andersen produces a
substitute father for Christian in the form of a rather uncanny
Norwegian Godfather (Andersen describes him as a musical genius,
reminiscent of both Paganini and Ole Bull), only to insert a scene
with the Godfather in which Christen falls into delirium and cramps
after finding himself inside a church bell. This tragic-comical scene
suggests to Kierkegaard that Andersen's lack of understanding of
(in this case musical) genius ultimately makes his protagonist into a
"sølle Skrog" [poor wretch], Andersen's own expression here
repeated ironically by Kierkegaard.[6]

If the novels did not produce fathers as major characters,
Andersen's own life, as explained in his autobiographies, letters, and
diaries, demonstrated a very conscious and strategic adoption of a

Father, namely Jonas Collin (1776-1861), one of the most influential figures of the Danish Golden Age. Andersen's own father had died in Odense after an aborted attempt at a glorious career as a soldier in the Napoleonic war. In Collin, Andersen, whose arrival in Copenhagen as a fatherless boy has been parsed extensively by scholarship, found a new cultural Father that could guide and center the oftentimes lost 'son.' Kierkegaard, Andersen's fierce critic, had deeper issues with fathers (ranging from the heavenly to his own biological father) and wrote extensively on the psychological, existential and religious impacts of fathers on sons.

To Kierkegaard, it is essential for an author to practice deception in order to produce credible novel characters. That is, an author must annihilate himself in order to deceive: a stratagem necessary for a literary work to be "on its own." Kierkegaard, we should recall, performs precisely this annihilation of self in his pseudonymous authorship, producing what he saw as a necessary formal and aesthetic distance between author and character. This strategy of deception is tied not only to Kierkegaard's understanding of novel characters, but also implicitly to his frequently fraught struggle with patriarchal concepts. To become a novelist of format, Kierkegaard implies, you must know the kind of anxiety that Abraham installs in Isaac; one in which you are familiar with the possibility that a father might or indeed must sacrifice his son to obey and please a higher law.

This incorporation of a different kind of anxiety than the one Andersen so often expressed (his was an anxiety of self-absorption) is necessary to install a "Livs-Anskuelse" [world view], Kierkegaard's term for that which he claimed Andersen lacked as a novelist.[7] Without a "world view," without comprehending that "Livet forstaaes baglæns gjennem Ideen" [life is understood backward through the idea][8], firm character contours disintegrate into soft sentimentalism. Or, in the words of Kierkegaard, we find a case of "lyrisk Selvfortabelse," [lyrical self-loss][9] if the author is unable to move forward to the "epical," that is, to a serious acceptance of, or engagement with, a given reality, where empirical (life) experiences are understood vis-à-vis higher powers (God).[10]

In his critique, Kierkegaard reduces Andersen both as a novelist and as a man, proposing that he is engaged in self-pollination like an androgynous flower. To Kierkegaard, what Andersen has not realized in life, he cannot realize in art (Kierkegaard took the consequence of this position in his own life, most famously in his broken engagement with Regina Olsen). His point is that, as a novelist, Andersen cannot depict a real character, since both he and his characters can be counted amongst the many fragmented and split personalities produced during the period of the nineteenth century that Kierkegaard's calls the "political time." Here the subject is irresponsibly freed of responsibility, Kierkegaard complains, and thus acquires a kind of perpetual care-freeness, which compromises and endangers any kind of authentic position on life. Without this authentic position in life, Andersen's novel character in *Only a Fiddler* stands in "endeligt og tilfældigt Forhold til Forfatterens Kjød og Blod" [finite and incidental contact with the author's flesh and blood].[11] In short, to Kierkegaard, Andersen becomes his own novel character and vise versa, and not a very good character at that. It is uncertain whether Andersen waited more than a decade to publish his next novel, in 1848, *De To Baronesser* [*The Two Baronesses*], because of Kierkegaard's devastating critique. Andersen, was after all, busy writing fairytales.[12]

Unlike the other five Andersen novels, The Two Baronesses offers a more direct engagement with fathers and patriarchal structures. But here the protagonist is no longer male. In fact, as the title suggests, we find two female protagonists, an old and a young baroness. The novel tells of the brutal torture by a feudal lord, the baron, of one of his serfs. The baron's son later marries the daughter of the brutalized serf, and she becomes the first of our new baronesses. The second of the two baronesses, an abandoned daughter of a decrepit traveling musician, marries her grandson. He in turn is conceived by rape and therefore originally rejected by our baroness after her daughter dies in childbirth. The novel's many

twists and turns clearly mimic Walter Scott's novels. But what is
important here is the way in which Andersen, by way of a female
protagonist, offers a far more radical 'questioning' of the father than
we find in his other novels.

Andersen's eye for the poetic value of material objects, as we
know it from his fairy tales, is unmistakable. At the end of the
novel, we learn that a wooden spoon in a small box hides the
painful 'secret' from the old baroness's past, her witnessing of her
father's humiliation. Cut out from the wooden horse [Træhesten]
on which her father had been tormented, the object has been
transformed from what it was (an instrument of torture) to
something quite different (an eating utensil). The transmutation is
ironic, even slightly comical; the eccentric baroness calls it
"Blomsten paa mit Stamtræ" [the flower of my pedigree], an ironic
mnemonics for coming generations.[13] More importantly, it is a
testament to the trauma of past patriarchal practices; the spoon
becomes a material witness to and a memento from a time in
history that—Andersen implies—needs to be retold and ultimately
reimagined. Hidden in the baroness' box but also concealed in the
text, and not unlocked and revealed until the last pages, the mute
utensil finally emerges as a rather eloquent if gloomy bridal gift to a
new generation whose task it is to remember, with every spoonful,
the story of historical and moral changes and the transformation of
power that is lodged so deeply and so inextricably in the modest
matter from which the spoon originates. The change from a brutal
patriarch to an eccentric matriarch is a change from the perversity
of blood nobility (the baron who tortured the female protagonist's
father on the wooden horse) to a new kind of nobility that is
allowed the excesses of an unconventional imagination that quite
manifestly cuts the emblem of patriarchal law into a spoon.

Kierkegaard did not review *The Two Baronesses*, but his nemesis
from the so-called Corsair affair (1845), Meir Goldschmidt (1819-
87), did, and in spite of the differences between Kierkegaard and
Goldschmidt, they agreed on the shortcomings of Andersen as a
novelist. Goldschmidt, himself a renowned novelist and author of

some of the best prose narratives in nineteenth century Danish literature, criticized Andersen's ability as a novelist while praising his genius for storytelling. In his fairy tales Andersen produces what Goldschmidt calls a kind of electricity that draws fortune ["Lykke"], like an Aladdin, and therefore

> ... behøver [han] blot at røre ved en Muur, ved en Gulerod, en Strikkepind, saa springer der en Aand ud. Han finder Poesien der, hvor Andre netop vogte sig for at søge den, i Gjenstande, som man anseer for uskjønne, i Kjelderen, hvor Grantræet ligger mellem Rotter og Muus, i Skarnbøtten, hvor Tjenestepigen har kastet et Par gamle Flipper o.s.v.

> [...he needs only to touch a wall, a carrot, a knitting needle, and a spirit springs forth. He finds poetry where others are loath to search, in objects considered horrid, in the basement, where the pine tree lies amongst rats and mice, in the trash bin where the maid has cast off a pair of old collars and so on].[14]

But the very qualities produced by Andersen's childlike Aladdin nature, the nervous electricity that makes things come alive, is a detriment to a novelist because a novelist must calmly reflect and produce an organic whole that follow what Goldschmidt calls "indre Nødvendighed" [inner necessity].[15] He asks: is Andersen's description of an eccentric old baroness's bequest of a wooden spoon to the next generation an organic inner necessity of the novel? Or is it in fact the novel itself and not just its protagonist that has turned eccentric? The goblin ["Nisse"] from his fairy tales has, Goldschmidt suggests, moved with the author into the novel so much so that Andersen in a ball scene in The Two Baronesses allows an ordinary button ["Knap"] to rule. In this case an overeager suitor, ready to propose to a young lady, loses a button on his suspenders and, so as not to drop his pants, must abort his proposal. The woman consequently accepts the proposal from another. This scene is narrated, Goldsmith notes, "i en Tone, der lader formode, at det egentlig var Knappen, som skulde fortælle ... Historien" [in a tone that allows us to presume that it was in fact the button that should have told ... the story].[16]

Andersen violates, Goldschmidt demonstrates, the formal requirement of the novel by pushing the boundaries between genres, not only to the fairy tale, but also to biography, autobiography and travel description. While Goldschmidt grants that Andersen has an eye like a daguerreotype for details, he includes too much nonsense ["Pjat"] and frivolous details in his novels.[17] Like Kierkegaard, then, Goldschmidt concludes that Andersen succumbs to a kind of electrical fever that might have power in real life but cannot have so in a novel without compromising the ramifications of the aesthetic.

For Goldschmidt, Andersen's lack of control over his material turns particularly problematic when he takes on larger questions of existence, as he does in his fifth novel "To Be or Not to Be," such as religion and faith vis-à-vis materialism and atheism. Here Andersen attempts to fold the question of immortality into his main characters. But, as Goldschmidt argues, in doing so he trespasses on the territory of the bible and thus implicitly suggests that if Christ had been a man, the bible would have been a novel. Since the novel's prime mission is to expose the workings of the human interior, not the divine human soul ["Menneskesjælen"] and its various inflections of passion, struggles, knowledge, fears and doubts, a novel's main protagonist must, Goldschmidt insists, embody a synthesis of aesthetic and ethical ideals. If, as is the case in *"To Be or Not to Be,"* the main character, the very naïve Niels Bryde, has "ingen Anfægtelser" [no doubt/scruples], no reservations or suspicions about the dangers of the human condition, he fails as a novel character. The postulated innocence and gullibility of Niels Bryde thus creates a shallow character. Or in Goldsmith's words:

Hvorfor bliver han i Grunden et lige skikkeligt Menneske, enten han troer eller ikke troer? - Fordi han er af Træ, intet virkeligt Menneske, intet Paradigma, hvorefter vi andre declineres eller conjungeres. Man har kaldt Niels Bryde 'en Pjalt'; men det synes os urigtigt; thi han er hverken svag eller feig; han er heller ikke stor og betydelig, men kold, træet, en Dukke ...

[How come he is in fact the same, an inoffensive human being, whether he believes or does not believe? Because he is made of wood, not a real human being, he is no paradigm according to which the rest of us can be modified and conjugated. Niels has been called a fool but that seems incorrect; for he is neither weak nor cowardly; he is neither grand nor significant, but cold, wooden, a doll ...].[18]

As we can see, the attacks on Andersen as a novelist resonate with terminologies that in Kierkegaard's case can be said to emasculate the author and in Goldschmidt's, infantilize him. His experiment with the novel genre, unlike his fairy tales, lacks, both Kierkegaard and Goldschmidt seem to agree, spine and format. The mutability of style, the lack of a central voice, they also seem to suggest (if not articulate), demonstrates the need to test a novel character against a firm antagonist. Such a firm antagonist during the age of "patriarchal self-perception" is, it goes without saying, often the father. When fathers are missing, the critics seem to infer, when the main characters do not have fathers to fight, they cannot become 'men,' that is to say believable characters. Instead they become, in the words of Kierkegaard and Goldschmidt, fools and weaklings. If we follow this logic, the only strong character in Andersen's novels is an eccentric woman (the old baroness).

If we return to his last novel, *Lucky-Peer*, published thirteen years after "*To Be or Not to Be*," we find a very different kind of novel character. In some sense Peer is not a novel character at all, but a peculiar myth-of-the-artist, fairytale-like figure, whose trials and tribulations are laid out like that of Aladdin's. Even Peer's death is mythical. He dies on stage after his piece de résistance, an opera piece on Aladdin, has concluded: "'Død!' gjenlød det. Død i Seiersglæden, som Sophokles ved de olympiske Lege, som Thorvaldsen i Theateret, under Beethowens Symphoni. En Aare i Hjertet var bristet, og som ved et Lynslag var endt hans Dage her, endt uden Smerte, endt i jordisk Jubel, i Kaldet af sin jordiske Mission." ['Dead!' it resounded. Dead at the moment of triumphant joy, like Sophocles at the Olympian games, like Thorvaldsen in the theater during Beethoven's symphony. An artery in his heart had burst, and as by a flash of lightning his days here were ended, ended without pain, ended in earthly elation, in fulfillment of his mission on earth].[19] Peer's fortune and his 'fortunate' death is obtained in spite of the social circumstances that he was born into; placing him amongst a pantheon of substitute cultural fathers like Sophocles and Bertel Thorvaldsen (1789-1838), the Danish neoclassical sculptor whom Andersen regarded as a cultural kin. Thorvaldsen's public death in the Royal Theater preoccupied Andersen immensely and in Peer's death scene he translated his anxiety into a triumphant finale where the moment of artistic accomplishment is cemented by a glorious death that guarantees that the artist is mythologized. By foregrounding mythological fathers (Sophocles and Thorvaldsen) and by using fairy tale structures in this final novel, Andersen deliberately seems to push the boundaries of genre that Kierkegaard and Goldschmidt wanted him to uphold and respect. But to him, ultimately, they did not have the authority and power to set the aesthetic agenda.

In conclusion, and returning to Ross Shideler's argument that the patriarchal father figure suffered a radical loss of power during the so-called Modern Breakthrough in Scandinavia, we can, as I hope to have shown, find an anachronistic instantiation of such a loss of power in the generation before, in Andersen's novels. This is not to argue or even suggest that Andersen's novels point toward the kind of "questioning" that Shideler had in mind, but rather to propose that Andersen offers a different inflection altogether, of fathers left out of the equation in a genre that still in the nineteenth century would focus a great deal of attention on negotiating this kind of authority.

Notes

[1] Møller Jensen, "Om bogværket," and "About the Print Work," accessed April 4, 2014.

[2] Kierkegaard, "Andersen som Romandigter," 45; "Andersen as a Novelist," 90.

[3] Kierkegaard, "Andersen som Romandigter," 43; "Andersen as a Novelist," 88.

[4] Kierkegaard, "Andersen som Romandigter," 45; "Andersen as a Novelist," 90.

[5] Kierkegaard, "Andersen som Romandigter," 54; "Andersen as a Novelist," 99.

[6] Kierkegaard, "Andersen som Romandigter," 54; "Andersen as a Novelist," 99.

[7] Kierkegaard, "Andersen som Romandigter," 32; "Andersen as a Novelist," 76.

[8] Kierkegaard, "Andersen som Romandigter," 33; "Andersen as a Novelist," 78.

[9] Kierkegaard, "Andersen som Romandigter," 26; "Andersen as a Novelist," 71.

[10] While Kierkegaard sees this weakness in *Only a Fiddler*'s Christian, he also notices how Otto in the novel *O.T.* is unable to embody a unifying

idea because he carries a "Pukkel" [hump] on his back, presumably referring to his scar/tattoo. "Andersen som Romandigter," 33; "Andersen as a Novelist," 78.

11 Kierkegaard, "Andersen som Romandigter," 36-37, "Andersen as a Novelist," 81.

12 Andersen's reaction came in the form of a dramatic satire called *Comedie det Grønne* [*A Comedy in the Open Air*] (1840) in which Kierkegaard is staged as a hairdresser that speaks nonsense, regurgitating too much Hegelianism. The same year as Kierkegaard's death, Andersen notes in his autobiography that Kierkegaard's Hegelian heaviness made his attack on Andersen difficult to read. See also Sanders, "Anxious Authors," 48.

13 Andersen, *De to Baronesser*, 524, my translation.

14 Goldschmidt, "Anmeldelse af De To Baronesser," accessed April 2, 2014. My translation.

15 Ibid.

16 Ibid.

17 Ibid.

18 Goldschmidt, "Anmeldelse af At være eller ikke være," accessed April 2, 2014. My translation.

19 Andersen, *Lykke-Peer*, 346-347. My translation.

Murdering the Father:
Hjalmar Söderberg's *Doktor Glas*

Susan C. Brantly

In his book, *Questioning the Father*, Ross Shideler tells us that he is interested in "the correlation between Darwin's displacement of God and the undermining of male authority figures in nineteenth-century literature" (1999, 13). Another part of the narrative enacted within nineteenth-century literature involves the impact that Darwin seems to have had in bringing attention to human sexuality, specifically female sexuality, which also undermined the status quo that had existed when God was in his heaven, Man was the head of the household, and Woman a decorative ornament to the parlor. Hjalmar Söderberg's novel, *Doktor Glas* (1905), enacts these tensions and conflicts in particularly intriguing ways. Söderberg called his novel a *tankebok* (a book of thoughts), and apparently wanted to write about the intellectual trends of his era, but in the form of a novel posing as the diary of a Doctor Tyko Gabriel Glas. Back in 1936, Ebbe Linde saw Dr. Glas's murder of Pastor Gregorius as a symbolic murder of religion itself (1978, 256). Along these lines, albeit more than seventy years later, Theresa Jamieson goes so far as to suggest "the death of the Rev. Gregorius at the hands of Dr. Glas can be seen as an allegory of the triumph of science over religion, which came to mark the twentieth century" (2009, 229).[1] Such an allegorical reading of Doktor Glas seems entirely worthwhile, and religion is an obvious loser, but one may question whether science does indeed emerge triumphant in the novel.

Helga Gregorius, and her sexuality, have been strongly impacted by the shifting ideas of her times. Helga, who is married to Pastor Gregorius, a man nearly twice her age, is a victim of the control that the religious world view claimed over women's bodies. She was raised in a religious household, and when a man, to whom she was attracted, tried to seduce her, she responded as she had been trained to: with terror and revulsion. Instead she rebounded into the marriage with Gregorius because he was a minister and she hoped "min längtan [skulle] slockna och mina begär dö bort" (1967, 32) ["my longing would vanish and my desire die away" (1998, 20)]. Gregorius turns out not to be as asexual as she had hoped, and instead, the marriage kills her faith.

Helga's thwarted desires eventually lead her into an extramarital affair with Klas Recke. She turns to science, in the form of Dr. Glas, for intervention. Pastor Gregorius insists upon his marital "rights," granted to him by God and their marriage vows. Helga cannot stand to be touched by her husband and asks Glas to help by giving her a gynecological diagnosis that might discourage Gregorius from claiming these so-called rights. Medical science becomes a weapon used to fend off the patriarchal "rights" guaranteed by the Church. Helga tells Dr. Glas that she dared to consult him on this matter because of a conversation she overheard between the pastor and the doctor, in which Dr. Glas argued that prostitutes were human beings and should be treated accordingly. Such a position, of course, is one of the major arguments of Modern Breakthrough writers. Christian Krohg, for example, argues in his novel *Albertine* (1886) that prostitutes are the victims of social circumstances, not innately depraved and sinful creatures as Gregorius' Lutheranism might suggest. Dr. Glas chooses to do as Helga asks and warns Pastor Gregorius that his wife's health is at risk, so he should leave her in peace, but this works for only a limited time. Gregorius rapes his wife one night:

> Han talade om att hans salighet stod på spel, han visste inte vilka svåra synder han kunde komma att begå, om hon inte gjorde honom till viljes. Det var hennes plikt att göra det, och plikten gick före hälsan. (1967, 28)

[He claimed his eternal soul was at stake---he didn't know what terrible sins he might commit if she didn't do his bidding. It was her duty, and duty came before health.] (1998, 18)

This rape only increases Dr. Glas's already strong dislike of Pastor Gregorius and, in addition, tends to set the reader's sympathy strongly against Gregorius as well.

Hjalmar Söderberg's own antipathy towards the Church is well known. The authority of the religious world view embodied by Pastor Gregorius is more than merely undermined in this novel: It is exposed as a hollow narrative meant to exert control over others. As Helga says, "[H]an har vant sig att begagna Gud till allt möjligt, som det bäst passar sig för honom. Det göra de alltid, jag jänner ju så många präster. Jag hatar dem" (1967, 28) ["(H)e's grown accustomed to using God for whatever suits his purposes. They always do—I know so many ministers. I hate them" (1998, 18)]. Helga's story is in some ways a cautionary tale about the power of narratives. She also says that when she was looking for answers about religion, she read lots of books both for and against: "Det finns människor som skriver så utmärkt väl, och jag tror att de kan bevisa vad som helst. Jag tyckte alltid att den hade rätt som skrev bäst och vackrast" (1967, 94) [There are people who can write so well that I think they can prove whatever they want. I always thought the one who wrote best and most beautifully was right" (1998, 67)]. Over time, Helga loses her faith and comes to see herself in a more Darwinian light: "Jag har lärt mig känna och förstå, att min kropp är jag. Det finns ingen glädje och ingen sorg och inte något liv alls annat än genom den. Och min kropp vet ju att den måste dö. Den känner det, liksom ett djur kan känna det" (1967, 94) ["I've come to the realization that my body is me. There is no joy and no sorrow, no life at all except through it. And my body knows it has to die. It can sense this, just as an animal can" (1998, 67)]. The master narrative of religion has given way to the master narrative of science. But even if one narrative has been replaced by another for Helga, it remains to be seen whether this more scientific view of life will sustain her.

Dr. Glas eventually murders Pastor Gregorius with a pill of potassium cyanide dropped in a glass of mineral water at a public café. He thinks he is murdering Gregorius in order to rescue Helga from her untenable situation and pave the way for her relationship with Klas Recke. Leading up to this act, Glas debates the ethics of such a deed with himself and talks himself into the rightness of his actions by appealing to a medical metaphor: "Din plikt som läkare är att hjälpa den som kan och bör hjälpas, och att skära bort det ruttna köttet som fördärvar det friska" (1967, 78) [Your duty as a doctor is to help the one who can and should be helped by cutting away the rotten flesh that infects the healthy tissue (1998, 55)]. This certainly seems to support the allegorical reading of science's triumph over religion: Religion, in the form of Pastor Gregorius, is more or less surgically removed. Even so, Dr. Glas's interest in both Helga Gregorius and her husband is not that of the disinterested scientist, even if he tries to convince himself this is the case. Glas's strong and complicated investment in this relationship can be illuminated using the tools provided by Dr. Glas's medical contemporary, Sigmund Freud.

In a newspaper article from 1936, Ebbe Linde seems to have been the first to have invoked Freud's name in conjunction with Doktor Glas, although it is apparently Hjalmar Söderberg who is put on the couch (1978, 252-63). In 1975, Tom Geddes suggested that the fictional Dr. Glas might suffer from an Oedipus complex (16-7). Lars O. Lundgren notes in 1987 that, although the famous psychoanalyst himself is never mentioned, Freud's ideas resonate throughout the novel. The following year, Egil Törnqvist produced an article which performed a detailed Freudian analysis of the character, Dr. Glas (1988). Whatever one's feelings about Freud, the fact remains that a Freudian analysis of the novel reveals a great deal. One can imagine, perhaps, how a session might go between the fictional character Dr. Glas and the original Freudian analyst.

What if, for example, Sigmund Freud were called in as a forensic psychologist to assess our character's involvement in the purported murder of Pastor Gregorius? Dr. Glas's diary would have been found and introduced as evidence. Dr. Glas is such a classic case, Dr. Freud might even want to analyze him in front of colleagues and medical students for their edification. The session might go like this (best, if imagined with a German accent):[2]

> FREUD: Welcome Dr. Glas. Thank you for agreeing to participate in this little demonstration. The police have supplied me with this diary that they found among your papers and I have found it very instructive.
>
> So, Dr. Glas, could you please tell me about your childhood...
>
> Yes, yes -- your Will. You seem to be very proud of this will of yours. You say as a child, you possessed much self control. You could suppress transient desires and focus your energies on your studies, where you excelled.
>
> (To the audience) Clearly a very repressed personality. His sexual energies were suppressed and through the process of sublimation, these energies manifested themselves in good grades. This repression is very dangerous, and might even express itself in an act of murder.
>
> (To Glas) And how did your parents feel about your achievements? Aha, they were very proud. What about your brothers and sisters? You had a brother, Ernst. You say your mother always liked him best. Where is he now? In Australia and no one knows whether he is dead or alive.

(To the audience) A case of sibling rivalry, I suspect. Glas became an overachiever in order to gain the attention and approval of his parents.

(To Glas) Now, what about your parents? I see. You were very fond of your mother... The two of you used to take walks together, and your father never came along, so you could have her all to yourself. -- You still like taking walks, don't you?

I see your mother's name was Marie. Did it ever strike you that this is also the name of the Madonna, the holy mother who gave birth through immaculate conception. I see...you have often thought of her this way.

What about your father? Ahem....you never liked your father. He beat you. I read in your diary that you felt a strong physical repulsion for your father, is that correct? You could not bear swimming with him, since it meant coming into contact with his naked body. And how do you feel about your mother and father's sexual relationship? Now Dr. Glas...calm yourself...do not get so upset!

(To the audience) Clearly, Dr. Glas suffers from an Oedipus complex. Oedipus, as you know, was a character in a Greek drama, who killed his father and married his mother. A very common desire. It is apparent that Glas worshipped his mother and relished the moments when he could get her away from his father. Honored colleagues, if you will look on page 88 of Dr. Glas's diary, you will see that he even compares himself to Oedipus.

(To Dr. Glas) What about any sexual experiences in your youth?

Yes, you've written here that you've never been near a woman, but what about this erotic encounter on midsummer's eve? You kissed the young lady and three days later, she was found drowned. How did you feel about this? You had nightmares about it. Did you feel as though you had been punished for this erotic advance? And ever since then, you have been attracted to women who are unattainable—women who were in love with other men—like your mother, for example. Now don't get upset, Dr. Glas!

Where is your mother now? She is dead. She died when you were 15 years old. She died too soon, rather like the young lady from midsummer's eve…

(To the audience) Glas most probably feels responsible for his mother's death. His erotic interest in a young lady, was followed by her early death. Glas's incestuous desire for his mother was also followed by her early death. A pattern has developed: sexual desire is punished by death. This is perhaps just another form of castration anxiety. Note that after his mother's death, Glas no longer hated his father. Once the object of desire, the mother, is gone, this particular Oedipus complex collapses: no need to fear punishment from the father or dislike him as a rival.

(To Dr. Glas) Now Dr. Glas, I want you to tell me how you felt about Pastor Gregorius.

You've hated him since you were a child, and
watched him from your family pew beside your
late lamented mother. You find him physically
repulsive. Would you say that he reminds you of
your father, whom you also found to be
physically repulsive? The strict church father and
your own father?

And what about Helga Gregorius, the pastor's
wife?

You find her attractive don't you? She is in love
with someone else, and so forbidden to you.

How do you feel about her marriage to Pastor
Gregorius? Abominable. Unnatural. Gregorius is
old enough to be her father. So, you feel there is
something incestuous about their marriage? You
felt you needed to protect Mrs. Gregorius from
her husband's unwanted attentions. Their sexual
relations upset you just as the knowledge that
your parents had sexual relations upset you.

(To the audience) The situation is quite clear. In
murdering Gregorius, Glas was acting out a
fantasy from childhood: A fantasy of murdering
his father, so that he could have unrestricted
access to his mother. Classic Oedipus complex.

(To Dr. Glas) Was ist das, Dr. Glas? Oh, you
object that you did not desire Helga Gregorius
for yourself?

Come, come now Dr. Glas. Just examine the
dream you recorded on page 31 of your diary.
You press a button on the wall and dispose of

Pastor Gregorius, just as one is to press a button to dispose of the rich mandarin you mention in the beginning of your diary. Mrs. Gregorius approaches you. She is completely naked and hands you a bunch of dark flowers. In dreams, flowers are obvious symbols of the female genitalia, so this symbolic gesture of handing you the flowers clearly represents sexual intercourse.

You yourself astutely observe on page 51 of your diary that dreams reveal wishes that you did not wish to wish, desires which you did not want to be conscious of. I myself have written a book about this. Obviously you desire sexual intercourse with Mrs. Gregorius, and you do away with Pastor Gregorius, who is the obstacle.

Conforming to your established pattern, however, you are immediately punished in the dream after this sexual contact. Klas Recke enters and declares you under arrest. A very revealing dream Dr. Glas.

Well, I see that our time is up. I think we have had a very productive session.

Despite Dr. Glas displaying a classic array of Oedipal symptoms, Hjalmar Söderberg explicitly denied any direct influences from Freud, since Freuds work was not really known in Sweden until much later. In 1940, when asked by Herbert Friedländer about the literary background of Doktor Glas, Hjalmar Söderberg responded:

Freud var 1905 knappast känd annat än möjligen i medicinska kretsar—annars skulle man naturligtvis sagt att jag var påverkad av honom. Just år 1905 gav han ut ett par av de böcker som

gjorde honom berömd. Jag anade på den tiden
inte hans existens. (Holmbäck 1988, 237)

[Freud was hardly known, except possibly in
medical circles—otherwise one would naturally
have said I was influenced by him. Just in 1905
he published a few books that made him famous.
At that time, I had no idea of his existence.]

This is simply a case of Zeitgeist. Glas and Freud would have been
in medical school at the same time.[3]

All things considered, it appears that Dr. Glas has murdered his
father in the form of Gregorius. This seems valid both in a
Freudian sense and in the allegorical sense that Dr. Glas has done
away with the symbolic representative of the Church. The real
trigger for Glas murdering Gregorius is the realization that Helga
Gregorius is pregnant, that Gregorius is about to become a false
father, displaying "hans äckliga fadersglädje" (1967, 96) ["his
disgusting paternal joy" (1998, 68)]. This cannot be allowed to
happen. The Church Father and his endorsement of the rules of
patriarchy are not just undermined, but handily dispatched.
However, in the Oedipal narrative, the son wishes to replace the
father. Although Dr. Glas might wish it, it does not seem as though
he is going to replace either Gregorius or Klas Recke as the object
of Helga's affections. Further, one might ask whether, from the
perspective of this novel, science can truly claim to have replaced
religion.

As a champion of science, Dr. Glas is somewhat
underwhelming. He confides to his diary that his patients die or get
well almost regardless of what he does for them. Medical science
appears to have an element of randomness about it, which is
actually the opposite of what science seeks to achieve: reproducible
results. On a number of occasions, Dr. Glas seems to be a lapsed
Romantic, for whom science has become a demoralizing substitute.
On these occasions Glas waxes quite poetic only to drag himself

back to a prosaic, scientifically sanctioned reality. For example, Dr. Glas sings the praises of love as a force that has driven us beyond a life as mere animals:

> Ur människornas längtan efter kärlek har ju hela den sidan av kulturen spirat upp, som icke direkt syftar till hungerns stillande eller försvar mot fiender. Vårt skönhetsinne har ingen annan källa. All konst, all dikt, all musik har druckit ur den. (1967, 11)

> [The longing for love has inspired all human culture that rises above the level of basic survival. Our sense of beauty has no other wellspring. All art, all literature, all music has drunk from it.] (1998, 4)

Then his mood shifts and Glas's medical training takes over: "Varför måste vårt släktes liv bevaras och vår längtan stillas just genom ett organ som vi flera gånger om dagen begagna till avloppsrör för orenlighet" (1967, 12) ["Why is our species preserved and our longing stilled by the same organ we use several times a day as a drain to remove impurities?" (1998, 6). Science has certainly taken the romance out of romance.

On another occasion, Glas momentarily swoons over the moon, another Romantic trope: "En blid och sentimental måne mellan björkar vid kanten av en sjö...Månen ilande genom dimmorna over havet...Månen på flykt genom rivna höstmoln...Kärleksmånen, som lyste på Gretchens trädgårdsfönster och Julias balkong..." (1967, 71) [A mild, sentimental moon between the birches at the side of a lake...The moon scuttling through broken autumn clouds...The moon of love that shone on Gretchen's garden window and Juliet's balcony...(1998, 49)]. But then science, this time in the form of astronomy, comes along to spoil the fun: "Och vad är månskenet? Solsken i andra hand. Försvagat, förfalskat" (1967, 71) [And what is moonlight?

Secondhand sunshine. Feeble, counterfeit (1998, 49)]. On another occasion, Dr. Glas begins his own hymn to the night: "Natten. Ett så vackert ord! Natten är äldre än dagen, sade de gamla gallerna. De trodde att den korta förgängliga dagen var född av den oändliga natten" (1967, 83) [Night. Such a lovely word. The night is older than the day, according to the ancient Gauls. They believed the short, transient day was born of the endless night" (1998, 58)]. This Romantic mood is once again spoiled by scientific knowledge:

> Vad är natten, vad är det som vi kalla natten? Det är den smala koniska skuggan av vår lilla planet. En liten spetsig kägla av mörker mitt i ett hav av ljus. Och detta ljushav, vad är det? En gnista i rymden. Den lilla ljuskretsen kring en liten stjärna: solen (1967, 83).

> [What is the night, that which we call the night? It's the narrow, conical shadow of our little planet. A small sliver of darkness in the midst of an ocean of light. And this ocean of light, what is that? A spark in space. The small circle of light around a small star: the sun.] (1998, 58)

The perspective of science renders everything insignificant. Humanity's realm is a little planet illuminated by a spark in space.

At one point, Glas reminisces about his reaction to Darwinism when he was but seventeen: "[J]ag satte mig på tvären mot darwinismen: med den tycktes mig allt bli meningslöst, dumt, tarvligt" (1967, 70) ["I refused to accept Darwinism: to me it made everything seem meaningless, stupid, insignificant" (1998, 49)]. He wants to argue against the classmate who seeks to persuade him: "Ty det som du säger kan inte, får inte på några villkor vara sant; då vill jag inte vara med längre, i en sådan värld har jag ingenting att skaffa" (1967, 70) [For what you're saying cannot, must not under any circumstances be true; if it is, then I don't want to be part of it any longer—I want nothing to do with such a world" (1998, 49)].

Glas loses the argument when it devolves into a physical scuffle—a Darwinian victory of the strongest: "Det gick ett år och det gick flera, men jag kände mig aldrig vuxen att överbevisa honom; jag fann, att jag måste låta den uppgiften ligga" (1967, 71) ["A year passed, and several more, but I never felt ready to disprove him; I found I had to let the matter drop" (1998, 49)]. If Dr. Glas is a Darwinist, he is so by default, just as he became a doctor because it was what he had been trained to do. He simply cannot come up with a better solution, but the result is that he holds the world to be meaningless.

Early in the novel, the historic rift between religion and science comes up in an almost comical way. Pastor Gregorius consults Dr. Glas about his heart, but before he gets to the point, he asks Dr. Glas's opinion regarding "Vad ska man göra för att förebygga smittoöverföring vid kommunionen?" (1967, 35) ["What can be done to prevent the spread of communicable disease when taking communion?" (1998, 23)] Gregorius himself, having read about it, suggests the possibility of taking communion in capsules. This is a splendid example of an age-old religious ritual being complicated by advances in medical science. The two are in conflict, and Gregorius is seeking a compromise. This elicits an epiphany on Dr. Glas's part:

> […] det stod med ens klart för mig, att han led av den sjukdom som kallas bacillskräck. Bacillerna stå tydligen i hans ögon på något mystiskt sätt utanför både religionen och den sedliga världsordningen. Det kommer sig av att de äro så nya. Hans religion är gammal, nära nitton hundra år, och den sedliga världsordningen daterar sig åtminstone från århundradets början, från den tyska filosofin och Napoleons fall. Men bacillerna ha kommit över honom på hans ålderdom, alldeles oförberett. (1967, 36)

[all of a sudden I realized he was suffering from a kind of phobia. In his eyes, germs in some mysterious way are impervious both to religion and to the moral order of the world. That's because they're so new. His religion is ancient, nearly nineteen hundred years old, and the moral order of the world can be dated back at least to the beginning of the century, to German philosophy and the fall of Napoleon. But germs have descended on him in his old age, completely without warning.] (1998, 24)

It is this point of vulnerability, the inability of Gregorius' faith to cope with the fears that modern medicine has inspired, that Glas exploits, first to get Gregorius to go to a watering hole for some time so he will leave his wife in peace, and then, when he murders Gregorius by offering him poison that he claims is a new treatment for heart trouble. Theresa Jamieson rather ingeniously posits that the swallowing of the poison pill "appears to be [...] representative of the discourses we so unthinkingly swallow and of the almost seamless exchange of Science for Christianity as the Grand Narrative of the Western world" (2009, 231).[4] But has the exchange been seamless? Has Glas committed the perfect crime and emerged as the triumphant victor and representative of the new Grand Narrative of Science?

There is some reason to question this. First of all, if Hjalmar Söderberg had meant to endorse Glas's actions and what he stands for, then he could have written a happy ending for this novel: Helga would have gotten her Klas, and perhaps even Glas would live happily ever after with Eva Mertens. As it is, the murder achieves nothing. In fact, it pretty much destroys any chances at all for a happy ending for anyone. Helga is not united with the man she loves, Glas's guilty secret will keep him from intimacy with anyone, and Pastor Gregorius has left behind an elderly mother who is now without support. Glas did not plan on any of these things. Moreover, Glas certainly seems well on his way to a nervous breakdown as he compulsively tests his lock: "Därför att jag har en känsla av att det oerhörda atmosfäriska trycket av andras meningar, de levandes, de dödas och de ännu oföddas, ligger samlat därute och hotar att spränga dörren och krossa mig, pulverisera mig" (1967, 101) ["Because I can sense the incredible atmospheric pressure of other's opinions—the living, the dead, the as yet unborn—that have accumulated out there, threatening to blow open the door and crush me, pulverize me" (1998, 72)]. The triumph of science over religion, the murder by Dr. Glas of Gregorius, has resulted in nothing good.

While at dinner with Markel, the prelude from Wagner's Lohengrin sparks another epiphany: "'Du skall icke fråga!' Icke gå till botten med tingen: då går du själv till botten. Icke söka efter sanningen: du finner den icke och förlorar dig själv" (1967, 117) ["'Thou shalt not ask!' Don't get to the bottom of things, if you do, you yourself will founder" (1998, 72)].[5] He reprises this theme, in good Wagnerian fashion, a few pages later: "Icke gissa gåtor! Icke fråga! Icke tänka! Tanken är en syra som fräter. Du tänker i början, att den blott skall fräta på det som är murket och sjukt och som skall bort. Men tanken tänker inte så: den fräter blint" (1967, 122) ["Don't try to solve riddles! Don't inquire! Don't think! Thought is corrosive acid. At first you think it will only corrode what's rotten and diseased and should be removed. But thought doesn't proceed that way: it corrodes arbitrarily! (1998, 88)]. Not only is Glas invoking his Wagnerian epiphany but he is also paraphrasing his own rationale for murdering Gregorius: he is simply removing what is rotten and should be removed. However, the acid of self-reflection continues to eat away at everything, blindly, and not necessarily according to plan. A few lines later, Dr. Glas repeats some fairly damning praise of science: "'Vetenskaperna äro nyttiga därigenom att de hindra människan från att tänka.' Det är en vetenskapsman, som har sagt det" (1967, 122) ["'The sciences are beneficial because they prevent human beings from thinking.' A scientist said that" (1998, 88)]. In other words, Glas does seem to realize that he has simply replaced one narrative with another, but that the new narrative is flawed too. It is not an unthinking substitution and that is part of Glas's problem. As he said earlier, Darwinism made the world seem meaningless, stupid, and insignificant, and to this, we might add arbitrary. Instead of a Master Explanation of Man and his Place in the World, science only reveals the inherent meaninglessness and arbitrariness of life. Dr. Glas finds himself staring into the Modernist abyss.

In the early days of the Scandinavian Modern Breakthrough, there was a certain optimism regarding science as an explanatory system. In August Strindberg's 1884 short-story rebuttal to Ibsen's famous feminist play, similarly titled "Ett dockhem" [A Dollhouse], a doctor exclaims confidently, "Det är vetenskapen, som avgör de stora frågorna i sista hand! Vetenskapen!" (148) [It is science that ultimately decides the big questions! Science!].[6] As a consequence of this great faith in science, Modern Breakthrough literature abounds with characters who happen to be doctors and who often play the role of truth-speakers. By the time Hjalmar Söderberg explores the theme, optimism has turned to pessimism. Dr. Glas does murder the Father and opens the door for a paradigm shift: science replaces religion. But the replacement is not satisfying. Science may have won, but not triumphed. The threat of Modernist meaninglessness and arbitrariness lies just around the corner.

Notes

[1] For an extremely detailed overview of the scholarship about *Doktor Glas* see Franke, 2004.

[2] I have, in fact, performed this sketch for my students for years, inspired primarily by Egil Törnqvist's analysis. Since Törnqvist's article exists only in Swedish, it can have value to go over some of the salient points here.

[3] In *Viljans frihet och mordets frestelse* (2003) [Freedom of the Will and the Temptation of Murder], a group of scholars looked at *Doktor Glas* in terms of its context within intellectual history and note that many ideas

that have come to be known through Freud flourished in other sources of the time. (Holmbäck et al., 2003).

[4] Jamieson actually makes this remark with regard to the postmodern reworkings of *Doktor Glas* that have appeared recently: Dannie Abse's *The Strange Case of Dr. Simmonds and Dr. Glas* (2003) and Bengt Ohlsson's *Gregorius* (2004). This seems to me a perfectly apt description of the moment in the original *Doktor Glas* as well.

[5] For further erudite reflections on the significance of the Lohengrin overture at this moment see Schoolfield, 2003, 300.

[6] See also Shideler 1999, 105, for a contextualization of Strindberg's "Ett dockhem."

Part II
Fathers: Cultural and Metaphorical

Cavafy, Debt, Translation

Stathis Gourgouris

There is a peculiar relation between the words "Cavafy" and "debt." On the one hand, there are the obvious and voluminous references to what the world of poetry generally (and certain poets specifically) owe to Cavafy: from practically the entire modern Greek poetic tradition from Karyotakis onward, to the broader sphere of poetry and literature worldwide, from Forster and Auden to Brodsky and Coetzee. The poetic debt owed to Cavafy has become something of a literary topos, even if, curiously, this has not been adequately addressed in the newfangled institution of the "world literature" canon, which has not managed to escape modern literature's nod to the hegemony of the novel. On the other hand, this literary topos should be contrasted with the fairly common ruminations (even if not quite as widespread) as to how Cavafy's poetry is indebted to no one, to no other poet or tradition that preceded him or is concurrent with his work. Of course, such judgments, on both sides, are how literary critics pay their dues (and occasionally even their debts), so they cannot serve as departure points for a substantial engagement with Cavafy's poetics and the world that enabled it or the worlds that continue to activate it—for no poetics exists outside of a history (or histories) of some kind. It's easy to say that Cavafy was unique; there are grounds for making such an argument, but I don't know what ground there is for arguing that Cavafy's uniqueness is unlike any other poetic uniqueness.

I mention all this in order to let it go. If I mean to address any notion of poetic indebtedness at all, this will have to respect an essential aspect of poetry: that it defies calculation. Nothing in the meaning of poetry can be counted (we're not talking prosody), which is why it is so difficult to determine what is it about poetry that counts as value that defies all measure. In speaking about poetic indebtedness, therefore, I should clarify that I hardly care to talk about poetic influence—a category of criticism that anyway I abhor. But I will address intersections and conjunctures, or more precisely encounters. As I argued recently, the supreme responsibility of literary criticism is to stage encounters, the requisite theatricality of which is most apt to convey the historical exigencies that lean on any manifestation of poiēsis in the natural sphere of human-being. As the radical creation of form, poiēsis is always transformative of the field in which it occurs, and in this sense, performative of the terms of engagement within that field, for no field in history is ever inert or given intact, but rather dynamic—a force-field of space and time, of movement and action, whereby things-as-they-are are altered.

So, rather than speaking of poetic ownership and literary propriety (and therefore, influence), the terrain of Cavafy's debt pertains more to how this poetic event encounters other poetic events in time and across languages, orientations, and geo-cultural spaces. Hence the rather elementary, but ever more profound than it always seems to be, problem of translation. Even if we were to address the issue of Cavafy's debt in the most traditional terms—as simply a matter of general influence on poetry and poetics—we cannot leave the matter of Cavafy's translations uncommented upon and unproblematized. In the English language alone, the abundance of translations is uncanny (more than fifty different translators in less than one hundred years), and yet very few—and I mean poems, not translators—are adequate to the Greek originals. This is not a matter of opinion. It seems to have been a problem since Cavafy's own ruminations on the translation of his work, as evidenced in his various responses or corrective advice given to his earliest translators, starting with his brother John, and it certainly seems to have preoccupied the full gamut of translators and literati who came into contact with his poetry since E.M. Forster. The crux of the matter points to a quandary: A poet from a minor language, complicated even more by being canonically minor in relation to this language in his lifetime, figures as one of the greatest poets in the entire history of poetry solely (and, of course, necessarily) on the basis of translation, which is nonetheless inadequate.

I am not making some fashionable point about the intrinsic impossibility of translation here—at the very least, because the Cavafy event would not exist without translation. The poet would have vanished along with the rest of colonial-cosmopolitan Alexandrian traces in the imperialist-turned-nationalist sphere of the Eastern Mediterranean in the 20th century, as Edward Said, a genuine Cavafy fan if there ever was one, inimitably documents in his memoir *Out of Place* (1999). Rather, I am staking an argument on something altogether specific: Cavafy's poetry is virtually untranslatable, and this goes beyond the simple axiom that, in the last instance, all poetry is untranslatable. To begin with, the defense of this claim cannot be relegated to the specific nature of the language. In other words, it's not a problem of not knowing Greek, as Virginia Woolf put it, although the resonance of her thought, despite the otherness of the occasion, should remain for us an object of close listening. That is to say, we would have to take very seriously what it means not to know Greek (or whatever) in the conventional sense, what it means to inhabit the far side of language, where language as reliable means to knowledge fails and another horizon of knowing opens up. Surely, Cavafy's poetic use of the Greek language is idiosyncratically complex, juxtaposing colloquialisms with archaisms, obsolete phrasings or mere linguistic inventions, and there is no doubt that rendering the multiple registers of Greek in his poetry (historically created but also made idiomatic by his own voice) fails at the point of transfer to another language with its own historical registers and trajectories.

But I am arguing that this failure is not a matter of lack of linguistic expertise; it's not a matter of language in the narrowest sense of the knowledge it takes for one to engage in translation. This is a failure about poetic language, which is to say—and I am putting it mildly—of language beyond language, of language that makes language, of language that makes an otherwise spoken language be differently and thus renders it unrecognizable. This making be, this process of giving language form (*poiein*), has always been for me less a matter of semantic deployment of words, even if in complex and oblique (poetic) fashion, and more a matter of rhythm—which is not, incidentally, to be restricted to metrics or rules of prosody—of rhythm in the simple sense that language always bears a particular sonority (so as not to say outright, musicality), a fact that poetry, as an archaic performative art, has always incorporated at its core, even when it claims to be entirely visual.

This is to say that even this specific argument about translation 'failure' at the level of poetic language cannot be exhausted in the usual arguments about poetic difficulty. Cavafy's poetic language is hardly characterized by poetic obscurity. In other words, he does not present the translatability problems of Mallarmé, Rilke or Celan (to stick with the dominant European languages). If Cavafy is virtually untranslatable, it is rather because the rhythm of his language has rarely been rendered successfully in another. His poetic fame (and influence) is based on his ideas, or perhaps the manner of his ideas. I mean this broadly to include not just his expressed ideas, but also his worldview of sensations and temporalities, his style of irony based on characterization, and in the contemporary world, his images of erotic being. Yet, for a reader of Greek, what makes Cavafy inimitable is an unmistakably idiomatic rhythm of words that are nonetheless ordinary, recognizable in verse as the mark of a historical world, even if not exactly in the way the national language speaks.

Occasionally, non-Greek readers speak of tone. In his introduction to Rae Dalven's translations of Cavafy, W.H. Auden attempts to explain how he came under the Alexandrine's influence—remember, this is not my interest here—by invoking the transference of "a certain tone of voice, a personal speech" which, in conclusion, he call more conventionally simply "sensibility."[1] But Auden withholds further examination of the musical underpinnings of tone, ultimately flattening the very point of his argument by invoking the inimitable in conventionally abstract terms: "I have read translations of Cavafy made by different hands, but every one of them was immediately recognizable as a poem by Cavafy; nobody else could have written it" (viii). In the end Auden argues

that what makes Cavafy recognizable in translation is the content—
perhaps a specific approach to the content, as I have already
mentioned, a manner—and by underlining Cavafy's lack of
preference for simile and metaphor, Auden thus corroborates the
standard view of Cavafy as a prosaic poet.

In the Greek world of letters, this now conventional judgment
about Cavafy's prosaic poetry was initiated in the 1920s by Kostis
Palamas, whose poetics is certainly incompatible with Cavafy's, but
it is George Seferis, in his classic 1946 essay on Cavafy and Eliot,
who famously wonders how this poet of profound sensibility (and
perhaps even sensuousness—*euaisthēsia*) could actually be so "dry"
(*stegnos*), arguing finally that, as a poet "who thinks with the senses"
(*skeptetai me tēn aisthēsē*), Cavafy is nonetheless "the most anti-poetic
or a-poetic [poet] I know."[2] Seferis' complexities, or perhaps
contortions, in relation to Cavafy make a topic of their own, but
what has prevailed in the world of Greek letters is a broad critical
repression of Seferis' ambivalence in favor of this pronouncement,
which has proved nearly impossible to overcome. Cavafy's
presumed anti-poeticity in Greek letters is often linked to an
understanding that his poetic language is idiosyncratically culled
from an array of quotidian idioms, which Forster, who may be said
to initiate literary criticism on Cavafy as early as 1919, corroborates
as an eyewitness. But, for Forster, this eclectic speech palette of the
"Greek gentleman in a straw hat, standing absolutely motionless at
a slight angle to the universe" is anything but prosaic:

> He may be prevailed upon to begin a sentence—
> an immense complicated yet shapely sentence,
> full of parentheses that never get mixed and of
> reservations that really do reserve; a sentence that
> moves with logic to its foreseen end, yet to an
> end that is always more vivid and thrilling than
> one foresaw. Sometimes the sentence is finished
> in the street, sometimes the traffic murders it,
> sometimes it lasts into the flat. It deals with the
> tricky behavior of Emperor Alexius Comnenus

in 1096, or with olives, their possibilities and
price, or with the fortunes of friends, or George
Eliot, or the dialects of the interior of Asia
Minor. It is delivered with equal ease in Greek,
English, or French. And despite its intellectual
richness and human outlook, despite the matured
charity of its judgments, one feels that it too
stands at a slight angle to the universe: it is the
sentence of a poet.[3]

Barring the specific content for a moment, we would recognize
here a description of the Proustian sentence (it is known that
Cavafy was enthralled by Proust), even if in resplendent Levantine
hue. But the Proustian sentence—this unprecedented gift to the
French language and to literature as such—is inconceivable without
the extraordinary skill of rhythm and the capacity to elevate (even if
by stretching without ever breaking) grammatical and syntactical
contours to the sensuous precision of a musical phrase. The
splendorous pages devoted to the memory of a particular musical
phrase (*une pétite phrase*) by Monsieur Vinteuil (a character in the
novel presumed to gloss Debussy, Fauré or Saint-Saëns) may be
configured as an over-the-top demonstration of the novel's entire
writing strategy. We may be talking about a novelist's language here,
but Proust's writing is what it is because it engages "the language of
a poet," a language that stands indeed "at a slight angle to the
universe"—a characterization equally apt to the Proustian
sensibility. Parenthetically, in closing this observation, I would argue
that what enables Cavafy to possess this acrobatic plasticity in his
spoken idiom is his profound knowledge of the multiple registers of
the Greek language (and indeed of katharevousa specifically, with
its capacity for baroque syntax), which in his hands was elevated to
a singular art form. That Forster, in the essay quoted above, goes on
to identify Cavafy with the demoticist literary movement is evidence
of his lack of knowledge, which the poet, with his typical irony,
politely indicates (by Forster's own account).

Having said that, Forster is otherwise correct to recognize "the language of a poet" even in quotidian speech. His view was ignored, however, in the broader literary criticism of Cavafy.[4] Indeed, this view of Cavafy as the prosaic ironist seems to have benefitted the poet's international reputation, and little effort seems to have gone into questioning it, until the claim of Daniel Mendelsohn's recent translations to render the tone and cadences of Cavafy's poetry, which is the impetus of his landmark effort to translate the entire Cavafy poetic corpus, including repudiated, unpublished, and unfinished texts. Mendelsohn does approach Cavafy's Greek as a language "whose internal cadences and natural music the poet exploited thoroughly. There is no question that Cavafy in Greek is poetry, and beautiful poetry at that: deeply, hauntingly rhythmical, sensually assonant when not actually rhyming."[5] That Mendelsohn only partially succeeds at the task of translating this recognition does not nullify the radical significance of his impetus, which goes against the grain of an iron-clad establishment of Cavafy's image as a prosaic poet.

However, the first to make this breakthrough, and without announcement but the sheer disruptiveness of poetic praxis, is James Merrill, who published only four translations of Cavafy's poems but whose encounter with Cavafy was profound in ways that elucidate the entire range of my concerns here: not just the matter of Cavafy's idiosyncratic rhythm, but those intangible aspects of the Greek language that bear a particular Greek sensibility—I would say, to raise the stakes, a particular lyric Greek sensibility in the post-Civil War years—which marks, in a substantial sense, Merrill's own poetics. This is the key encounter I want to stage, and here I can do so only partially. But let me return for a moment to Cavafy and to another signifying range of "Cavafy's debt."

I quote here another one of Forster's well-known reminiscences of Cavafy at a much later phase, in 1951:

> Half humorously, half seriously, he once
> compared the Greeks to the English. The two

peoples are alike, he argued: quick-witted, resourceful, adventurous. "But there is one unfortunate difference among us, one little difference. We Greeks have lost our capital—and the results are what you see. Pray, my dear Forster, oh pray, that you never lose your capital." That was in 1918. British insolvency seemed impossible then. In 1951, when all things are possible, his words make one think—words of a very wise, very civilized man, words of a poet who has caught hold of something that cannot be taken away from him by bankruptcy, or even by death.[6]

I reproduce the passage in full because it has led to various interpretations and perhaps misreadings. An interesting evocation of it occurs in the concluding paragraph of Giorgio Agamben's *Means without End* (1995):

E.M. Forster relates how during one of his conversations with C.P. Cavafy in Alexandria, the poet told him: "You English cannot understand us: we Greeks went bankrupt a long time ago." I believe that one of the few things that can be declared with certainty is that, since then, all the peoples of Europe (and perhaps all the peoples of the Earth) have gone bankrupt... Every people has had its particular way of going bankrupt, and certainly it does make a difference that for the Germans it meant Hitler and Auschwitz, for the Spanish it meant a civil war, for the French it meant Vichy, for other people instead it meant the quiet and atrocious 1950s, and for the Serbs it meant the rapes of Omarska; in the end, what is crucial for us is only the new task that such a failure has bequeathed us. Perhaps it is not even accurate to define it as a task, because there is no longer a people to undertake it. As the Alexandrian poet might say today with the smile: "Now at last, we can understand one another, because you too have gone bankrupt."[7]

It's not unusual for Agamben to think on the basis of misquotation or mistranslation, although here one wonders about the ease with which a Forster quotation in English can be so radically changed. Certainly, how Agamben quotes Cavafy in the language of Forster not only diverges from the source text but actually inverts the original point. Forster's Cavafy begins with an equation of Greek and English sensibility, which is then meant to be disrupted by the historical condition of "the loss of capital." Agamben's Cavafy— though in (mis)quotation of Forster's language—begins with a divergence, a lack of understanding, between Greek and English sensibility, which is to be overcome by the common experience of bankruptcy. Agamben's point may be determined by Forster's own remark about British post-WW2 insolvency, which he then takes as a departure point for a narrative of the postwar years all the way to the present (1995) as a procession of an ultimately common fate of sovereign insolvency by different means. To say that "Every people has had its particular way of going bankrupt" sounds a bit like saying everyone has a particular way of using language, but we all have language all the same. It is a relativist phrase, a phrase of equivalence at the very moment of articulating difference.

Interesting as it may be to argue that the common experience of sovereign insolvency forges an understanding between peoples who have gone bankrupt and are thereby (similarly or commonly) disenfranchised, Agamben's remark makes a rather flaccid political point. What may be the political horizon of peoples whose common link is the loss of their sovereignty isn't really articulated here, other than the rather bleak insinuation that there may not be any such people left to undertake the task of overcoming their loss of sovereignty. Forster, on the other hand, for all his colonial sensibility, focuses his thinking, not on the British and their postwar economic troubles, but on the Greek poet.

It is important to note here that in Cavafy's remark, as quoted by Forster, inheres an ambiguity on the very basis of language, which Forster disregards.[8] "Capital" is word with two different meanings, and it is altogether possible that Cavafy's lament of Greeks having lost their capital refers, just as well, to the loss of Constantinople, the capital of Hellenism, which would then insinuate a warning about the British Empire's possible demise-to-come. According to Forster, the conversation took place in 1918. This places it four years before the Asia Minor catastrophe (1922), which was the nail in the coffin of the historical expanse of Mediterranean Hellenism that Cavafy exemplified, an ironic conjuncture, for Cavafy's poetry is utterly alien to anything prophetic; rather, it means to read historical reality with utmost precision.

But this date is also well within range of Greece's sovereign bankruptcy of 1893, which ended the first aspirations for Greek industrial modernization. To this national economic disaster we could add the personal condition of the Cavafy family bankruptcy in the late 1880s, and we cannot ignore Cavafy's well-honed understanding of the permutations of speculative capital, as he was a frequent (and not altogether unsuccessful) trader in speculative commodities in Alexandria's stock market, which he favored as often as he did various joints of ill repute. Forster was well aware of Cavafy's ease with economics as a topic of conversation, so his conclusion should not be so easily dismissed. Whichever way, even if we judge that Forster errs in the direction of one interpretation of "capital" over another, he still holds on, even if unwittingly, to the decisive condition of poetic ambiguity: "words of a poet who has caught hold of something that cannot be taken away from him by bankruptcy, or even by death." Poetic language defies the order of calculation. Which is to say, and for Cavafy's poetry all the more, that even if the discourse of economics is presumed to be an interesting angle of literary analysis, it must be engaged in an altogether other language.

The word in Greek for "debt"—χρέος—occurs only twice in Cavafy's poetry. One of these occasions is famous and it means not debt at all, but rather the other significance of the term in Greek: duty, obligation. It marks the beginning of the poem "Thermopylae" (1901-03): "Τιμή σ' εκείνους όπου στην ζωή των/ώρισαν και φυλάγουν Θερμοπύλες./Ποτέ από το χρέος μη κινούντες·" ["Honor to those who in their lives/Determined to guard a Thermopylae/Never moving away from duty"]. The other occasion is from a prose poem, "Το Σύνταγμα της ηδονής" ("The Regiment of Pleasure"), written in 1877 and kept hidden: "Don't believe you're bound to any obligation [υποχρέωσις]. Your duty [χρέος] is to give in, to always give in to your Desires, which are the most perfect creatures of perfect gods. Your duty is to enlist as loyal soldier, with simplicity of heart, when the Regiment of Pleasure passes by with music and banners." Not a particularly good poem, not because of its prose, but rather because of its unpoetic disclosure of the erotic condition that otherwise permeates some of the best Cavafy poems. Its frankness explains why it was hidden, but its directness may have served as a sort of personal manifesto for the poet, which is why he may have chosen to preserve it even if concealed.[9] Panagiotis Roilos makes an interesting, if not fully thought through, observation that these early hidden prose poems, which he calls sketches of "extravagant" or "inflated lyricism," are in a sense inversely analogous to the lyrically reticent erotic verses that make up much of the best of the published oeuvre.[10] Perhaps to call this poem lyrical at all is an abusive invocation of the category of lyric, conventionally speaking, not so much because it is so obviously prosaic, but because it is indeed so extravagantly transparent that it doesn't even work as allegory, strictly speaking.

In any case, in the invocation of χρέος vs. υποχρέωσις, we see here, if anything, the opposite of indebtedness—duty opposes obligation in the very same way that an ethical decision opposes a moral command: "All moral laws—badly understood, badly implemented—are nothing and cannot even stand for a moment when the Regiment of Pleasure passes by with music and banners." This is because hedonistic pleasure, in this poem, is not some sort of decadent pastime, bought or sold illicitly and lived parasitically, but rather an overt and conscious responsibility to the self, a chosen way of life that cannot be gained in the market of exchange, where values are measured by external means, by what society rewards or denigrates. *Hedonē*, the poet tells us, is like life itself, inherited—and, in that sense, inherent—in one's very being. It's important, however, that we don't see this notion of inheritance as a mark of privilege, as entitlement, in the abusive way the term tends to be used nowadays. *Klēronomia*, the common Greek word for inheritance, is best understood here in its literal composition: *klēros* being the accidental element of life, one's lot in life in the most rigorous sense, which at once bears a law (*nomos*), yet not as transcendental command but as whatever is specifically imparted into one's being according to *nemein*—the operative verb of *nomos*, which means partitioning, distributing, and indeed allotting. So, although this poem does not deserve the sort of attention most of Cavafy's poems do—for, as I said, it is unpoetically transparent—it serves as a clear-cut demonstration of Cavafy's repudiation of the language of debt and indebtedness, marketable valuation and exchange, as a personally didactic manifesto for all of the poet's subsequent evocations of a life stance in his poetry, not just erotic but indeed, literally, political.

A couple of other poems from this era, which Cavafy either kept hidden or repudiated and removed from subsequent circulation, lay out more sharply and with more subtle poetic skill this life stance. The first is intriguingly titled "The Bank of the Future" (1897):

> To make my difficult life secure
> on the Bank of the Future, I shall
> issue but a handful of draft notes.
>
> I doubt it possesses many assets

and on the first crisis, I've come to fear
its payments will suddenly altogether cease.
(trans. Mendelsohn, 293)

If economics is the blatant metaphoric language of this poem, its impetus is self-reflexively poetic with a kind of clarity that may be said to go beyond the simple but lithe rhyme: the value of the poet's life is banked entirely on the basis of poetry; there is no other resource. This life is entirely precarious. It does not lend itself well to the security of time, to investment in some future fruition. It is a difficult life, with doubtful assets, and therefore vulnerable to the minutest crisis. We understand the double entendre of the word *krisis* in Greek—all poetry is always subject to crisis, to judgment and critique, and whether it can yield its wealth or wither is not something one can safely bet on, for, I repeat, poetry—and the poetic life—remains incalculable.

The second poem, written just a month later (February 1897), is one of my favorites of Cavafy's poetics manifestos. It elucidates precisely this incalculability of poetry and is appropriately titled "Addition":

If I have good fortune or misfortune I don't examine.
Except one thing joyfully I always mind –
that in the grand addition (addition I detest)
which bears myriad numbers, I do not count
as one of their many units. In the sum total,
I'm not a number. And this joy is just enough for me.
(Mendelsohn, 295)

With its peculiar verse breaks, which strain but do not quite hold on to the 15-syllable line, and an uncommon (in Greek) rhyming scheme (a-a-b-c-b-c), the very structure of the poem doesn't quite add up. No doubt, an explicit poetic sensibility that resists the violence of depersonalizing calculation or quantification grants this poem a strong poetic voice, but although the lyric "I" registers an unabashed presence, the poem rejects individualist achievement as much as it rejects inclusion in some impersonal plurality—any kind of aggregate collective: society, nation, culture, group of poets, anthology, literary marketplace, etc. Of course, the most conventional thing to say about Cavafy is that he performs a poetry that refuses numeration and calculation, which is why he so persistently kept its publication outside the marketplace. In the end, the poet speaks of the sufficient pleasure of remaining within one's own terms, of escaping the heteronomy of being counted and discounted. I would go so far as to say that this includes the erotic world of men, if it were to be seen as a collective. The illicit homoeroticism in Cavafy's poems is always singular and itinerant; it belongs to the moment as moment—as real eroticism must, after all. It has only become an addition of moments—an enumeration, a collective—in the anthologies of editors and publishers, translators and critics.

But it is important, nonetheless, that in this rejection of calculation, we do not get beguiled by romantic convention and read in this poetic stance some sort of heroic defiance—of bourgeois society, moral propriety, or what have you. With this poem specifically—which, let us recall, Cavafy withdrew from circulation in his folios even though it had been published—we have the rare advantage of the poet's own critical observations regarding its translation into English by his brother John. Without least hedging and rather sternly, Cavafy corrects John's choice to translate the sentiment of the first verse in terms of not having "the smallest care": "Once and for all this 'smallest care' must be removed. It is something I never said in my poem, I never had the intention to say, and I believe I shall never write. It is a dangerous statement [in English]... and a profession [in English] that in no way I would want to commit. What I wrote is 'I do not examine whether I am happy or unhappy'... I do not examine, not I do not care."[11] There is, in other words, a perfectly self-aware coolness of mind that refuses to underline an affective investment in the One at the same time that it refuses to accept the privilege of the Many. It seeks to discredit the quantification of life altogether, and it does so regardless of the pressure of any personal care, of the pressures of the Ego upon one's desire, pressures which in an epistolary moment of kinship the poet acknowledges. It is perhaps impossible not to care whether you are counted or discounted in life, but it's important nonetheless to learn to live with the sufficient joy of your decision to excise yourself from this numbers game. This is the succinct poetics of this poem. For this reason, Cavafy's ironic and defiant play with the language of economics in his poetry cannot be reduced to a metaphoric indication of an illicit and unproductive life, whether erotically or otherwise. This is a great blind spot of Roilos' otherwise painstaking analysis of "the economics of metonymy" in Cavafy. His attempt to link the poetic invocation of economics in Cavafian verse to an economics of desire—essentially homoeroticism and unproductive sexuality, but also a generally unproductive life stance of an Alexandrian aristocratic class in decline—suffers from the facility of an obvious semantic association.

Roilos practices a literary criticism that seeks what he calls Cavafy's "anti-economic aestheticism" or "non-productive existence" in poems that treat this as a theme. But because this economics of desire cannot be calculated or measured, its literary analysis cannot be conducted along the lines of a metonymy of economic signs. Cavafy's powerful poetic eroticism cannot be reduced to a literary critical account of eros denied, eros hidden, eros imagined, eros illicitly bought and sold in real life, whereby a personal situation is merely sublimated into art, but rather as eros lyrically fictionalized, in histories of the past and of the present and in topoi imagined even when claimed to be remembered, whereby the poetic art itself suffices as life. If there is something to learn from Cavafy's correction of his brother's translation it is just that: the decision to disregard personal sentiment and put forward an ironic performative persona that thinks entirely within the terms of the poem alone, even in a poem of personal sentiment enacting a poetics.

"To sound personal is the point" says James Merrill somewhere, not to be personal in one's poems. From Cavafy's scant private notes and hidden poems, we see how much of a struggle this was for the poet—how could it not be? It isn't that he doesn't care; it is that he chooses not to examine—but if there is a great lesson from these traces it is not to read in his poems for the language of evidence: "Πάω άδικα, αισθητικώς. Και θα μείνω αντικείμενον εικασίας· και θα με καταλαμβάνουν το πληρέστερον, απ' τα όσα αρνήθηκα." "I am dealt an aesthetic injustice. And I will remain an object of speculation. And I will be understood more from what I have refused."[12] The poet Cavafy is not indebted to his own life.

Notes

[1] W.H. Auden, "Introduction" to *The Complete Poems of Cavafy*, trans. Rae Dalven, vii-xv.

[2] George Seferis, *Dokimes* I, 344-345.

[3] E.M. Forster, *Pharos and Pharillon*, 91-92.

[4] It is worth noting Arnold Toynbee's letter to Forster in 1924: "I admire the way in which he makes his point by a series of flat colourless statements." In the same letter, we may find the first judgment that separates Cavafy's poems into the two groups that have become conventional, "erotic and historical." See Peter Jeffreys ed. *The Forster-Cavafy Letters: Friends at a Slight Angle*, 72. Jeffreys also reminds us of Richard Clogg's discovery that among the first candidates for the Lectureship in Modern Greek at King's College, London, which became the Koraes Chair with first occupant being Toynbee, was C.P. Cavafy: "A Greek man of letters 'de l'école d'Alexandrie... qui est un ésprit remarquable, un Monsieur Cavafis'." (quoted in Jeffreys, 26n).

[5] Daniel Mendelsohn, "Introduction" to *C.P. Cavafy: Collected Poems*, xviii.

[6] E.M. Forster, "The Complete Poems of C.P. Cavafy" in *Two Cheers for Democracy*, 237.

[7] Giorgio Agamben, *Means Without End*, 142.

[8] Maria Margaronis, in her review of Mendelsohn's translations, mentions this often discussed ambiguity: "Mixing History and Desire: the Poetry of C.P. Cavafy" in *The Nation*, August 3, 2009.

[9] An extraordinary rendition of this poem by the legendary Greek punk avant-garde/electronica group Lost Bodies actually shakes off this poem's problems. Which, in the end, goes to show that the performativity of poetry–and its intimate relation to musicality/theatricality–goes way beyond the author, the text, and the page. It can be viewed at http://www.youtube.com/watch?v=_XdAmIk-TQo

[10] Panagiotis Roilos, *C.P. Cavafy: The Economics of Metonymy*, 42-44.

[11] C.P. Cavafy, *Peza* [Prose Works], 239.

[12] (http://www.kavafis.gr/archive/texts/content.asp?id=13) Isn't this the case with another classic manifesto of poetics, the famous poem "Che fece... il gran rifiuto"?—"The one who refuses does not repent. If asked again/ he would still say No. But this great No –/ the right No—wears him down his whole life." Refusal is a decision against the interests of a productive future, but more than that a decision that underwrites a life stance.

A Promise Concealed, Revealed, and to be Fulfilled: On Some Affinities between Figural and Political Interpretation

Efrain Kristal

In 1981 Fredric Jameson published *The Political Unconscious* when he was firmly established as the premier American Marxist literary theorist. As this landmark book was making its impact in the history of literary theory writ large, Jameson had some involvement in the publication of Erich Auerbach's posthumous edited volume *Scenes from the Drama of European Literature* for which he wrote a famous blurb. Auerbach's volume appeared in 1984 in the prominent "History and Theory of Literature" collection of the University of Minnesota Press, and it featured the first English translation of "Figura," widely acknowledged as one of Auerbach's seminal essays, originally published in 1938, during Auerbach's exile from Germany in Turkey. [1] Auerbach published *Mimesis*, his most important book, six years later 1946, shortly before moving to the United States where he took up several academic positions. He taught at Yale University from 1950 until his death in 1957. Jameson worked on his Ph.D. at Yale from 1954 to 1959, and Auerbach was one of his mentors, and had he not died before Jameson finished his Ph.D. he might have been his dissertation advisor. According to a statement attributed to Jameson in an internet link, Jameson considered himself to be Auerbach's student:

> I was Auerbach's student at Yale, but not believing in hierarchies (usually), we became comrades as well. Dr. Auerbach—er, Erich—was a little angel on my shoulder as I wrote my dissertation on no less a thinker than French existentialist Jean-Paul Sartre. Auerbach—that German master of mimesis—introduced me to tons of ideas he imported from Germany (he was

exiled by Nazis). Anyway, Auerbach taught me
that realism matters.[2]

Although Auerbach was not a Marxist literary critic, his
approach to literary analysis has some affinities with Marxist
approaches to literature such as his interest in Hegel's dialectic, his
keenness to stress the connections between literature and reality, his
emphasis on literary realism, and his preference for approaches to
interpretation grounded in historical processes and even in what he
has called "material historical facts."[3] In *The Political Unconscious*,
Jameson cites Auerbach's *Mimesis* among the "greatest modern or
modernizing literary histories"[4] while making the suggestive, albeit
undeveloped, point that these commendable sorts of literary
histories are of significance in what they "have sought to do in their
critical practice, if not in their theory."[5] Jameson makes an equally
suggestive claim about "Figura" when he calls it "a very significant"
theoretical statement that has not aged."[6]

There are homologies of structure between Auerbach's
approach to literary exegesis in the "Figura" essay, and those of
progressive theorists, like Jameson, for whom the task of literary
criticism is grounded in a period of transition highlighted by the
development of a method of interpretation that makes binding,
holistic claims in a historical process where humanity moves from
an undesirable state of affairs to a more desirable one. Both figural
interpretation (in Auerbach's account) and Marxist interpretation (in
Jameson's account) share the view that their own critical practices
are as grounded in history as the works they analyze, and that their
claims are strong enough to understand the present in ways that the
past was not able to understand itself. Indeed, the new method is, in
some sense, decisive: it warrants a reassessment of the past based
on a compelling anticipation of things to come. What is at stake for
both figural interpretation, and the kind of political literary theory
Jameson champions, is not just the grounding of a better theory of
interpretation, but the grounding of a theory of interpretation that
subsumes all other forms of interpretation under the historical
destiny of humanity.

In the case of figural interpretation, the absolute horizon involves a Christian view of spirituality grounded on the premise that every human being is worthy of salvation, and in the case of Jameson's critical theory, it involves the primacy of a political interpretation grounded in Marxist philosophy, according to which no human being should be subject to exploitation. In the case of figural interpretation, humanity is living a historical moment in which the truths of Christian salvation have been revealed, even though they have not been fully grasped, and certainly not fully realized because the true fulfillment of figural interpretation can only happen after the Last Judgment. In the case of Jameson's approach to political interpretation, humanity is living a historical moment in which the truths of human liberation have been revealed by Marxist philosophy (even if they may require revision or further theorization), but not fully grasped, and certainly not fulfilled.[7] It is only through the vantage point of figural interpretation that the significance of the past before the advent of Christ can be truly appreciated, and for Jameson "only Marxism can give us an adequate account of the essential mystery of the cultural past."[8] Although Jameson does not explicitly cite the "Figura" essay in *The Political Unconscious* he does recognize, and we will return to this matter at the end of this essay, "the methodological interest in Christian historicism" as an antecedent to a genuine philosophy of history.[9] The kind of political interpretation Jameson advocates is not just a hermeneutical approach among others, but the hermeneutical approach par excellence, one that will replace all others, or under which all others must be subsumed. For Jameson political interpretation is not "an optional auxiliary to other interpretative methods current today—the psychoanalytic or the myth-critical, the stylistic, the ethical, the structural—but rather as the absolute horizon of all reading and all interpretation."[10] This is analogous to the claims of figural interpretation that its approach brings together the past, the present and the future of humanity. Jameson's bold affirmation in favor of a Marxist approach to literary exegesis, therefore, has some structural affinities with the figural approach according to which biblical and literary hermeneutics are to be subsumed under a historical process involving the anagogical realm, that is to say, the explanation of texts in function of what is to come for all of humanity, most notably in the afterlife, after the Final Judgment. In the case of the political approach, liberation is the end-point and the *raison d'être* of interpretation, and in the case of figural interpretation the end point is salvation.

In "Figura" Auerbach offers an impressive philological history of terms, concepts and categories, all of which he presents as vague, imperfect or insufficient in the light of their fulfillment in figural interpretation. Auerbach does not hide his admiration for Christian modes of exegesis and their power to inspire, engage or address the circumstances of both the learned and the unlearned; and he insists that figural interpretation is the necessary tool to fully grasp the complexities of Dante's *Divine Comedy*, something he recognizes he may have vaguely intimated but not fleshed out in Dante. Poet of the Secular World, his first major book originally published in 1929. The main foil against which Auerbach measures the subtleties of figural interpretation is any kind of allegorical hermeneutics according to which an algorithm or predetermined code of some sort or another leads the interpreter from a text, to what it is supposed to mean. Auerbach's skepticism regarding the preeminence of allegorical interpretation resonates with Jameson's own skepticism of any "system of allegorical interpretation in which the data of one narrative line are radically impoverished by their rewriting according to the paradigm of another narrative, which is taken as the former's master code or Ur-narrative and proposed as the ultimate hidden or unconscious meaning of the first one."[11] It is not that Jameson is against a master approach to literary interpretation. On the contrary, Jameson is an advocate of Marxism as the master approach to literary interpretation, one that is historically grounded while encompassing the political destiny of humankind. From this vantage point the allegorical approaches Jameson rejects involve reductive, misleading or partial codes with which a critic can translate one set of terms into another set of terms, circumventing historical considerations. And it is in an analogous spirit that Auerbach prefers the figural method over allegory because figural interpretation engages the past, the present and future in a dialectical relationship whereby past anticipates the present, and the present confers the past with its true significance, as it articulates clear hopes for the future.

Auerbach's other foil to Christian modes of interpretation is an approach he attributes to some religious practices of non-European peoples according to which a symbol can be endowed with magical qualities, as a primitive mode of exegesis. In short, Christian exegesis is superior to pagan exegesis, to allegorical exegesis, and to the exegesis of non-European peoples. In Auerbach's "Figura," Christian exegesis is apparently also superior to Jewish exegesis, or at least to the examples of Jewish exegesis that Auerbach quotes in the essay. The most sophisticated form of Jewish exegesis Auerbach cites in "Figura" is that of Philo of Alexandria who was able to go beyond the literal elements of biblical texts understood as historical documents, in order to discern moral truths, but this form of exegesis is inferior to Christian exegesis, according to Auerbach, because it is ultimately a-historical, even as it addresses historical events:

> Following the Jewish tradition, Philo [...] saw in the fate of Israel in general, as well as in the lives of the individual actors in Jewish history, as an allegory of the movement of the sinful soul in need of salvation from its fall through hope to its final redemption. This approach was clearly based on spiritual and extra-historical interpretation.[12]

What Christian exegesis has that these other non-Christian approaches lack is a powerful historical grounding that links the experiences of individuals and communities to a historical past, a present situation, and a future that is yet to be realized.

The paradigmatic example of figural interpretation is the story of Moses taken as a historical event: Moses leads the Jewish people from slavery in the land of Egypt to freedom in the promised land, and in so doing Moses is also prefiguring the historical advent of Christ who can redeem humanity from original sin, offering eternal salvation. In this context the lack of clarity regarding the meaning of the Incarnation has significant consequences in matters of salvation, especially for those who continue to live according to the laws and paradigms that have been superseded by the advent of Christ, which gives them a new meaning: "the Old Testament was transformed from a book of laws and national history of Israel into a series of figures of Christ and Redemption."[13]

Figural exegesis, according to Auerbach, is not a simple allegorical move from a text to a meaning but a view of history, in three steps according to which (1) a promised was concealed, (2) a promise has been revealed, and (3) a promise is to be fulfilled. The three steps correspond to three historical moments that involve (1) the history of the world until the advent of Christ, (2) the Christian era, and (3) the final judgment that is yet to come.

Figural interpretation can only take place in a specific historical moment, which endows a transforming, retrospective meaning to a past one, as it anticipates a future one, that is to say after the promise of Christian salvation has been revealed but before it has been fulfilled. In short, figural interpretation depends on faith in Christian truths that supersedes anything that may have been held as true in the past, in the assumption that historical events in the past prefigure historical events in the future, and in the expectation that the Christian promise concealed in the historical events of the past and revealed in the historical event of the Incarnation, will be fulfilled. Auerbach does not hesitate to argue that this hermeneutic approach is "dialectical" in Hegelian terms: "This dialectic is especially obvious in the figure of Christ ... which shows us in its purest form the figures of what is present to our senses, what is provisionally veiled and what is—from the very beginning—beyond all time."[14] In Auerbach's view the first element of the dialectic involves "history" as accounted for in the Old Testament whereby Moses is the historical figure that prefigures Christ; the second element is the advent of Christ, which is the era in which we are living, and the final element is the final judgment, which is ahead of us. In a first abstraction Auerbach underscores that "Figura is something real and historical that represents and proclaims in advance something else that is also real and historical,"[15] or in another formulation, "the prophetic figure is a material historical fact and is fulfilled by material historical facts."[16] Auerbach spells out the dialectic of figural interpretation as follows:

> The first event points to the second, the second fulfills the first. To be sure both remain concrete events that have taken place within history. Yet, when seen from this perspective, both also have something provisional and incomplete about them. They point to one another and both point to something in the future that is still to come.[17]

> In figural interpretation facts are always subordinated to a meaning that is fixed in advance; they orient themselves according to a model of events that lies in the future and that thus far has only been promised.[18]

It is possible to detect some affinities between the Christian figural program and the Marxist program. If we were to substitute Marxist modes of production for what Auerbach calls first and second events, and the word "political" for "figural," the previous two quotes would yield the following:

> **Feudalism** points to the **Capitalism**, the second fulfills the first. To be sure both remain concrete **modes of production** that have taken place within history. Yet, when seen from this perspective, both also have something provisional and incomplete about them. They point to one another and both point to something in the future that is still to come.

> In **political** interpretation facts are always
> subordinated to a meaning that is fixed in
> advance; they orient themselves according to a
> mode of production that lies in the future and
> that thus far has only been promised.

In the case of figural interpretation what lies in the future is
salvation after the final judgment, and in political interpretation
what lies in the future is liberation after the final mode of
production is established, namely Communism.

In the case of figural interpretation Exodus points to the
Incarnation when the Laws of the Old Testament are annulled, but
both Exodus and even the Incarnation are provisional until the final
judgment, which is what lies in the future, and has only been
promised. Until the promise is fulfilled, however, the old Law has
been annulled and it has been substituted by higher hopes:

> Paul, in whom the practical and political
> combined in exemplary fashion with faith
> endowed with a high level of poetic creativity,
> managed to transform the Jewish idea of the
> resurrection of Moses in the Messiah into a
> system of historically real prophecy, in which
> Christ resurrected simultaneously fulfills and
> annuls the work of his predecessor. Whatever the
> Old Testament had to sacrifice in legal authority
> and in historical-national autonomy, it gained in
> new and dramatically concrete contemporary
> relevance.[19]

The analytics of political interpretation has some analogies to
figural interpretation, if one were to substitute the advent of
dialectical materialism in the bourgeois era for the figure of Christ,
and Lenin (or an individual or collective analogue to Lenin) for
Saint Paul, as the agent able to mobilize humanity towards the ideal
(of salvation in the case of Christianity or liberation in the case of

Marxism). Thus, the bourgeois revolution anticipates the socialist revolution when bourgeois law is annulled, but both the bourgeois revolution and the socialist revolution are provisional until the true ideals of Communism are realized. The ease with which it is possible to substitute terms signals some of the compatibilities between figural and political interpretation. In short, the advent of Christ and the Gospels would be to the former what the advent of Marx and dialectical materialism would be to the latter. Indeed, Auerbach's account of Saint Paul's figural intervention can be paraphrased in Marxist terms:

> **Quote**: Obedience to the old law is pointless, even harmful after Christ has brought fulfillment and salvation to humanity by His sacrifice. Christians are justified not by works in accordance with obedience to the Law, but by faith.[20]

> **Paraphrase**: Obedience to bourgeois law is pointless, even harmful after Marx's program for the liberation of humanity from oppression has been articulated. Marxists are justified in their circumvention of bourgeois law, according to a program of liberation.

In his account of figural interpretation Auerbach also offers a program for literary interpretation—not just for biblical exegesis of the Old Testament and the Gospels—grounded in history, that recalls the objectives of ideological criticism: "in the creation of art, the artist produces an imitation of a shadowy figuration of a true reality that is also a sensuous reality."[21] It is the role of the figural interpreter of literary works to give clarity and transparency to the shadowy figurations of artists, and this thought anticipates the role of literary critics who are able to identify the ideological underpinnings of a text, or its "political unconscious." The role of the literary critic and historian for Jameson would be, as Steven Venturino has summarized it, "[to reveal] a disjunction between a text's meaning (as defined by any given interpretation) and 'the repressed and buried reality' of the 'fundamental history' of class struggle."[22] For both Auerbach and Jameson allegorical exegesis is an inferior kind of hermeneutics to one grounded on the destiny of human redemption from original sin in the case of "Figural" interpretation and from oppression in the case of the kind of political interpretation favored by Jameson.

The move from Auerbach's pagan world before the advent of Christ to a bourgeois world before the advent of Marx; from the advent of the doctrine of Christian salvation to the advent of dialectical materialism; and from the hopes of Christian fulfillment in the apocalypse to the political hopes of the fulfillment of Communism after the revolution gives way to a classless society, could be read as analogous. Auerbach's account of the figure concealed, the figure revealed and the figure fulfilled, itself prefigures a kind of literary exegesis, with some theoretical currency today, that is both critical in its political approach, and friendly to the rhetoric of Christian exegesis.

The invitation to draw the parallelisms between the kind of interpretation that Auerbach calls figural, and the kind of interpretation that Jameson calls political, is spelled out in *The Political Unconscious* where Jameson makes connections between Christian exegesis and his own approach to Marxist analysis. He underscores that Christian modes of exegesis—precisely of the kind that Auerbach outlines in the "Figura" essay—are a prehistory of sorts to his own approach to political interpretation, and he suggests that his own approach to political interpretation is an invitation to rethink the significance of Christian interpretation. Jameson, therefore, is arguing that the kind of interpretation Auerbach has called "figural" is a "figure" of sorts that "prefigures" his own mode of exegesis. He is therefore using figural analysis to reframe in Marxist terms the kind of figural interpretation that Auerbach has elucidated:

> Any comparison with religion is a two-way street,
> in which the former is not necessarily discredited
> by its association with the latter. On the contrary,
> such a comparison may also function to rewrite
> certain   religious   concepts—most   notably
> Christian historicism and the 'concept' of
> providence, but also the pretheological systems
> of   primitive   magic—as   anticipatory
> foreshadowings of historical materialism within
> precapitalist social formations in which scientific
> thinking is unavailable as such.[23]

Jameson explicitly offers a coming together of Christian and
Marxist patterns of interpretation in *The Political Unconscious* when he
makes the connection between Christian interpretation and
ideological analysis:

> The interpretation of a particular Old Testament
> passage in terms of the life of Christ—a familiar,
> even hackneyed, illustration is the rewriting of
> the bondage of the people of Israel in Egypt as
> the descent of Christ into hell after his death on
> the cross—comes less as a technique for closing
> the text off and for repressing aleatory or
> aberrant readings and senses, than as a
> mechanism for preparing such a text for further
> ideological investment, if we take the term
> ideology here in Althusser's sense as a
> representational structure which allows the
> individual subject to conceive or imagine his or
> her lived relationship to transpersonal realities
> such as the social structure or the collective logic
> of History.[24]

Jameson specifically compares the anagogical (defined as the
interpretation of scripture in a spiritual level) as a tool for political
exegesis:

[in the anagogical sense of a text] the text undergoes its ultimate rewriting in terms of the destiny of the human race as a whole, Egypt then coming to prefigure that long purgatorial suffering of earthly history from which the second coming of Christ and the Last Judgment come as the final release. The historical or collective dimension is thus attained.[25]

In the letter to the Can Grande of Verona attributed to Dante, the anagogical is defined as "the leave taking of the blessed soul from the slavery of this corruption to the freedom of eternal glory."[26] Jameson offers a political corrective, when in *The Political Unconscious*, he defines that anagogical as a "political reading (collective 'meaning' of history)."[27]

Notes

[1] The essay was retranslated by Jane O. Newman in 2014, a testimony to its significance, and to the need to update a translation to eliminate misunderstandings that may arise from the state of contemporary theoretical discussions. In her splendid translation Jane O. Newman generously acknowledges the work of her predecessors and she predicts "there will be subsequent Auerbach translations too." Jane O. Newman, "Translator's Note," *Selected Essays of Erich Auerbach. Time, History, and Literature*, xlviii.

[2] http://www.shmoop.com/frederic-jameson/comrades-rivals.html

[3] Auerbach, Erich, "Figura," *Selected Essays of Erich Auerbach. Time, History, and Literature*, 80.

[4] Jameson, *The Political Unconscious*, 12.

[5] Jameson, *The Political Unconscious*, 12.

6 From Jameson's blurb to *Scenes from the Drama of European Literature*: "A major collection of important essays on European literature, almost all classics, and almost all required reading for their various centuries - thus the book is indispensable for the medieval period, the seventeenth and nineteenth centuries; in addition, the 'Figura' and the Vico essays are very significant theoretical statements. The book is lucid and far more accessible for undergraduates than current high theory. Nor has Auerbach's own work aged--all of his varied strengths are in evidence in this collection, which is a better way into his work than *Mimesis*."

7 It goes without saying that for Jameson the hopes of Marxism have not been fulfilled in capitalist society, but Jameson is also a strong critic of Stalinism.

8 Jameson, *The Political Unconscious*, 19. Jameson expands the thought and quotes from Marx's Capital following this thought: "These matters can recover their original urgency for us only if they are retold within the unity of a single great collective story; only if, in however disguised and symbolic a form, they are seen as sharing a single fundamental theme—for Marxism the collective struggle to wrest a realm of Freedom from the realm of Necessity."

9 Jameson, *The Political Unconscious*, 18.

10 Jameson, *The Political Unconscious*, 17.

11 Jameson, *The Political Unconscious*, 22.

12 Auerbach, "Figura," 97.

13 Auerbach, "Figura," 95.

14 Auerbach, "Figura," 101.

15 Auerbach, "Figura," 79.

16 Auerbach, "Figura," 80.

[17] Auerbach, "Figura," 100. This will be the actual, complete, real and final event. This is the case not only for Old Testament prefiguration, which points to the Incarnation and the proclamation of the Gospel. It is also the case for the Incarnation and the Gospel themselves. For these two are not yet the final fulfillment but rather also a promise of the Last Days and the true Kingdom of God to come.

[18] Auerbach, "Figura," 100.

[19] Auerbach, "Figura," 95.

[20] Auerbach, "Figura," 94.

[21] Auerbach, "Figura," 104.

[22] Venturino, Stephen, "Jameson, The Political Unconscious," http://aprofessorintheory.com/notes-on-theory-texts/jameson-the-political-unconscious/

[23] Jameson, *The Political Unconscious*, 284.

[24] Jameson, *The Political Unconscious*, 30.

[25] Jameson, *The Political Unconscious*, 30.

[26] http://www.feedbooks.com/book/4237/the-epistle-to-can-grande

[27] Jameson, *The Political Unconscious*, 31.

Ach Grete!
A German Tutor in 19th Century Brazil

Ricardo da Silveira Lobo Sternberg

Let me begin with a short bio-bibliographical note: a few weeks after Elizabeth Bishop passed away in 1979, I was called by her partner, Alice Methfessel, and asked whether I would like to take a look at Elizabeth's Brazilian books. I made the trip to Boston and, for the last time, to Lewis Wharf where Bishop had lived until her death. Alice had arranged piles of books in Portuguese on the floor and I quickly realized what a treasure trove it was. No need to triage and I told Alice I would take them all. (I believe I did with one exception. The poet Frank Bidart who was there that day must have recognized the name of Vinicius de Moraes. Perhaps from stories told by Bishop—Vinicius had visited often in Ouro Preto the colonial town where Bishop lived after Lota's death—and Bidart kept two or three of Vinicius's books dedicated to Elizabeth Bishop and I took the rest back to Toronto.)

If one went simply by the name scribbled on the insides, the books belonged some to Bishop and others to her Brazilian partner, Lota Macedo Soares. The authors? Manuel Bandeira, Mario de Andrade, Carlos Drummond de Andrade, Clarice Lispector: in short, the Pounds, the Eliots and the Hemingways of Brazil were all there. Many with dedications to Elizabeth. (One I recall was from the poet Manuel Bandeira and read: para Elizabeth Bishop, de um tradutor perplexo. To Elizabeth Bishop from a perplexed translator.) Amongst such riches, I paid little attention to a small volume with the title *Alegrias e Tristezas de uma Educadora Alemã no Brasil*. (Joys and Sorrows of a German Tutor in Brazil) by one Ina von Binzer.[1] The book carries Elizabeth Bishop's name written in her own handwriting and below it in parenthesis "from Rosinha Christmas 1958." Rosinha, I assume was Rosinha Leão, a friend of

Bishop and Lota who had accompanied Elizabeth on a trip down the Amazon.

No doubt bedazzled by those signed first editions of so many major Brazilian writers of the 20th century, it would be years before I read Binzer's book. But I remembered the title as I prepared a course called "Foreign Mappings" that traced the foreign gaze in Brazil, from the famous first letter written in 1500 by Pero Vaz de Caminha to Richard Burton's *Explorations of the Highland of Brazil* to Maria Graham's *Journal of a Voyage to Brazil* to the poetry of Bishop herself and of P.K. Page (a Canadian poet whose stay in Brazil as the wife of the Canadian Ambassador in the 1950s overlapped with Bishop's. She is the author of a delightful *Brazilian Journal*).[2] Ina von Binzer's book takes its place alongside a numerous collection of travel literature by foreign visitors to Brazil, a canon that we could say begins with that letter of 1500 announcing the discovery of Brazil but that becomes numerous and gains popularity only in the 19th century, a century that saw a great increase in the number of travelers not just to South America but throughout the world.

The accounts of travelers to Brazil came to fill a void for the Portuguese themselves, who after the initial flurry of texts, many of them written by missionaries in the early days of colonization, showed very little interest in writing about Brazil. But the canon gains impetus after 1808 when the Portuguese Royal Family, better yet, the entire Portuguese court, one step ahead of the invading forces of Napoleon, abandon Lisbon and sail to Rio de Janeiro, turning that city into the only city in the New World that was, for a brief spell, the very centre and court of a large European Empire.

Portugal had, since 1591, prohibited the presence of "foreigners" in Brazil, closing the ports to all non-Portuguese vessels. Only then, in 1808, and in response to pressure from England, are the ports opened and a degree of liberalization in commerce takes place. From then on, a great number of foreigners, scientists, artists, artisans, some invited by the Royal Family itself, made their way to Brazil and many left a written record of their journey. It is said that between 1500 and 1808 there are only about 100 texts that can be considered travel literature and that that number doubled within fifty years of the Royal Family's arrival in Brazil.

By an overwhelming margin the collection of Brazilian travel literature is comprised of texts written by men. (I have no reason to believe that Brazil was unique in this respect.) I know of no account written by a woman visiting Brazil before the 19th century. And there are only a few in that century. Men came in the course of their work (as missionaries, engineers, scientists) while women tended to travel accompanying their men. Ina von Binzer's book stands out not only because the author is a woman but also because she is a woman traveling to South America on her own.

After completing her Governess's exam and teaching a few years in Germany, Ina Sofie Amalie von Binzer sailed to Brazil in 1881 at age 25 to take up a prearranged position as tutor to a Brazilian family. She remained in Brazil until 1884. She left her first employer, the Rameiro family, for health reasons and lived in Rio for a period teaching at a private girls' school. She left that school and went to work for the Costa family in the Province of São Paulo. We do not know how the initial hiring was done but Brazilian newspapers were full of ads of families looking for tutors or tutors looking for families. She might, for instance, have placed an ad such as this one, published in a Brazilian newspaper at the time:

> A Tutor, with German certificates desires to find employment with a family or a school to teach the following subjects: Conversation and Grammar in French, English and German, piano, drawing, painting both with watercolours or oil, History, Geography and Arithmetic. Leave message at the German School.

The book, gathering letters written by Ulla van Eck, for so Ina von Binzer called herself in these letters to her friend, Grete, is perhaps slightly fictionalized though many of the details narrated in the letters have been confirmed. It appeared in Germany in 1887 and the Brazilian translation, the very book included in my Elizabeth Bishop's collection, appeared in 1956. A second Brazilian edition would come out in 1980 under a different title: *Os Meus Romanos* (My Romans) a reference to the Greco-Roman names of the children in her third job: Lavinia, Caius Gracchus, Tiberius, Cloelia and Cornelia, etc.[3]

Two characteristics make von Binzer's book worthy of our attention. The first is the very unique position she holds and that informs her text. The many scientists and travelers who left journals behind were people in transit, moving through areas as they collected flora and fauna. Though in Brazil, they truly look at Brazilian life from a distance. Von Binzer, as the letters make clear, wrote from what I would call a very intimate, quotidian perch inside the very houses and alongside the families she worked for. There are details in her letters that are truly singular. The second characteristic is the voice in these letters: she is funny, observant, intelligent. (And one can only imagine how much these letters delighted Elizabeth Bishop.) Yes, she sees Brazil with foreign eyes and often with foreign prejudices but never, I would say, with malice. The letters are also quite varied in tone. She can describe a landscape objectively, with precision, almost as a scientist would, or she can wax romantic about Brazilian scenery. She can speak with some authority on the pedagogical problems facing Brazil or pour out her soul to Grete, especially when a certain English Engineer, Mr Hall, conquers her heart. It is perhaps no accident that the title of her book evokes that quintessential romantic novel also written in epistolary form: The Sorrows of Young Werther.

Von Binzer's first letter to Grete is remarkable for betraying how little this young woman knew about Brazil, discovering, for instance, only on arrival, that Portuguese not Spanish was spoken. But the letter also speaks of the shock between her romantic expectations of what Brazil and Brazilians would be like, drawn from literature or from opera, and the reality on the ground. She would note for instance, that Dr. Rameiro, her first employer could not be considered an elegant man and "bears no resemblance with the beautiful Brazilians of the Operattas of Friderich Wilhelmstadt. How disappointing"(p.21).

Fazenda São Francisco, May 27 1881

My dear Grete!

> Fazenda means plantation. I am sorry not to write"hacienda," for you are all probably still convinced that this is how it is said and I am sorry to disappoint you in the very first lines of my letter. Console yourselves: the same thing happened to me but I still think it adorable that we innocently confused Spanish with Portuguese. Thus, one loses one illusion after another (p.19).

Another illusion lost is mentioned in the same letter:

> A second disappointment awaiting you will be my travel from Rio de Janeiro to here: I will not be able to tell you of any assaults by indians, not even a struggle against tigers, when, at the very least, you were expecting giant snakes. Having arrived here without any accidents I recognize from the start my position of inferiority vis a vis other travellers in the tropics" (p.19).

She goes on to say how disappointed she was to be picked up by her employer, Dr. Rameiro in a "very comfortable European carriage"(p.19). In explaining the Dr. in Dr. Rameiro, she suggests much about the patriarchal nature and class stratification of Brazilian society that, accurate in the 19th century, is still to a certain extent valid today: (doutores sem doutorados/doctors without doctorates)

> I do not know why they call him "Doctor" and I doubt that he himself could give a reason for this treatment. The only logical explanation would be that every Brazilian well placed in life is already born with the right to the title, and if, on the one hand, it would appear to be a lack of humility, on the other it would be simply stupid to demand that they go out and conquer such title by actual studies that would prove as difficult as they are unnecessary (p.19).

As she very quickly understood there was no necessity of a doctorate to be a doctor: all one needed was property, land and slaves, and of course, to be white.

Whatever expectations Ina had prior to arriving, the reality of her position as tutor was quite different. She writes to Grete:

> Free time! Oh my dear Grete how these words had the power to make me almost elegiac. Do you remember when we decided between us as a fact that Brazilians did nothing beside worry about their elegance and smoke? Their ladies, wrapped in vaporous dresses, rocked in the hammocks being fanned by interesting negro girls dressed in red and white...? How orange and banana trees, through the mist of our fantasy, had the unique tendency of growing through the windows right into the house while multicoloured parrots and gracious hummingbirds flew around us like the pigeons in Lilli Park? Naturally people that romantic would never demand of a tutor, excessive work but rather would allow them to rest with their pupils

under the shade of orange trees, teaching, almost
as if playing, the mother tongue, tasting fruits,
taming parrots, writing poetry, decorating each
other with garlands of flowers...

Ah Grete, what can I say except Ach! (p.21).

Her life as a tutor in the Fazenda was indeed far from the imagined
dulce far niente :

The family had 12 children and 7 of them under
her tutelage. These seven would be divided into
two groups. Ina had brought from Germany a
pedagogical manual by Karl Bormann with the
faith that it would solve whatever issues she
encountered in Brazil. Ach. The oldest three,
young ladies of 19, 21 and 22, (only a little
younger than their German tutor) were habitually
late to every class so that Ina, following the
guidelines set out by Karl Bormann demanded
they arrive on time. They do so only to sit
indifferent, morose, hostile. Ina:"Ah Grete this
trio is horribly paralyzing. The appearance of
these three remind me of the Holy Inquisition,
and the judges sitting on the bench would
certainly not show themselves more belligerent
than these three"(p.23). The younger pupils are
nicer but impossible to control. "Ach Grete!
They are so provoking" (p.24).

Ina would teach different subjects and different configurations of
pupils from 7 in the morning to 5 in the afternoon with a short
break for breakfast and a short break for lunch. Brazilian pupils
would prove challenging in all three jobs.

Part of the problem was the informal, domestic, unstructured
space where classes were held. And she notes this was especially

deleterious for the education of girls as the boys were often sent to boarding schools, and some even to Europe, to further their education. For the girls, a varnish of education was all that was required: a little foreign language, the ability to play something on the piano, a dabbling in drawing and painting. Very little importance or priority was given to the work of tutors brought in from Europe such as von Binzer. Teaching in the midst of a busy, large household proved extremely difficult what with the noise, the interruptions, the effort spent in keeping the students focused. Here she writes of a piano lesson gone astray:

> The Piano lessons are given in the Mistress's Workroom since the children are not to use the Grand Piano at the Salon. This so called work room is at the very centre of the house with doors opening to several other rooms: to the pantry, to the bathroom, to the children's bedroom, to the bedrooms of the older girls, to a dressing room and to the sewing room. You can already imagine the level of noise under normal conditions...(p.48).

She then goes on to describe the day during one of her classes when all the contents of the Pantry were emptied into the work room as the Mistress and several slaves searched for mice. All while she is trying to teach. And, she adds, "to top it all a young negro girl that is being taught to read by one of the daughters posted herself behind me reciting in a monotonous tone: b-a ba; b-e be; b-i bi. That was it. I got up furious, picked up the music, called to Leonila and finished the class in the Salon. They did not approve of my attitude and at the end I was the one considered to be at fault" (p. 49). Even at the school in Rio, Ina did not have what she considered adequate space for teaching. She shared her classroom with another teacher and notes "while at one end they are reciting poems in Portuguese at the other I try to explain to my inattentive ladies the complicated declinations of German" (p.65).

The Karl Bormann Manual, on which she had placed so much confidence, proved of little use south of the equator. Here she tries to apply it to a situation in the girls' school in Rio. She tells Grete:

> As for discipline! The word itself brings blood to my head. Imagine this: the other day, I entered and found the class noisy and unruly and in my confusion I again had recourse to the Bormann manual. When I managed to silence them so as to be heard, I ordered them to rise and then to sit five times in a row—what in our country would always be shameful to the entire class. But here—Oh Sancta Simplicitas—when I finally made them understand what I wanted from them, the children were incapable of seeing it as a punishment and thought it was a fun game and noisily stood up and sat down, stood up and sat down—up and down they went like automatons, having themselves a grand time. Since then, Grete, the Bormann has been definitely retired (p.67).

The lack of discipline and insubordination by the students was in part caused by the close contact that children had with parents, relatives and slaves during class time. This confusion between public and private space in the education of children is noted by other travelers and by Brazilians themselves. "Rico se educa em casa" goes the saying. The rich are educated at home. The other factor making these Brazilian children hard to teach was their exacerbated sense of entitlement. These were children of the Master, at the very top of their society, some of them, as one of Ina's younger pupils, themselves owners of slaves given to them as birthday gifts. Children, in short, used to lording over adults and not much inclined to show respect to a young German tutor. And though the two translators of the Brazilian edition criticize Ina for being too rigid, too Germanic, too anti-Brazilian, Ina, having finally put her Karl Bormann manual away, is actually quite reasonable when she concludes:

> I recognize that the adoption of a pedagogy here is indispensable– but it should be a Brazilian pedagogy and not a German one, based on Brazilian realities, and adapted to the character of the Brazilian people and to the domestic conditions where it takes place. Brazilian children should not be educated by Germans: it is a waste of time (p.67).

Another rich vein of observations in the letters are the tutor's comments on slavery. She arrives in Brazil as the country makes it slow, cynical, piecemeal moves towards abolition. By the time she arrived the so called Free Womb law had been passed in 1851 that would eventually free every child born of slaves after that date. The Law of the Sexagenerians of 1885 would be enacted after her departure and abolition itself came only in 1888.

Her attitude towards the African slave is, especially at first, simply informed by the run of the mill 19th century European racist attitudes and European sense of racial superiority. Her first impression of slaves is one of almost physical revulsion. This will change with time but she will maintain in her letters that the African did not understand freedom and therefore was not yearning for it. When Dr. Rameiro speaks of a slave who had enough money to buy her freedom but chose not to, von Binzer notes in her letter, "One cannot expect of that race, enslaved for so many generations, a view of self proper of highly civilized people, nor intend that they adopt our concept of freedom, in terms of man or of honor in terms of women; that would simply be useless poetic aspiration" (p.40). As she spends time in Brazil she recognizes that abolition is inevitable, and here she is quite perceptive in describing how little prepared the country is for the transition to the next stage.

Throughout the letters Binzer notes the Brazilian economy's total dependence on slave labor and its deleterious effect on Brazilians, especially the disdain it creates for work, seen as something shameful. She notes "the Brazilian does not work and when he is poor prefers to live as a parasite in the house of family or rich friends rather than search out for an honest profession" (p.34). She is describing, of course, the custom of "agregados," (household retainers—not quite employees, not quite family) a very typical Brazilian social arrangement in the 19th century. The agregados with their ambiguous social status would be of great interest to novelists such as Machado de Assis. O agregado Dias, for instance, plays an important role in one Machado's greatest novels, *Dom Casmurro*. She is also very cognizant of the fact—and the future consequences—that no effort was being made to prepare the slaves for freedom: no provision for their education or their training in a trade.

The unique perspective afforded Binzer is well demonstrated in her description of two incidents concerning slaves in the two different fazendas where she lived. It would be hard to imagine a foreign visitor not living in the master's house being able to experience at first hand these episodes. Both of them are written with a sense of immediacy and of drama that my summary here cannot duplicate.

In the first, written almost entirely in dialogue, evening tea is interrupted by the arrival at the door of two slaves, runaways from a neighboring farm owned by a Dr. Albus, famous in the area for his cruel treatment of slaves. The two begged Dr. Rameiro to buy them from Albus. Mrs. Rameiro explains to Binzer that "Dr. Albus is known to mistreat his slaves. All my husband has to do when faced with an insubordinate slave is threaten to sell him to Dr. Albus to make him immediately meek" (p.38). Dr. Rameiro points out that he cannot afford to allow the slaves to spend even the night and will have to deliver them back to their owner. When Binzer asks whether there are then still places where the conditions described in *Uncle Tom's Cabin* still exist, Rameiro gives a typical Brazilian answer:

> The Brazilian is kinder than the north-american
> and among us the negroes have a very different
> life. Look: when a slave is freed, he is given equal
> rights with whites: we have professors, artists,
> doctors, deputies and even ministers of color.
> And Princess Isabel also dances with negroes.
> The disdain on one side and the anger on the
> other are not as deep here as they are among our
> brothers in the North (p.39).

To loop back to Elizabeth Bishop: she would refer to the episode of the princess dancing with a black man in her famous or infamous Life World Library book on Brazil. There she notes that Brazilians often point to this incident to illustrate their different attitudes towards race. When ladies at the court of Pedro II refused to dance with the famous black engineer, Andre Rebouças, Princess Isabel crossed the room and asked that he dance with her.[4] As to what will befall the two runaways, Rameiro explains to Ina: "--They will receive a good beating and will from now on be treated with even greater severity" (p. 39).

The second incident is described in a letter written from the household of the Costas in São Paulo on 21st of April of 1882. It tells with some amusement the story of a young slave who, sent into town on an errand, never returned. Dr. Costa, considering him a runaway, published a note in the newspaper seeking his return. He then received a letter from an abolitionist society, informing him that they had been approached by his slave Tiberius, who presented himself to the society asking to be freed and depositing with the society the amount of 200,000 cruzeiros, (about 400 marks). The society was thus offering that amount to Dr. Costa. Binzer notes that Dr. Costa yelled, screamed, blamed himself for not sending the slave to work at the plantation earlier and then made a counter offer demanding 2,000 marks for the slave's freedom. Ina then writes:

> This morning was the deadline when a doctor
> and another specialist had to decide on the value

of this human merchandise. If yesterday, our
dear Mr. Costa was furious, today he was like a
man possessed, yelling loud enough to shake the
walls. What could have happened? In the days
since his disappearance, the abolitionists had
plied Tiberius with purgatives, one after the other
so that this strong young man, so healthy in the
recent past, appeared at as a miserably weak
human being, wobbly in the legs and in such a
sad shape that the doctor and the evaluator could
not estimate him being worth beyond 200
cruzeiros. What do you think of this case?
Certainly not an honest behaviour but it contains
a good dose of humor (p. 81).

In letters written from the Costa's farm, von Binzer begins to
tell Grete of a British Engineer, Mr Hall who courted her
cautiously, at times perhaps too timidly for Ulla's liking. She first
speaks of him in April of 1882 where among people she met at the
house of German friends is a "a very attractive man that spoke
almost exclusively with me and praised my English as being very
good. He is called Mister Hall" (p.77). She ends that letter: Ach
Grete, how happy I am here! So happy (p.77)! Several letters from
then on will mention Mr. Hall.

The last letter in the book, and not coincidentally the end of
my talk, is a note of joy dated January of 1883 where she announces
their engagement and their forthcoming departure from Brazil. It
lists their two names: Ulla von Eck and George Hall followed by
Engaged, and continues: Sweet Grete! It happened at the ball! I've
always loved balls. I will no longer be writing to you since we will
soon be there. Your more than happy—and trying here her future
name for the first time—Ulla Hall (How funny to hear it!)(p. 137).

As it turned out, according to what records we have, it was not
to be. Binzer would not leave for another year. Perhaps during that
time, the ever-reticent Mr. Hall backpedalled. The fact is that on her

return Ina von Binzer marries not the English Engineer but a German judge. Ah Grete! What can I say but ach!

Notes

[1] Ina von Binzer, *Alegrias e Tristezas de uma Educadora Alemã no Brasil*, trans. Alice Rossi, Luisita da Gama Cerqueira de Carvalho. São Paulo: Editora Anhembi, 1956. All citations of the letters are from this edition and translated into English by the author. Subsequent parenthetical references will refer to this edition.

[2] Paulo Roberto Pereira, introduction to *Os tres únicos testemunhos do descobrimento do Brasil*. São Paulo: Lacerda Ed. 1999; Sir Richard Francis Burton, *Explorations of the highlands of the Brazil: with a full account of the gold and diamond mines, also canoeing down 1500 miles of the great river São Francisco, from Sabará to the sea*. New York: Greenwood Press, 1969; Maria Graham, Journal of a voyage to Brazil. New York: Praeger, 1969; P.K. Page, *Brazilian Journal*. Toronto: Lester & Orpen Dennys, 1987.

[3] Ina von Binzer, *Os Meus Romanos: Alegrias e tristezas de uma educadora alemã no Brasil*. São Paulo: Anhembi, 1956.

[4] Elizabeth Bishop, *Brazil*. New York: Time, Inc. 1962, p.113.

Part III
Gender Identities

Gender is the Real Queer: Gender Wars in Contemporary Poland

Joanna Niżyńska

The Letter

On December 29, 2013, on the Sunday of the Holy Family, a holiday celebrated in the Catholic liturgical calendar, a pastoral letter of the Bishops' Conference of Poland (Episkopat Polski) was read in Polish churches. The bishops—or "the Shepherds of the Catholic Church in Poland," as the letter was signed—examined a theme appropriate to the holiday, namely the importance of marriage and the family and the challenges facing these old institutions in modern society. It was this letter that catapulted to the front page of every Polish newspaper a foreign word that most Poles had never heard before: gender.

The notion of gender appeared in the letter as part of the phrase "gender ideology" ("ideologia gender"), a phrase as confusing for the average churchgoer unfamiliar with the term as it was for those familiar with the notion's complex cultural semantics. The letter barely hinted at a definition of the term; it kept the meaning suspended, forcing listeners to recreate its sense from the description of increasingly damaging effects that this foreign phenomenon supposedly exercises on Polish society and its collective identity. Threatening the "Christian vision of marriage and family that transpires from the interpretation of human nature," gender ideology, according to the pastoral letter, "attempts to impose a different definition of marriage and the family," which "inevitably leads to the breakup of families and the defeat of the human being."[1] Gender ideology "promotes principles that are totally contrary to reality and to an integral understanding of human nature. It maintains that biological sex is not socially significant and

131

that cultural sex, which humans can freely develop and determine irrespective of biological conditions, is paramount."[2]

According to this ideology, the letter explains, "humans can freely determine whether to be men or women and freely choose their sexual orientation." The freedom to "voluntary self-determin[e]" one's sexual identity leads society, in turn, to "accept the right to set up new types of families, for instance, families built on homosexual relations." Gender ideology is, hence, an ideology that fractures the system of fundamental Christian values. Moreover, the bishops warn that because society is not aware of its inherent danger ("a decisive majority has no idea what this ideology is about and consequently does not feel threatened by it"), gender ideology surreptitiously permeates the deepest societal tissues; the more surreptitious its mode of spreading, the letter seems to suggest, the more damaging its effects.

Hence, gender ideology renders imperceptible the dissolution of the values that define the contemporary Polish collective. Without religious intervention, the Polish family will fall into the trap of de-spiritualization, into which other modern societies have already plunged. This imported de-spiritualization that gender ideology represents threatens hence both religious and national identity, inextricably interwoven in the discourse of the Polish Catholic Church (and best expressed in the stereotype "Pole, the Catholic" [Polak katolik]). The sustenance of national identity depends, according to the Church, on adherence to the teachings of the Catholic doctrine cemented by centuries of Poland's (self-)image as antemurale christianitatis (the Bulwark of Christianity).

Gender ideology is culturally and spiritually foreign to the very core of Polishness, but in the letter read on the Sunday of the Holy Family it is not clear whether it is a fifth column sent from the "West" (i.e., the EU and its liberal policies) or whether perhaps it has something to do with things local, since it is related to "some radicalizing feminist movement" and Poland can boast quite a good one. Regardless, gender ideologists neither understand nor respect the values that kept Polishness alive throughout numerous historical misfortunes and long periods of foreign oppression. In the context of a post-communist allergy in Poland to historical materialism, the genesis of gender ideology as a "product of decades of ideological and cultural changes [...] deeply rooted in Marxism and neo-Marxism endorsed by some feminist movements and the sexual revolution" marks it as foreign as well. It's foreign because, like Marxism, it was imposed on Poles by an external force and it belies the essence of Polish collective identity.[3]

Only one sentence of the letter suggests that "gender" may have something to do with cultural analysis: "There is nothing wrong with research on the impact of culture on sex,"[4] the bishops affirm, but they immediately follow this affirmation with the warning that "what is dangerous, however, is to argue on the basis of ideology that biological sex ("płeć biologiczna") has no significance in social life." The first sentence ("There is nothing wrong with research on the impact of culture on sex"), thanks to the fact that it was translated mechanically into English, reveals the problems of rendering in Polish the categories related to gender and sexuality, which may easily escape one's attention in the Polish original. Since the only word given in Polish is "płeć," the translator worked on autopilot and assigned it the direct equivalent "sex." "Płeć" indeed denotes "sex" (this is the word used, for instance, on birth certificates), but in Polish when talking about biological and cultural aspects of sexual identity one needs to resort to modifiers to distinguish between "gender" and "sex." Hence, the adjective "cultural" before the word "sex" denotes "gender," whereas the word "biological" before "sex" denotes "sex" (literally, sex means "biological sex" ["płeć biologiczna"] and gender means "cultural sex" ["płeć kulturowa"]).

The bishops are aware of this distinction, and they use the necessary modifiers in the original. Since they view sex and sexuality as immutable biological categories, they didn't intend to suggest that research on the cultural modification of sex is harmless; hence, the lack of "cultural" before "sex" must have been unintentional. We can assume, however, that for many in the audience who were oblivious to the pitfalls of analytical vocabulary, the word "płeć" without the modifier claimed by default its traditional biological semantics. One way or another, even though "gender" and "sex" as distinct yet mutually dynamic notions are a staple of global academic discourse, including Polish academia, public discourse in Poland frequently conflates the two.

The appeal to "all people of good-will"[5] to courageously defend the truth about marriage and the family strengthens an exhortation to educational institutions to resist pressure from "the few but vocal groups with considerable finances" who "in the name of modern education carry out experiments on children and young people." Nomina sunt odiosa—names are hateful—and just as we do not learn the definition of gender ideology, neither do we learn the names of these mysterious groups. An informed audience can guess that the considerable financial resources refer to the money Poland receives from the European Union to implement so-called gender mainstreaming ("polityka równościowa"), that is, various political, educational, and cultural strategies to promote gender equality (particularly equality in the political sphere including the gender distribution of parliamentary seats). The bishops' letter is intended to warn, then, that although "some media portray this ideology in a positive way: as a means to counteract violence and to aim for equality" it is in fact a way to conduct experiments on the young (let us not forget that the letter was read on the holiday celebrating family) and on society in general. The bishops' counsel becomes all the more critical, as "without public knowledge or Poles' consent for many months now the gender ideology has been slowly introduced into different structures of social life: education, health service, cultural and education centres and non-governmental organisations." Signaling that "gender ideology" is a subject of financial and institutional manipulations for the few vocal groups makes this more than a Polish affair; what is suggested is the larger context of the EU and its social and cultural politics.[6]

Finally, to conclude my brief discussion of this version of the letter (as there will be another), I would like to signal the issue of homosexuality linked in the bishops' message to the notion of family structure. Gender ideology, with its disregard for the biological and emphasis on the free choice of gender and sexuality, promotes "new forms of family, for instance those built on homosexual relations." Although "the Church will never agree to debasing persons with a homosexual inclination, at the same time it strongly underscores that homosexual activity is profoundly disorderly and that marriage as a community of a man and a woman as a social phenomenon cannot be put on a par with a homosexual relationship." Note that the bishops do not talk about the homosexual relationship as countering heterosexual marriage but rather qualify it under the group of alternative forms of family life.

The episcopal letter hence outed, so to speak, what it considered to be hidden from the eyes of most of society: the deeply damaging effects of a seemingly beneficial cultural strategy and its surreptitious dissemination. Practically overnight, "gender" became the subject of numerous public debates. What followed in the media was a national-scale frenzy around an empty signifier. For the opponents (it turned out that it was possible to be an opponent or a proponent of "gender"), "gender" and "gender ideology" became a space onto which everything could be projected: the destabilization of family values, a culture of oversexualization, and a disregard for the value of traditional gender roles. The foreignness of the word, no doubt, facilitated this projection of gender as an import from the "West," a view of sexuality and family that threatens to obscure the blueprints of Polish society and its collective identity. Clearly, the notion became a useful tool in the culture wars: it could be either demonized by its adversaries or simplified by its advocates. In both cases the picture was painted with broad brushstrokes.

"Gender" was on everyone's lips and in every type of media. It appeared on the front pages of every newspaper in Poland; it was the topic of endless TV debates, talk shows, radio programs, and

Internet blogging. Remember that in addition to a sizeable audience of declared and practicing Catholics (these categories actually rarely overlap in Poland), the Church exercises a strong influence on public discourse through its media, such as popular TV and radio stations. Until now used mainly in academic discourse, "gender" became a keyword of the contemporary Polish cultural lexicon. Its pervasiveness was so thorough that it was chosen as the 2013 word of the year in Poland by a committee of leading linguists and the Polish Language Foundation, beating, for instance, "Euromaidan," a notion that pertained to the vital interests of the Polish state in Ukraine. The language of gender has become a useful tool of political visibility and manipulation. As the specter of gender came to haunt the Polish parliament, a group was formed to fight gender ideology ("Stop ideologii gender": 1 woman, 15 men).[7] Public discourse in Poland's young democracy thrives on polarization, and what better instrument of polarization than a foreign word whose meaning is unclear?

"Queer" versus "Gay"

The earlier debate on the use of a foreign term took place nine years ago and it concerned the notion of "queer," for a Polish audience a notion with a much more complicated foreign provenance. How "queer" entered public circulation and how it circulated may provide a refreshing perspective on the career of "gender." "Queer" emerged onto the public arena in 2005 following the publication of "the first queer novel," *Lubiewo*, by Michał Witkowski (*Lovetown* in the English translation[8]). There were others queer novels before *Lovetown*, but none deserved the designation "breakthrough" in terms of their popularity, publicity, or the significance of their reception. Since its publication, *Lovetown* has been reprinted in Poland seven times, has undergone five different editions with the text significantly adjusted each time, has been translated into several languages, and has won major literary awards. It was staged in Cracow's theaters, got its own graphic novel edition, and became a blogging phenomenon. Its author, self-fashioned as a celebrity "queen/ciota" (this is how Witkowski refers to himself, after his main characters), has been garnering media attention ever since in a style that has remained subversive and unique in Poland's celebrity and literary cultures alike.

Because no other novel that takes sexual minority as its subject had triggered this kind of intense public debate in Poland before, the vocabulary used in this debate was symptomatic of the conceptual framework at the critics' disposal and had a consolidating effect on that vocabulary. The novel triggered a substantial discussion on the visibility and representation of gay communities in Polish culture; the representation was fictional, yet in its reception by Polish audiences (culturally accustomed to socially engaged literature) it acquired the status of almost a documentary, albeit flamboyant, portrayal of queer life under communism. In other words, Witkowski's fiction became naturalized and historicized.[9] The bottom line is that *Lovetown*'s criticism played both a descriptive and a prescriptive role: it discussed the subject of representation but in the process of discussion produced this very subject in the first place, particularly for audiences beyond academia. After *Lovetown*, no author or critic could write the way they had before its publication.

Let me in a few words describe what's going on in *Lovetown*. Employing colloquial, campy, brazen, at times shocking, at times poignant language, Witkowski writes about both the homosexual circles of communist-era '70s Poland and their twenty-first-century post-communist edition. The novel's primary narrator functions (in the book's first and best-known part) as listener to the recollections of two aging cioty (Polish jargon for queens or faggots), and he occupies the role of mediator between the two homosexual subcultures, which Polish critics labeled as pre-emancipated and emancipated (problematic terms when applied to the context of Polish minorities under the communist and post-communist political regimes). The pre-emancipated group consists of the aging cioty who speak about themselves in feminine forms, cross-dress, talk with nostalgia about the communist-era cruising grounds and public toilets, and celebrate their own abjection. The emancipated group (known as "the group from Poznań") showcases Poland's new geopolitical standing—its assimilating, westernizing gays play volleyball on the beach, frequent the gym, shop at Sephora, and contemplate fighting for their rights to marry and adopt. The narrator articulates his awareness of his own ambivalent position: he is young, well-educated, gay, and although in the beginning of the novel he is disgusted with the communist-era cioty, he gradually begins to valorize their exploits, identify with their creativity; above all, he is enchanted with the scope of their imagination to perform their otherness. A cosmopolitan, doctoral-dissertation-writing (an important fact given the novel's sarcastic, self-conscious take on queer studies) narrator from the book's opening chapter ends up ironic towards the new Poland's assimilating gays. In the words of Western academia, he travels—via the '70s queens—from "gay" to "queer."

The book's reception proliferated sets of binaries, which were expressed in the reviews as sets of questions: is this a pro- or anti-gay novel; emancipatory or anti-emancipatory; pre-emancipatory or emancipatory; emancipatory or post-emancipatory; first or not first in the historical trajectory of the subject, and so on and so forth. Each of these binaries is imbued with fascinating cultural idiosyncrasies, which deserve a separate treatment, but I would like to turn my attention to the case of conflating in Polish criticism two fundamental notions: "queer" and "gay." In 2005 the use of these terms in most of the reviews of the novel is interchangeable. When *Lovetown* is called a queer novel, it simply means that it is a pro-gay and emancipatory novel. Clearly, this is a serious de-contextualization of what we know about the gay–queer trajectory in the United States, where the queer formation separates itself from the gay agenda of gaining political capital via a structural assimilation into the institutions of civil society. This assimilation— such as gay marriage and adoption—presupposes that, as long as we bracket out the uncomfortable issue of desire, in civil society we are all the same. In the American social, cultural, and political context, queer emerges as the result of a long history of emancipation; only because it benefited from this history of emancipation could it afford to turn against it. Transplanted into Polish ground, the notion lost its inherent hyper-self-consciousness of subversion. The larger question to ask, however, is this: Could Poland have its own "queerness" if it didn't have its own capital of "gayness" that could be subverted? Can there be queer before gay?

Interestingly, when Polish critics of *Lovetown* resorted to foreign terms, that is, to the notions of queer and gay, they tended to conflate them. Both terms were used in the same way for both sides of the (communist and post-communist) historical divide that the novel so suggestively constructs. When a Polish term would enter the discussion, it created the reverse trajectory (from queer to gay), although critics themselves did not seem to be aware of what they were suggesting. Paweł Dunin-Wąsowicz, for instance, wrote about the novel: "*Lubiewo* is about the world that is in the process of transformation from faggot-ness (pedalstwo) into gayness (gejostwo)."[10] With the use of the local term of exclusion ("pedalstwo" comes from "pedał," and is an equivalent of "ciota," the governing term of *Lovetown*), the notion of gay maintained its emancipatory distinctiveness.

A thought-provoking reversal emerges if we wanted to translate the Polish term "pedał" (or "ciota") in the spirit of the novel back to English. Since the characters of *Lovetown* perform their otherness in a hyper-aware style, rather than "faggot" or "fagotness," which carries only the charge of derogation, not resignification, we should use, precisely, "queer." And if so, Dunin-Wąsowicz's statement would read that "*Lovetown* is about the world that is in the process of transformation from queerness into gayness." A trajectory from "queer alla Pollacca" to a universalized gay emerges: under communism we had our local "ciotas," and now we have Westernized gays.

I say "queer alla Pollacca" because the resignification of "queer" in American English has a specific historical trajectory and is connected with the history of feminist, gay, and LGBT activism. Cultural theories of queer studies and the hyper-self-awareness of the field inherently relate (even if in an act of defiance) to the history of social activism. This is not the case in Poland. What happens in Polish academia often precedes what happens on the level of civil society. As a rule, imported notions such as queer circulate decontextualized and dehistoricized.

Just a few years after the publication of *Lovetown*, books on queer studies in Poland addressed this earlier tendency to conflate "queer" and "gay." Many agreed that the conflation indicated that the distinction between the identity politics of LGBT movements and the post-identity politics of the queer remains superfluous in the context of Polish society, in which minorities struggle to generate various forms of social visibility, in most cases with the goal of emancipation in mind. In other words, the American trajectory, "from gay activism to queer theory," did not glocalize well. The notion of "queer" as a return to irreducible difference, and the performance of this difference through a positionality (David Halperin's approach, for instance) that is par excellence subversive and oppositional (and not just counter-narrative but always already open-ended), cannot be well accommodated by a society in which sexual minorities still battle for recognition and visibility.

This incompatibility of the notion of "queer" with the Polish social context finds its reflection in the functioning of the very word "queer," which even for those Poles who know English well cannot carry the same charge of resignification or palimpsestic signification of simultaneous abuse and subversive affirmation. The mere fact that the radicality of "queer" is lost in the mouths of foreign speakers might explain why it has been adopted as an institutional label for programs in Queer Studies. If the discipline wanted to preserve the residue of the original shocking value of the term it would have to valorize a native term of abuse. The most direct equivalent of queer studies—"teorie pedalstwa" (to translate back the translation: "faggot theories")—was, however, too drastic a proposition for Polish academia, and the attempts to circulate it quickly died out. Hence, Polish Queer Studies could come into being institutionally only with the name, which marked it as a foreign transplant, adding to it an intriguing cosmopolitan flair. The punch of the "limp-wristed slap in the face of normativity"[11] of the American "queer," in its Polish edition—and I am discussing the name only, not the field's activities—became neutralized through the foreignness of the label. This foreignness plays an ambivalent role: for those who are familiar with the term, it still allows subversion of the normative; for those who are not, its foreignness closets that which it is supposed to celebrate—the Polish "faggot-ness."[12]

Back to Gender

The circulation of "gender" and "queer" in Poland is an example of convoluted trajectories of glocalization. The social and cultural implications of "queer" and "gender" are future-oriented and emancipatory. In both cases emancipation requires a revision of national constructs, myths, and traditions that generate resistance. It would be relatively easy to demonstrate to many Poles how gender issues are related to professional advancement, job markets, glass ceilings, and the practical aspects of the private/public divide (it is enough to mention the ongoing struggle of a few generations already with child care), indeed, from time to time a public discussion indicates that gender-related issues are at the heart of Polish culture. The country's national meta-narrative, that is, the narrative that has most distinctly shaped collective imagination from the times of lost sovereignty at the end of the 18th century, through the series of uprisings, two world wars, and the hardships of the communist period, has been Romantic. This essentially compensatory narrative was martyrological; it fetishized suffering and elevated it to the level of the sublime. In its most iconic, albeit most simplistic version, the meta-narrative gendered Polish experience into that of women in the role of sacrificial *Mater Dolorosa* (or, to refer to the title of a famous Romantic poem, "Polish Mother") and men in the role of heroes whose action, regardless of how doomed to failure, deserved cultural glorification. Or perhaps precisely because this heroic action was doomed to failure it was venerated for what Polish culture configured as the pathos of faithfulness to oneself.

How sensitive this meta-narrative is to destabilization by, say, the wild card of homosexuality can be shown by another heated debate over a book published in 2011 by a female academic and visual artist, Elżbieta Janicka. Janicka in *Festung Warschau* explores the "mythical imperative" (another way to address the fatal power of the Romantic paradigm) of Polish national memory and discusses two young iconic fighters of the Polish anti-Nazi underground, suggesting a homoerotic love between them.[13] The homoerotic undertones of their relationship in no way undermine the accomplishments and sacrifices of these Warsaw's Achilles and Patroclos, in Janicka's comparison. Their elevated cultural standing is not disputed, and their love more than anything else only underscores the sense of loss and fragility of life in the midst of the horrors of wartime Warsaw. But the suggestion of a homoerotic relationship deprives the two young men of the essence of traditional masculinity, and only within the parameters of this traditional masculinity could Polish culture conceive of heroism. Heroism proper requires proper gendering, which in this case means—and here the Polish rendering of the English distinction between sex and gender as biological and cultural sex respectively makes for an ironic pun—biological sex aligned with cultural sex (sic!) according to the blueprints of the patriarchal society.

What threatens is not so much that which is foreign and radical—the bishops, after all, showed no reaction to the provocative poses of *Lovetown*'s queens. What threatens is that which may pass imperceptibly because it is linked to something that connotes familiarity and cultural respectability—heroic, but homosexual soldiers potentially evolving into socially respected couples; homosexual marriages accepted on par with their heterosexual equivalents: in other words, structural assimilation of otherness into the very fabric of the traditional society, its present and its past alike. Hence, "queer" as long as it preserves its queerness doesn't register on the broad public radar. Its complexities and its foreignness remain limited to the circle of activists and theorists and their sympathizers, all groups more often than not associated with the academic circulation of ideas. No matter how resonant and extensive the scandal of Lovetown, no matter how numerous the copies sold, the novel stands no chance of matching the power and range of the bishops' cannon (and canon). However loud, *Lovetown* performs for a self-selective demographic; the bishops' letter for the broad public and mass media. The scope of the two is incomparable.

Interestingly, the two mechanisms I suggested in the ways the imported notions of "queer" and "gay" circulated—first that of a conflation of the two terms and second their reversed trajectory ("from queer to gay")—could be found in the Church's strategy towards "gender." In the former case, the conflation and reversal were symptomatic of, on the one hand, what was culturally useful and hence absorbable, and on the other, how the social history of the sexual minorities embedded in these terms could get displaced by the historical idiosyncrasies of the local. In the bishops' announcement one can also observe the rhetoric of conflation and displacement, but this rhetoric becomes visible only when we compare the letter publicized in churches with its earlier online version.

It turns out that the bishops' letter read on the Sunday of the Holy Family was a second version of the document that was in circulation as an official statement issued by the Episcopate for just a few hours. Posted online on Friday, December 27, 2013, at 11:40 a.m. by the Catholic Information Agency (KAI), an official news platform of the Episcopate, it was taken down at 3:30 p.m. the same day. It is not clear why it was posted in the first place, whether it was intentional, a mistake, a misinformation, or something else altogether. The Episcopate claimed that the first version of the letter was meant for bishops' personal information and enlightenment whereas the second was meant to be distributed in churches. As it turned out later, the first version was not to be publicized because some bishops found it unacceptable, and even the second one was not univocally accepted. The decision whether to read it or not to read it to the faithful was left to the regional clergy.[14]

The main difference between the first and the second (longer) version is that the first spells out what the second seems only to suggest. *Tygodnik Powszechny*, a liberal Catholic weekly that published the texts of both letters in the form of editorial comparison, calls the first "radical" and the second "a bit milder," but the aggressive and accusatory tone of the first document can actually be, paradoxically, less damaging that its supposedly softer version.[15] Just as the assimilation of "gay" threatens more than the radicality of "queer" so does the milder rhetoric disseminate anxieties more effectively than the frontal attack.

Both versions stress that gender ideology rejects biological determinants of, to use Polish terminology, biological sex (sex) and claim that cultural sex (gender) can be chosen on a whim, but the first version emphasizes the claim that gender ideology makes on homosexuality as inborn sexual orientation (hence something we have no control over). The inherent irony of this accusation, according to which homosexuality is validated by being taken back to nature, must have been lost on the authors. After all, nature (i.e., the ultimate unshakeable order of things) serves the Church as the main argument against the cultural relativization of traditional values. Validating homosexuality as "natural" results in reconfigurations of social structure: "gays and lesbians are given the right to establish relationships, which are to form a new type of the family and even the right to adopt and raise children."[16] Children are also the main victims—education in the spirit of gender ideology cleverly disguises its main goal, which is sexualization of children, who later, as a consequence of such an upbringing, become "clients of pharmaceutical, erotic, pornographic, pedophilic, and abortion industries."[17] Nota bene, many Poles interpreted the pedophilic reference as both outrageous and preemptive; it was a popular conviction that the gender wars served as a smoke screen deflecting public attention from what really mattered, i.e. the numerous pedophilic scandals shocking the country in the spring of 2013 and earlier, and displacing guilt from the priests to parents and children.[18]

Both letters emphasize that gender ideology circulates in society without Poles' permission—"gender ideology without society's awareness and Poles' permission has been for months advanced in various structures of social life," the letter read in churches complains.[19] The first letter, however, delineates clearly these structures of social life where the corruption takes place, first of all the "legislation, which superficially aims at protecting the citizen while surreptitiously damaging them,"[20] and where the second letter only suggests the demoralizing influence of the European Union, the first one spells out specific institutions as responsible for it. The first letter shows the institutional distribution of gender ideology from the Council of Europe Treaty, which "although dedicated to an important problem of violence against women, promotes nevertheless so-called 'non-stereotypical sexual roles' and deeply interferes with the education system making it obligatory to educate and promote homosexuality and transsexuality among others things."[21]

The World Health Organization is to be blamed for establishing the parameters of sexual education that leads to the "profound demoralization of children and the youth." They promote, among other things, "masturbation at the kindergarten age and discovering by children the joys and pleasures coming from touching their own body and the bodies of their peers."[22] The prime example of such practices in early childhood education became, to translate literally, "equality kindergarten" (przedszkole równościowe), an EU-subsidized institution where supposedly what is taught—"without the parents' permission and awareness"—is an acceptance that gender roles are fully exchangeable and a disregard for the biological determinants of sexual and gender identity.[23] All of this ultimately leads to, according to the pastoral letter, a destabilization of healthy identity formation, "a human being deprived of a stable sexual and gender identity loses a sense of his/her existence."[24]

Gender studies at Polish universities are accused in the first version of the letter of "producing the propagators of this ideology that claims that a traditional family is anachronistic and that it doesn't matter whether a child is raised by lesbians or gays because the child can be as happy in these structures and developing as well as a child brought up in a traditional family."[25] Finally, the heaviest cannons are trained on gender ideology and its influence in medical fields. The ideology "promotes right to abortion, contraceptives, in vitro fertilization, surgical and hormonal sex changes and also the gradual introduction of the 'right' to euthanasia and eugenics, that is to the possibility of eliminating those who are sick, weak, mentally disabled, who, according to the gender ideologists are 'of damaged value.' What transpires from this is that human being does not count, what counts is economic-financial gain."[26] We can easily understand how gender ideology in this context "presents a threat worse than Nazism and Communism combined."[27] Yet, it is the passage about immoral medical advancements in the fields of eugenics and euthanasia that was entirely eliminated from the second version of the letter.

The first letter strikes with a tendency to conflate different social phenomena and anxieties—eugenics, homosexuality, financial conspiracy—under one label. "Gender" becomes an all-governing agent of civilizational evil stretching from identity-confused kindergarteners to aborted fetuses of the mentally disabled. The second letter does not aim so much for shock value, and in this sense it is indeed milder. However, its rhetoric is more damaging because it leaves most of the agents and their actions unclear. The EU is not present, no specific institutional names are dropped, eugenics and euthanasia are not mentioned. Yet, without foreign agents to blame for the import of corruption, the second letter suggests that the agent can be anywhere, and, if so, it will hide most likely in the guise of something familiar and acceptable—"a decisive majority does not know what this ideology is hence is not able to register any danger."[28] The fear of homosexual marriages replacing heterosexual marriages becomes in the second edition of the letter the fear of destabilization of traditional family roles and hence gradual demoralization of children, yet demoralization too subtle to be noticed by disoriented parents.

The danger now is that like in *Lovetown*, where flamboyant queens a generation later become middle-class gays, the otherness becomes domesticated and naturalized. The non-normative may surreptitiously begin to function as another form of norm (the "alternative families" from the second letter may with time become simply "families"). The bishops would probably prefer *Lovetown*'s queens to the well-educated, self-aware, emancipation- and assimilation-oriented gays. The real danger of gender ideology is not the striking perversion of social engineering, but an all-permeating, odor-free subversion of a clear understanding of what is normative and what is not and, ultimately, the establishing of the non-normative as a new default position. In this sense, Poland is much better off if queer remains marked as queer rather than as gay, which is constituted as early as in kindergarten when a boy wears a wig and an apron.

Hence, the bishops intend to out "gender," so to speak, by disclosing its "real" ideological danger—the imperceptible assimilation of subversion (and perversion). In its power to surreptitiously subvert, gender is the real queer. Society should then be vigilant so that the virus of non-normativity won't spread through different forms and levels of social interaction and communication. The fact that it is hard to recognize instances in which "gender" threatens the order of things only increases its corruptive power. "Gender ideology" progresses from the destabilization of traditional family dynamics through the valorization of alternative forms of family building to the dissolution of the "very integrity of the human being, as a spiritual and bodily creation." Disregard for the rhetorical distinction between "biological sex" and "cultural sex" results in a conflation of the two into an unclear, yet essentialized, entity; the lack of definition of gender facilitates the rhetoric of impending danger.

Thus, gender ideology, like carbon monoxide, can be only experienced through its damaging after-effects; it cannot be reasoned or debated, it can only be resisted or succumbed to. But because it is not easily localizable one needs to be keen and distrust even the reasonable-sounding claims of gender equality. An old imperial strategy of rege et divide becomes conflate—various often incompatible phenomena under the same label—and alienate your audience by making them feel disoriented and with a sense of having little control over a cultural conspiracy so clever that only a constant vigilance enables one to differentiate it from innocuous forms of societal life.

It is tempting to look at this rhetoric and see it as just another example of the backwaters of Eastern Europe unable to digest the advancements of the liberal West (a persisting topos in Western media).[29] But Poland has a fascinating tradition of local feminist movement and thought; it had its own theorists of gender and sexual identity long before "krytyka genderowa" (in this form most Polish academics described a gender approach to cultural analysis—literally gender criticism—English roots, Polish suffix and case) had started to circulate in academic discourse and long before departments and programs in Gender Studies acquired their cachet and boasted high enrollments. The reaction in academic circles, particularly feminist circles, to the Episcopal letter mirrored the bishops' warnings about dissolution of family structure with the warning against dissolution of state structure and relied on legal arguments and constitutional rights. This reaction shows that many Polish academics are no longer interested in playing nice and that they choose a non-reconciliatory strategy and a civic action rather than a pseudo-pedagogical mission of getting involved in pointless discussions with an opponent who refuses to define the language of the subject. This in itself is a sign of the advancement of the local critical and social tradition. The bishops meant to bring to the surface hidden dangers of "gender ideology," but as a side effect they brought to the surface a different type of academic opposition. If they meant to redefine "gender," so did these communities redefine their actions and reactions.

I find it significant that the Church did not choose to make a stronger link between Polish feminism and "gender." Considering how various emancipatory movements are conflated in Poland and how often they join forces in order to gain greater visibility for their political and social agenda, it would seem to have been much easier to point a finger at well-known public figures and circles and show the extension of the "gender" agenda of Polish feminists to a "gender" agenda of sexual minorities. It would be easy to remind the faithful of the strategies of these movements because they were visible, sometimes literally (as in a billboard campaign showing homosexual couples and captioned "may they see us"). But that's precisely the point. Keeping the agents of the enemy less visible, so to speak, and suggesting that they come from the outside and that they have nothing to do with a broad public by claiming that "gender ideology" spreads through a few groups (yet "vocal and with considerable financial resources") is to construct "gender" as something that a healthy Polish psyche cannot absorb. But it may also mean that those in Poland who know a thing or two about "gender" present too formidable an enemy to throw down the glove to. If this is so, then the bishops' "gender" is a success of Polish feminism.

Notes

[1] The text of the letter comes from the official website of the Polish Bishops' Conference (Konferencja Episkopatu Polski): "List pasterski na Niedzielę Świętej Rodziny 2013 roku [Pastoral Letter of the Bishops' Conference of Poland to be Used on the Sunday of the Holy Family 2013]," n.d., http://bit.ly/1JQdatu (accessed January 18, 2015). In spring 2014 the letter was posted on the same website in both English and Polish versions. Unless noted, the translation of the letter read in churches comes from this official version.

[2] Ibid.

3 As an aside, it is ironic from the Polish perspective to hear about Marxism in this context—the Stalinist propaganda in the 1950s preached Lysenkoism (from the name of Trofim Lysenko, a Soviet biologist [Łysenkism in Polish])—a Soviet rejection of classical Mendelian genetics and its theory of chromosome inheritance in favor of exclusive environmentally acquired inheritance. The very same Stalinist propaganda outlawed sociology as a bourgeois competition to Marxism Leninism, and quantum theory to historical materialism. See Piotr Bratkowski, "Normalność 2.0," *Newsweek*, 20–26.01.2014, p. 37.

4 "Nie jest czymś niewłaściwym prowadzenie badań nad wpływem kultury na płeć."

5 Ironically, "people of good will" (ludzie dobrej woli) was a topos of communist propaganda speeches.

6 While the Church in Poland was exorcising gender, the Vatican and Pope Francis had a different reaction. When the Congress of Women (Kongres kobiet), a well-known movement and organization gathering activists, public intellectuals, and regular women alike to work on issues of gender equality, sent a letter to the pope in late November 2013 (hence, before the bishops' frontal attack on gender) about its concerns regarding the damages that the attack on "gender" may cause in many aspects of gender equality, the pope sent Celestino Migliore, a papal nuncio to Poland to discuss the situation with the leaders of the Congress. During the meeting on March 4, 2014, the nuncio reminded the Congress of the heterogeneity of the Church and condemned creating an atmosphere of fear by the local Church authorities; he noted the need to be aware of the demands of the modern world, and also admitted that the letter sent to the pope was received with great displeasure by the highest officials of the Catholic Church in Poland. He reassured the Congress that the pope was aware of the situation and that he was committed to supporting gender equality. In a reconciliatory gesture, he interpreted the current "misunderstandings" in Poland as a result of the ignorance of many about the meaning of the notion. Zuzanna Radzik, 2013, "Odpowiedź na list Kongresu Kobiet do Franciszka w sprawie gender: radość i pytania," March 5, http://bit.ly/1n21SI2 (accessed January 25, 2015).

7 Distribution of seats according to gender in the 2011 (October) parliamentary elections resulted in 24% held by women. A gender quota (in Polish "parytety") was instituted in January 2011. The next elections, in October 2015, should increase the percentage of female parliamentarians. Inter-Parliamentary   Union,   n.d.,   Poland   Sejm   (Sejm), http://bit.ly/1Px1RD2.

8 Michał Witkowski, 2010, *Lovetown*, trans. William Martin (London: Portobello Books).

9 It is important to remember that Polish sexual minorities did not experience such unifying experiences as the AIDS epidemics and the ACT UP action that followed it, which were also, the tragic dimension of AIDS aside, the events that gave the homosexual subculture greater visibility. The publication of the scandalous *Lovetown* suddenly gave a celebratory visibility not so much to contemporary gays but to their communist counterparts, actually the Polish equivalent of the AIDS and the ACT UP generation on the American continent.

10 "Witkowski opisuje świat ... przekształcający się z pedalstwa w gejostwo." Paweł Dunin-Wąsowicz, 2005, "Oldskulowe pikiety [Books: Reviews]," July 29, http://bit.ly/1Rrad4Z (accessed January 15, 2015).

11 I am paraphrasing here Andy Medhurst's picturesque definition of camp. See "Camp" in Andy Medhurst and Sally R. Munt, eds., 1997, *Lesbian and Gay Studies: A Critical Introduction* (London: Cassell), 276.

12 Inga Iwasiów, a leading Polish feminist and a main signatory of the protest letter to the prime minister in response to the gender wars, categorized queer studies in Poland as the field closest of all Polish intellectual formations to its American counterpart (private conversation). This proximity, however stimulating intellectually, may be at times politically limiting. Theoretical sophistication does not always match what needs to be done *in situ*.

13 Elżbieta Janicka, 2011, *Festung Warschau* (Warszawa: Wydawnictwo Krytyki Politycznej).

[14] For the distribution of the letter, see Błażej Strzelczyk, 2013, "Biskupi byli podzieleni w sprawie listu o gender. 'Wielu wyraziło zastrzeżenia," *Tygodnik Powszechny*, December 23, http://bit.ly/1UWl45d (accessed January 25, 2015).

[15] *Tygodnik Powszechny* published both letters with the editorial markings showing how the original text was modified (what exactly was eliminated, added, rephrased) to reach the form that was eventually distributed in churches. *Tygodnik Powszechny*, 2013, "Dwie wersje listu KEP na Niedzielę św. Rodziny. Porównujemy oba dokumety," December 20, http://bit.ly/1STcdCG (accessed January 25, 2015).

[16] "Według gender homoseksualizm jest wrodzony, zaś geje i lesbijki mają prawo do zakładania związków będących podstawą nowego typu rodziny, a nawet adopcji i wychowywania dzieci." http://bit.ly/1STcdCG (accessed January 15, 2015).

[17] "Bardzo sprytnie pomija się fakt, że celem seksualizacji genderowej jest w gruncie rzeczy seksualizacja dzieci i młodzieży (...). W następstwie takiego wychowania, realizowanego przez młodzieżowych edukatorów seksualnych, młody człowiek staje się stałym klientem koncernów farmaceutycznych, erotycznych, pornograficznych, pedofilskich i aborcyjnych." Ibid.

[18] In other words, pedophilic affairs put parents at fault for raising their children in a highly sexualized atmosphere (and, by extension, we may continue with this logic and make children responsible for tempting priests with their uncontrollable sexuality, rather than vice versa).

[19] "ideologia gender bez wiedzy społeczeństwa i zgody Polaków od miesięcy wprowadzana jest w różne struktury życia społecznego" http://bit.ly/1STcdCG (accessed January 15, 2015).

[20] "Ideologia gender jest wprowadzana na różnych płaszczyznach życia społecznego. Dokonuje się to najpierw przez prawodawstwo. Tworzone są dokumenty pozornie służące ochronie, bezpieczeństwu i dobru obywateli, które zawierają elementy mocno destrukcyjne." Ibid.

[21] "Konwencja Rady Europy przeciwko przemocy wobec kobiet, która choć poświęcona istotnemu problemowi przemocy wobec kobiet, promuje jednak tzw. 'niesteoretypowe role seksualne' oraz głęboko ingeruje w system wychowawczy nakładając obowiązek edukacji i promowania, min. homoseksualizmu i transseksualizmu." Ibid.

[22] "do głębokiej deprawacji dzieci i młodzieży. Promują one między innymi masturbację dzieci w wieku przedszkolnym oraz odkrywanie przez nie radości i przyjemności, jakie płyną z dotykania zarówno własnego ciała, jak i ciała rówieśników." Ibid.

[23] "Elementy tych tzw. standardów są aktualnie wdrażane—powtórzmy: najczęściej bez wiedzy i zgody rodziców—np. w projekcie Równościowe przedszkole, współfinansowanym przez Unię Europejską. Autorki Równościowego przedszkola proponują między innymi, by w ramach zabawy chłopcy przebierali się za dziewczynki, dziewczynki za chłopców, a reszta dzieci zgadywała, kim są i tłumaczyła, dlaczego tak uważa. Projekt ten zawiera wiele innych podobnych kontrowersyjnych propozycji." Ibid. [A standing example for gender experiments before the bishops' letter started to circulate became a group of kindergartens whose educational programs encouraged children to exchange gender roles, but which was condemned as confusing children's understanding of their own biological sex. The icon of these programs became a little boy in an apron and a wig whose photograph without any description was repeatedly used to support the claims against gender ideology. As it turned out, the boy was not performing an underage edition of drag-queening, but was playing a hairdresser (a profession dominated in Poland by women) in a game that was showing that both genders can perform the same profession.]

[24] "Człowiek pozbawiony stałej tożsamości płciowej, gubi bowiem sens swego istnienia." http://bit.ly/1STcdCG (accessed January 15, 2015).

[25] "Na wielu uniwersytetach w Polsce niemal nagle powstały kierunki studiów na temat gender (gender studies, czyt. dżender). Kształci się na nich nowych propagatorów tej ideologii i głosi, że rodzina jest już przeżytkiem i nie ma znaczenia, czy dziecko jest wychowywane przez gejów czy lesbijki, bo jest w takich strukturach równie szczęśliwe, rozwijając się tak dobrze, jak dziecko wychowywane w tradycyjnej rodzinie." Ibid.

[26] "Na polu medycyny mamy do czynienia z działaniami promującymi prawo do aborcji, antykoncepcji, zapłodnienia in vitro, chirurgicznej i hormonalnej zmiany płci, a także stopniowego wprowadzania 'prawa' do eutanazji oraz do eugeniki, czyli możliwości eliminowania osób chorych, słabych, upośledzonych, które—zdaniem ideologów gender—są 'niepełnowartościowe.' Wynika z tego, że człowiek w ogóle już się nie liczy, a ukrytym motywem są ostatecznie korzyści ekonomiczne." Ibid.

[27] An expression by Bishop Tadeusz Pieronek quoted in Sławomir Sierakowski, 2014, "The Polish Church's Gender Problem," *New York Times*, January 26, http://nyti.ms/1Qct2Yo (accessed January 17, 2015).

[28] Zdecydowana większość nie wie, czym jest ta ideologia, nie wyczuwa więc żadnego niebezpieczeństwa.

[29] See, for instance, Agata Pyzik, 2014, "Poland Is Having a Sexual Revolution in Reverse," *The Guardian*, February 11, http://bit.ly/1RUZE9b (accessed January 15, 2015).

Champagne Seduction and Sewer Putrefaction: Homosexuality and August Strindberg

Brian Martin

On March 18, 1885, August Strindberg wrote to Isidor Kjellberg that he intended to write about—and even advocate for—homosexual men. In his letter to the Stockholm journalist, Strindberg writes: "Mankind should learn to look upon this as an unfortunate whim of nature, without considering it a crime! I believe that they are very unfortunate, these poor wretches...When I become a little more courageous, I intend, at the risk of being considered a pederast...to put in a compassionate word for them!"[1] Strindberg's characterization of homoerotic desire as "an unfortunate whim of nature" reflects the pervasive homophobic discourse of both France (where he lived intermittently from 1883 to 1887) and Sweden during the 1880s. However, his call for decriminalization, empathy, and compassion demonstrates a remarkably sympathetic view of homosexuality in late nineteenth-century Europe.

Strindberg's sympathies in this 1885 letter were echoed by Émile Zola in 1896. During the 1890s, an anonymous homosexual man had sent an autobiographical text to Zola, hoping to convince the novelist either to publish this manuscript or advocate for greater understanding for homosexual men. Reluctant to publish this text, Zola sent it to Dr. Georges Saint-Paul who published the manuscript as *The Novel of a Born Invert* in 1896. In Zola's preface to this text, he writes: "When I received this curious document a few years ago, I was struck by the great psychological and social interest it offered. I was touched by its absolute sincerity, for one can feel the passion or...eloquence of truth...which very few men have dared to create."[2] Having admired the anonymous author for his honesty and courage, Zola nevertheless regrets that he is unable to take the project any further: "I first had the desire to use the manuscript and give it to the public in a form that I looked for in vain, and that finally made me abandon the project" (1). However, Zola had already written several sympathetic male characters—in his twenty novel series titled the *Rougon-Macquart* (1871-93)—who share great emotional and physical intimacy with other men: notably the Parisian valet Baptiste in *La Curée* (1871) and the military buddies Jean Macquart and Maurice Levasseur in *La Débâcle* (1892).[3]

Like Zola, whom he admired, Strindberg would go on to write about homosexual characters with alternating sympathy and disdain. Strindberg's homophobic writing on lesbians demonstrates this ambivalence, and must be understood within the larger context of his simultaneous attraction to and misogynist criticism of powerful women, from his wives Siri von Essen, Frida Uhl, and Harriet Bosse, to his protagonists Laura, Julie, and Tekla in *The Father* (1887), *Miss Julie* (1888), and *The Creditors* (1889). Strindberg's jealousies over Siri von Essen's intimate relationship with the Danish actress Marie Caroline David—which was later dramatized in Per Olov Enquist's *The Night of the Tribades* (1975)—led to a series of homophobic characterizations of lesbians in Strindberg's texts, from Gurli and Ottilia in "A Dollhouse" (published in the first volume of his short-stories titled *Getting Married*, in 1884), to Maria and Helga in his semi-autobiographical novel *A Madman's Defence* (1895). In "The Perverse" (from his second volume of essays titled *Vivisections*, in 1894), Strindberg's attack on lesbians evokes his marital jealousy and contempt for his ex-wife and her female lover: "For young girls, it is more difficult to define the line between perversion and friendship...Unhappy is the man who discovers one fine morning that he has married one of these and doesn't have the power or brutality to break this contemptible bond."[4] Having indeed been such an unhappy man in his marriage with Siri von Essen, Strindberg extends this personal contempt to an even broader condemnation of other women in intimate relationships "between perversion and friendship" with one another.

Like his writing on lesbians, Strindberg's texts on homosexual men also focus on perversion. But several of these texts demonstrate an ambivalence between homophobic judgment and humanistic sympathy. In "The Reward of Virtue" from the first volume of *Getting Married* (1884), the young Theodor Wennerström struggles with a degenerative abstinence from his own (homo)sexuality. In "Nature the Criminal" from the second volume of *Getting Married* (1886) and in the semi-autobiographical novel *The Son of a Servant* (1886-87), Strindberg features frank portraits of men trying to negotiate the strict limits of their homoerotic desire in late nineteenth-century Sweden. And again in "The Perverse" (1894), Strindberg recounts both in anecdote and in theory his ideas on homosexuality. Collectively, these texts document Strindberg's thoughts on what he unashamedly calls the "extraordinary phenomenon...of sexual perversion."[5]

I first discovered these texts as a graduate student in Comparative Literature at UCLA in 1994-95, when my mentor Ross Shideler encouraged me to research and write about them for his Strindberg seminar. After two years of study in Comparative Literature and Scandinavian Studies with Professor Shideler (as well as with Kathleen Komar, Mary Kay Norseng, Tim Tangherlini, and Emily Apter), Ross invited me to present my work on Strindberg at the MLA Convention in Washington DC in 1996, and encouraged me to publish this work afterwards. Ever a delinquent student, I neglected to complete this assignment. With this essay, I hope to thank Ross for his mentorship during those formative years, and for his encouragement, inspiration, and friendship during the past two decades. In returning to Strindberg, I also hope to honor Ross's expertise in Scandinavian Studies and Comparative Literature, to congratulate him for his decades of teaching and service at the University of California, and to celebrate his lifetime of engaging scholarship on writers from Henrik Ibsen, to Émile Zola, and Tomas Tranströmer, and particularly on the poetry, drama, and fiction of Gunnar Ekelöf, Per Olov Enquist, and August Strindberg.[6]

During the past twenty-five years since the publication of Eve Kosofsky Sedgwick's *Epistemology of the Closet* and Judith Butler's *Gender Trouble* in 1990, Queer Studies have inspired new generations of Strindberg scholars and new investigations of his texts. During the last fifteen years, a great deal of research has been done on homosexuality in Strindberg's work, notably by Matthew Roy, Göran Söderström, Eva Borgström, Anna Westerstahl Stenport, and Ann-Sofie Lönngren.[7] To this body of work, I would like to add this modest essay. More specifically, I want to discuss Strindberg's alternating sympathy and disdain for male homosexuality in texts from 1884 to 1894. From *Getting Married*, to *The Son of a Servant*, to *Vivisections*, Strindberg writes about male homosexuals in terms that are frequently homophobic, but that vacillate between (what I would describe, using discourse borrowed from Strindberg himself, as) a kind of champagne perversion (of sparkling nightlife and erotic seduction) and sewer putrefaction (of public scandal, humiliation, and abjection).

Champagne Seduction

In "The Perverse," Strindberg characterizes homosexuality as a perversion and disorder to be diagnosed and corrected, but nonetheless expresses a willingness to engage in open debate: "Why, my dear moralists, do we forbid ourselves from discussing the extraordinary phenomenon of sexual perversion? How do we expect to correct this disorder without proper diagnosis?" (152-153). Despite its homophobic focus on perversion, this discourse on disorder and diagnosis is consistent with entire fields of research on homosexuality in sexology, psychology, and criminology in nineteenth-century Europe, from the pioneering scholarship of Karl Heinrich Ulrichs, Karl-Maria Kertbeny, and Richard von Krafft-Ebing, to the research and advocacy of Havelock Ellis, Paul Näcke, Sigmund Freud, Gustav Jäger, and Magnus Hirschfeld.[8] To this eminent list should be added the work of several Swedish pioneers, who led what has been called the "homosexual breakthrough" in turn-of-the-century Sweden, including the Stockholm physician

Anton Nyström, the Swedish journalist Victor Hugo Wickström, and the Uppsala philosopher Pontus Wikner.[9] While Strindberg characterizes male homosexuality as perverse, he nonetheless takes part in this broader discourse on male homosociality and homoerotic desire, and thus bears witness to the lives of homosexual men in late nineteenth-century Europe.

In what might be characterized as the lighter side of his writing on homosexuality, Strindberg describes homosexual men in Stockholm bars and Berlin balls, where alcohol creates opportunities for emotional and physical intimacy. In these descriptions, Strindberg focuses on relationships between older and younger men, whose champagne seductions are framed in terms of alcoholic and pederastic perversion. Despite such homophobic discourse, these texts nonetheless document the existence of a sparkling and effervescent homosexual subculture during the 1880s and 1890s.

In "The Perverse," Strindberg writes, "The young man meets one day at a party or in a café an older man of higher social standing. The older gentleman seeks the intimate company of the younger, listens to his ideas with an approving smile; the young man is flattered, imagines he has extraordinary qualities to attract a superior man like this. The older one invites him to dinner, gives him lots of champagne, and ends by placing his hand on the young man's knee" (154-155). With this example, Strindberg implies that such scenes of seduction, initiated by older and wealthier men, are based on social inequality, manipulation, and exploitation, in which younger and less privileged men are seduced with flattery, food, and champagne.

Describing a homosexual drag ball in 1890s Berlin, Strindberg speculates on the role of alcohol (as well as physical intimacy in male homosocial settings) in creating the conditions for homosexual seduction: "The majority of [these men] were barbers, waiters, and bathhouse attendants. It seems that in the lower classes, the phenomenon seems to present itself as a professional illness...Perhaps it is barbers' and bath attendants' occupational necessity to touch bodies that plays a role in their mischief. For the waiters, maybe it's the old men, the drinks, the alcoholic vapors, the temptation of the clients, and the lack of women among the clientele" (164-165). Here, Strindberg reasons that while older and wealthier men seduce with flattering conversation and champagne suppers, younger working-class men are prone to homosexual perversion because of the hypnotic proximity to alcohol and nude male bodies.

In "Nature the Criminal," Strindberg offers two more examples where men who work in homosocial environments are susceptible to what he characterizes as the occupational hazard of homoerotic intimacy. Describing an athletic coach who "taught gymnastics and swimming" and whose sexless marriage effectively forced him "to live as a celibate for...fifteen years," Strindberg recounts how "after fifteen years there was a rumpus at the swimming pool" (254-255) which led to a homosexual scandal. Rather than judge the coach for seducing his swimmers, Strindberg searches for explanations and "contributory factors: professional disease, or opportunity offered, and...the lack of a proper outlet" (255). Just like barbers, waiters, and bathhouse workers, athletic coaches are—in Strindberg's assessment—vulnerable to homosexuality as a professional risk or occupational hazard.

This focus on homoerotic athletics recalls the popularity of the *Flottans badhus* in Stockholm, a floating bathhouse and open-air gym on the island of Skeppsholmen that was created for sailors but became a homoerotic hotspot from the 1880s to 1910s, and the subject of several paintings by the homosexual Swedish painter Eugène Jansson, including *Flottans badhus* (1907), *Badtavla* (1908), *Badsump* (1911), and his celebrated *Självporträtt* (1910).[10] Jansson's homoerotic images of nude swimmers, boxers, and gymnasts reflect an entire genre of nineteenth-century paintings of male bathers, from Georges Seurat's *Baignade à Asnières* (1884), Frédéric Bazille's *Scène d'été* (1869), and Paul Cézanne's *Baigneurs* (1875-1906) in France, to Thomas Eakins's *The Swimming Hole* (1885) in the United

States, and both German and Scandinavian celebrations of nudist *nacktkultur* and open air *vitalism* in such works as Max Beckmann's *Junge Männer am Meer* (1905), J.A.G. Acke's *Östrasalt* (1906), and Edvard Munch's *Badende Menn* (1907-08). In visually documenting the muscular homosociality of the *Flottans badhus*, Jansson dramatizes the homoerotic potential of athletics that Strindberg describes in *fin-de-siècle* Stockholm. And like Jansson, Strindberg broadens this analysis from swimmers to sailors.

Comparing naval life to "the life of the monk and the prisoner," Strindberg argues in "Nature the Criminal" that homosexuality can be "a professional risk for monks and sailors" (247). Here, Strindberg cites the case of a young naval cadet who was invited to his superior officer's cabin, where the officer's "manner became progressively more intimate" (251). Having offered the cadet "a glass of punch," the officer tells the young man: "You've a pleasing exterior…Do you know that you're good looking?" (250-251). Recalling Pierre Loti's fraternal sailor novel *Mon frère Yves* (1883) and presaging Jean Genet's overtly homoerotic naval narrative *Querelle de Brest* (1947), Strindberg's tale of shipboard intimacy in the Swedish navy culminates one evening when, the cadet reports, "I was held fast by two arms, and felt a kiss on my lips that might have come from the rough tongue of a bull" (252).

Here again, Strindberg cites the familiar tropes of an older man seducing a younger one with alcoholic drinks and affectionate kisses. Rather than condemn this naval officer, Strindberg defends such intimacy as "one of the most remarkable phenomena of our time" that "has always existed" (246), just "[a]s Socrates loved Alcibiades" (252). Even though he categorizes homosexuality as unnatural—going so far as to call homosexuals "freaks of nature" (252)—Strindberg also calls for tolerance, lamenting that in Sweden "they have to go about like lepers, consumed by the constant fear of being suspected or discovered" (247) and arguing that "It may be a crime on the part of Nature…but by this time human beings should be enlightened enough not to punish disabilities" (146). Despite this discourse on criminality and disability, Strindberg again advocates for tolerance, insisting "I know that such a relationship can be innocent" (147). And later in this text, Strindberg nuances his argument on the unnatural, to suggest that homosexuality may in fact be a natural alternative to heterosexual desire: "Don't tell me that there's anything new or unnatural about these manifestations. They're all part and parcel of Nature who, when denied free passage, will find another way out" (253).

In *The Son of a Servant*, Strindberg yet again returns to the figure of the older man who seduces younger men with champagne toasts and kisses. Describing homosexual life in Sweden in the late 1860s and early 1870s, Strindberg recounts the story of an anonymous German diplomat named Herr von X, whom the protagonist Johan and his friend Fritz meet in Stockholm following their graduation from Uppsala University: "Johan found himself at [the] Hasselbacken [café]. There they had been introduced to the diplomat [Herr von] X who sat down next to them. He was an old man with…very kind and friendly eyes. He drank a few toasts with the lads…Everyone drank more than they should."[111] Having enjoyed the complimentary drinks and conversation with the kind diplomat, Johan and Fritz decide to remain in his company: "He took a cab and Johan and Fritz came along…On the way, Herr von X said: 'Now you will come up to my place and share a glass of champagne with me.' Johan didn't exactly understand, 'What the hell is this all about?' he asked. 'Oh he's just an old pig,' said Fritz" (177). While Johan is confused, Fritz seems more aware of Herr von X's seductive intentions.

When Fritz and Johan meet Herr von X again, it is in the same café landscape of champagne toasts and handsome young men: "We returned to the city and had dinner in a private room of the inn. Champagne was set on ice, and the best of everything was ordered. The champagne gave way to conversation…When everyone was drunk and the conversation had changed to the subject of eternal friendship, visits with friends abroad, and so on, everyone began hugging and kissing each other on the cheek, according to the custom of Herr von X's home country" (178).

Here again, the old aristocrat tries to seduce young men with chilled champagne, sparkling conversation, and bubbly affection, as is the custom of his native Germany, or his symbolic home of Sodom, which Marcel Proust later describes in *Sodom and Gomorrah* (1921-22) as both the origin and extension of an entire homosexual male subculture stretching across turn-of-the-century Europe, from London and Paris, to Berlin and Stockholm.

In "The Perverse," "Nature the Criminal," and *The Son of a Servant*, Strindberg initially characterizes these older men as harmless, since their attempts at champagne seduction have little effect on young men like Fritz and Johan. What is more alarming to Strindberg is when younger men reciprocate these older men's affections. In "The Perverse," Strindberg reports, "Unfortunately, there are young men who stay at this table of dishonor. The devil has shown them the world in all its delights and splendors; he has offered his protection along life's difficult road, he has paved it with gold and glory" (154-155). In *The Son of a Servant*, Strindberg recounts, "Johan remembered later a mystifying story that he heard when he was in the Vidala Parish clerk's office about a young man who received a gold watch and as much money as he wanted from an 'older gentleman.' Why? No one seems to know" (178-179). While some young men go no further than champagne conversation, others are seduced by golden gifts. Despite his initial defense of male homosexuality as merely "an unfortunate whim of nature," Strindberg is troubled by the champagne seduction of vulnerable youth in the company of older and wealthier men. "The Perverse," "Nature the Criminal," and *The Son of a Servant* thus offer a judgmental but nonetheless sparkling and golden glimpse into the champagne world of male homosexuality in late nineteenth-century Europe, from the Stockholm of Strindberg's youth, to the Berlin of his later travels.

Sewer Putrefaction

Champagne seduction, however, leads to what Strindberg later qualifies as sewer putrefaction. In "The Reward of Virtue,"

Strindberg recounts the slow decline of Theodor Wennerström who, on the deathbed instructions of his pious and overprotective mother to avoid the masturbatory pleasures of "youth's most dangerous enemy," quickly degenerates into a frightened and frail young man.[12] Bereft of judicious masculine guidance (from his timid academic father and macho military uncle), Theodor is forced to rely on his mother for "information about…the procreation of the species" (51). Faithful to both his mother's dying wish and the stern warning of his pastor to abstain from onanistic "self-abuse" (67), Theodor represses his adolescent sexual development and becomes sickly and weak. This self-abnegation is exacerbated by self-abjection, when Theodor represses his erotic dreams with physical mortification: "He jumped out of bed, threw the featherbed and the sheets onto the floor, and lay down on the horsehair undermattress with nothing over him but a thin blanket. He was cold and hungry, but the devil must be destroyed" (70). Like a self-flagellating medieval monk, Theodor submits his body to literal self-abuse and masochistic torture rather than give in to his natural desire for erotic release: "He lay down once more, this time on the bedstead, and derived a strange pleasure from feeling the iron bars cut into his arms, his thighs, and shins" (71).

In this text, for which he was prosecuted in a Stockholm court on charges of blasphemy and indecency in 1884, Strindberg is critical of both religious austerity and the familial dysfunction that has left Theodor with "too much soft metal from his mother, and too little hard from his father," which in turn leads to Theodor's emotional and psychological "conflicts and an uneven swing" (54).[13] Strindberg is most critical, however, of social conventions that impose sexual abstinence.[14] He thus advocates for a healthy expression of human sexuality in the forms of masturbation and heterosexuality, as preventatives for alternative outlets such as homosexuality that, he argues, is perverse but should be both tolerated and understood.

In addition to the crippling effects of abstinence, Theodor Wennerström's homosexuality is also linked—Strindberg suggests—to the long-term effects of narcissism. "The Reward of Virtue" thus takes part in a larger body of sexological, psychoanalytic, and literary discourse on homosexuality and narcissism in turn-of-the-century Europe. In fact, Strindberg's story predates the seminal essays on homosexual narcissism by Havelock Ellis (1898), Paul Näcke (1899), and Sigmund Freud (1905, 1910, 1914).[15] And Theodor Wennerström presages the appearance of other narcissistic literary dandies, such as Joris-Karl Huysmans's Jean des Esseintes in *À Rebours* (1884), Oscar Wilde's Dorian Gray in *The Picture of Dorian Gray* (1891), and Marcel Proust's Baron de Charlus in *À la recherche du temps perdu* (1913-27), who became archetypes for the narcissistic homosexual in *fin-de-siècle* literature.

In the decades preceding and following the invention of the word "homosexuality" in 1869, a vast body of sexological, psychological, and criminological research focused on the notion of sexual "inversion," in which a man who erotically desired another man was said to have a female soul trapped in a male body.[16] However, Havelock Ellis, Paul Näcke, and Sigmund Freud argued in a series of essays published between 1898 and 1914 that homosexuality is linked to auto-eroticism, self-love, and narcissism. In his *Three Essays on the Theory of Sexuality* (1905), Freud writes that "It comes as a great surprise to learn that there are men whose sexual object is a man and not a woman...People of this kind are described as having 'contrary sexual feelings,' or better, as being 'inverts,' and the fact is described as 'inversion.'"[17] Freud goes on to define inversion as a process of inverted (or diverted) desire, in which a boy looks to himself (and other males) as a source of sexual stimulation: "[F]uture inverts...pass through a phase of very intense but short-lived fixation to a woman (usually their mother)...[A]fter leaving this behind, they identify themselves with a woman and take themselves as their sexual object...[T]hey proceed from a narcissistic basis, and look for a young man who resembles themselves and whom they may love as their mother loved them" (144-145). For Freud, sexual inversion thus operates as a function of narcissism.

In a later essay in 1910, Freud explains the mythological origins of narcissism and describes the role of narcissistic object choice in the development of the male homosexual: "He finds the objects of his love along the path of narcissism...for Narcissus, according to the Greek legend, was a youth who preferred his own reflection to everything else and who was changed into the lovely flower by that name."[18] Freud then traces a connection between narcissism, auto-eroticism, and homosexual desire: "The boy represses his love for his mother; he puts himself in her place, identifies himself with her, and takes his own person as a model in whose likeness he chooses the new objects of his love. In this way he has become a homosexual. What he has in fact done is to slip back to auto-eroticism" (100).

Finally, in his essay "On Narcissism" (1914), Freud explicitly associates narcissism with sexual inversion: "The term narcissism...was chosen by Paul Näcke in 1899 [and Havelock Ellis in 1898] to denote the attitude of a person who treats his own body in the same way in which the body of a sexual object is treated, who looks at it...strokes it and fondles it till he obtains complete satisfaction."[19] Beyond masturbation, Freud argues, this narcissistic desire for auto-eroticism extends to homoerotic desire: "We have discovered [in] perverts and homosexuals, that in their later choice of love-objects, they have taken as a model not their mother but their own selves. They are plainly seeking themselves as a love-object which must be termed 'narcissistic'" (88). From Ellis to Näcke to Freud, narcissism thus entered sexological and psychoanalytic discourse as a way of understanding sexual inversion and homoerotic desire.

In "The Reward of Virtue," Theodor's narcissism is triggered by his reading of Ovid's *Metamorphoses* and his admiration of a narcissus flower in a Stockholm park: "He paused opposite a clump of narcissi, broke off a flower, and sniffed it until his temples throbbed. He had never looked closely at this flower before. But last term in his Ovid he had read the story of a beautiful youth who had been changed into a narcissus" (56). For Theodor, this is a moment of delayed literary illumination and unconscious self recognition: "He had not discovered any particular meaning in the myth. A youth who, because he fails to requite love, becomes the object of his own passion, and is finally consumed by its flame, in love with his own image, which he sees reflected in a spring" (56).

Just as Ovid's Narcissus recognizes himself in the reflective pool, Theodor unconsciously sees his own pale face (as well as that of a consumptive classmate) reflected in the petals of the narcissus flower: "Now as he gazed upon the white petals, the cup, waxen-yellow, like the cheeks of an invalid, with the delicate streaks of red one sees on the face of a consumptive, whose constant cough forces his blood into the minutest vessels of his skin, he began to think of one of his schoolmates" (56). Here, Theodor is looking not only at a substitute for his sickly schoolmate, but at a mirror image of himself. Theodor has become Narcissus, a young man so starved by his own sexual repression that he has degenerated into a sickly and frail young man: "He grew sickly. His face fell in, so that you could see all the more prominent bones of his skull. His skin became a yellowish-white of a pickled embryo, and always looked damp...His eyes were lusterless, his hands so thin that all his joints projected through the skin. He looked like an illustration from a didactic work on human vices, and yet he was pure" (79).

Like the delicate petals of the narcissus flower, Theodor's skin is pale and translucent. Though beautiful on the flower's petals, this pallor underscores Theodor's physical weakness and decline. In contrast to the masculine virility and muscular vitality of Eugène Jansson's swimmers, boxers, and gymnasts, Theodor is a wilting flower, a withering man, a weakling. In struggling to please his mother and pastor by remaining sexually abstinent, Theodor has remained "pure," but he has also starved himself of sexual expression, which has led to his physical decline, his emotional degeneration, and—as Strindberg suggests—both his psychological and moral depravity.

Theodor's degeneracy culminates in his final recourse to homosexuality. As a young professor of theology at Uppsala University, he is accused of soliciting a male student: "People began to whisper that Theodor Wennerström, in a fit of frenzy, had assaulted one of his fellow students at his home, and made shameful proposals to him. For once what they whispered was true" (80). Having once been a vulnerable young man who submitted to the strict admonition of his pastor on sexual abstinence, Theodor has now become the older man who invites younger men to his home for a very different kind of sexual instruction. While Strindberg had once described such scenes between older homosexuals and younger men in terms of champagne toasts and sparkling conversation, he characterizes Theodor's seduction of a young student as a case of shameful perversion.

This in turn leads to a public scandal described as a kind of infectious pestilence: "[A] rumor began to circulate in Uppsala, a horrible rumor, which spread over the horizon like a dark cloud. It was as if someone had forgotten to shut the lid of a sewer, and that a frightful stink was suddenly reminding the population that their city...rested upon a foundation of putrefaction, which might at any time burst its pipes, and poison the whole community" (80). Despite his condemnation of abstinence and his advocacy for healthy sexuality in "The Reward of Virtue," Strindberg describes Theodor's recourse to homosexuality in terms of darkness, sewerage, stench, putrefaction, and poison. Reflecting the complexities of Strindberg's broader engagement with gender and sexuality in his collected work, these contradictions are exemplified in this volume of stories titled *Giftas*, which means both "married" and "poisoned." If Theodor's homosexuality has "poison[ed] the whole community," his hasty marriage to a sympathetic German *Fräulein* named Sophia Leidschütz is not an effective antidote. While his heterosexual marriage may satisfy the good people of Uppsala, Theodor is newly poisoned (*gift*) from the effects of being married (*gift*), and "Thirteen months later, Theodor Wennerström was dead" (81). Far from the champagne seduction and golden gifts of

Stockholm bars and Berlin balls, this tale of homosexual perversion and poison in Uppsala concludes with sewer putrefaction, a rotting corpse, and moral decay.

Conclusion

After his acquittal in the Stockholm blasphemy trial against *Getting Married* in November 1884, Strindberg might have been more cautious and even more pessimistic about writing and advocating for greater tolerance towards homosexuals. But as his March 1885 letter to Isidor Kjellberg demonstrates, Strindberg continued—even amid his contradictory discourse on homosexual perversion—to "put in a compassionate word for them" during the next ten years, from his second volume of *Getting Married* (1886), and *The Son of a Servant* (1886-87), to the second volume of *Vivisections* (1894). While "The Reward of Virtue" led to public scandal for both Theodor Wennerström and August Strindberg, the sewer putrefaction of this text did not poison the champagne seduction of Strindberg's later work on homosexual men.

Despite his continuing sympathies and contradictions, his competing discourses on tolerance and perversion, and his alternating sympathy and disdain, Strindberg's writing on late nineteenth-century homosexuality features several visionary moments that herald late twentieth-century tolerance and early twenty-first century acceptance. In "The Perverse," Strindberg recounts his meeting with another Swedish writer, an elegantly dressed dandy who speaks openly about his homosexuality over dinner and drinks: "I once met a man...who revealed himself to me completely [d]uring a trip to Sweden...As he was a very well-known writer, I invited him to my hotel. In front of me stood a man of 35, perfectly dressed in the latest fashion, perhaps a little too neat. A fresh complexion, a full beard, medium height, in short a man like anyone else, except with a little too much sway in his hips" (158-159). Critical of his fellow writer's fastidious appearance and effeminate style, Strindberg is nonetheless delighted when "He invited me to dinner" and discovered that "[t]he champagne was already there" (158-159). Like the young Johan and Fritz with Herr von X in *The Son of a Servant* or the young naval cadet with his superior officer in "Nature the Criminal," Strindberg enjoys the champagne hospitality and sparkling conversation of his homosexual host who, when asked by Strindberg for "an explanation of the phenomena" of homosexuality, explains: "It is what it is. Each person comes to the world as he is" (160-161). Amid the vast and complex debates on the sexological, psychological, and criminological origins of sexual inversion, perversion, narcissism, and homosexuality in turn-of-the-century Europe, the utter simplicity of this reply belies its profound modernity, suggesting a move from narrow investigations of homosexual desire to a fuller explanation and expression of queer identity and diversity.

In his conclusion to "The Perverse," Strindberg offers a final anecdote that goes even further. Against those who argue that homosexuals are "defective" and thus should not "propagate their rotten lineage," Strindberg replies that "this seems false to me, since I have seen perverse men with beautiful children" (168-169). He then cites the case of an intriguing "ménage à trois" in which the older male lover of a young man (who later weds a woman) becomes an integral part of the marital and family life of the young married couple: "A young artist of my acquaintance, the lover of an older gentleman, gets married...After a year, [the older gentleman] entered the conjugal household on friendly terms, became godfather to the child, renewed the relationship with the friend, and became lover to his wife...After the young couple, who did not love their child, experienced some financial problems, the old friend adopted the child and became its father" (168-169). With this final story, Strindberg describes a happy threesome (and indeed foursome) that must have shocked many of his readers in 1894, but which represents a radically progressive vision of queer sexuality, family, complexity, and diversity that is increasingly familiar—if not wholly uncontroversial—today.

Notes

1 August Strindberg, *August Strindbergs Brev*, 56. Unless otherwise noted, all English translations (from Swedish and French) in this essay are mine. Parts of this letter are also cited by Mary Sandbach in her notes to: August Strindberg, *Getting Married*, 374-375n4.

2 Émile Zola, Preface, *Le Roman d'un inverti né*, in Georges Saint-Paul [Dr. Laupts], *Tares et poisons: perversions et perversité sexuelles, une enquête médicale sur l'inversion*, 1. See also: Daniel Grojnowski, ed., *Confessions d'un inverti né: suivi de Confidences et aveux d'un Parisien*.

3 For more on the *Novel of a Born Invert*, see: Karl Rosen, "Émile Zola and Homosexuality," *Excavatio* 2, 111-115; Vernon Rosario, *The Erotic Imagination: French Histories of Perversity*, 89-98; Christopher Rivers, "Improbable Prescience: Émile Zola and the Origins of Homosexuality," *Excavatio* 14.1-2, 49-57; Brian Joseph Martin, *Napoleonic Friendship: Military Fraternity, Intimacy, and Sexuality in Nineteenth-Century France*, 259-263. For more on homoeroticism in Zola's *La Curée* and *La Débâcle*, see Martin 229-254.

4 August Strindberg, "De Perversa," *Vivisektioner II*, 156-157. Originally written and published by Strindberg in French as "Les Pervers" in 1894, this text was first translated into Swedish in 1958. All English translations of this text (which I have called "The Perverse") in this essay are mine.

5 Strindberg, "De Perversa," 152-153. To this list, Matthew Roy adds Strindberg's *Black Banners* (1907) and A *Blue Book* (1907-12), in which Strindberg's homophobia—following his *Inferno* (1897) crisis—becomes more virulent. Matthew Roy, "August Strindberg," *Who's Who in Gay and Lesbian History: From Antiquity to World War II*, 504. While Strindberg uses the word "perverse" to describe homosexuality, Freud uses "perversion" to describe a broader category of sexual practices outside of normative heterosexual intercourse. In "The Sexual Aberrations" (1905), Freud writes: "Perversions are sexual activities which either a) extend, in an anatomical sense, beyond the regions of the body that are designed for sexual union, or b) linger over the intermediate relations to the sexual object which should normally be traversed rapidly on the path towards the

final sexual aim"; Sigmund Freud, "The Sexual Aberrations," *Three Essays on the Theory of Sexuality* (1905), *The Standard Edition of the Complete Psychological Works of Sigmund Freud*, vol. 7, 16.

6 Ross Shideler, *Questioning the Father: From Darwin to Zola, Ibsen, Strindberg and Hardy; Per Olov Enquist: A Critical Study; Voices under the Ground: Themes and Images in the Early Poetry of Gunnar Ekelöf; The Hour of the Lynx: A Play by Per Olov Enquist*, trans. Ross Shideler; *The Night of the Tribades: A Play by Per Olov Enquist*, trans. Ross Shideler.

7 Matthew Roy, *August Strindberg's Perversions: On the Science, Sin, and Scandal of Homosexuality in August Strindberg's Works*. Göran Söderström, *Strindberg: Ett Liv*; and "Strindberg och homosexualiteten: En biografisk studie," *Lambda Nordica* 1, 22-44. Eva Borgström, "Emancipation och perversion: Strindberg och den besvärliga (homo)sexualiteten," *Res Publica* 62-63; *Kärlekshistoria: Begär mellan kvinnor i 1800-talets litteratur*; and "'Jag hatar henne eftersom jag älskar henne': Strindbergs *En dåres försvarstal*," *En Bok om Strindberg*. Anna Westerstahl Stenport, *Locating August Strindberg's Prose: Modernism, Transnationalism, and Setting*. Ann-Sofie Lönngren, "Triangular, Homosocial, Lesbian: A Queer Approach to Desire in August Strindberg's Novel *A Madman's Manifesto*," *Contagion* 19, 205-229. To these titles, I would also add: Göran Söderström, Fredrik Silverstolpe, Greger Eman, et al., *Sympatiens hemlighetsfulla makt: Stockholms homosexuella 1860-1960*.

8 To this list of eminent German, Austrian, Hungarian, and English sexologists, psychologists, scholars, and activists, one should also add the work of François Carlier, Auguste Ambroise Tardieu, and Georges Saint-Paul in France, and Edward Carpenter and John Addington Symonds in England.

9 Greger Eman, "1907: Det homosexuella genombrottet," in *Sympatiens hemlighetsfulla makt*, 149-64. Eman's discussion of the "homosexual breakthrough" is of course an homage to the "Modern Breakthrough" in Scandinavian literature at the end of the nineteenth century, famously articulated by the Danish literary critic Georg Brandes in his book *Hovedstrømninger i det 19de Aarhundredes Litteratur* (1871-75). For more on nineteenth-century European sexology, research, and advocacy, see: Eman

149-164; Martin 259, 323n67, 325n15; Westerstahl Stenport 136; and notes 15 and 16 below.

[10] For more on Eugène Jansson, see: Nils Wollin, *Eugène Jansson Måleri*; Kirk Varnedoe, *Northern Light: Realism and Symbolism in Scandinavian Painting, 1880-1910*, and *Northern Light: Nordic Art at the Turn of the Century*; Inga Zachau, *Eugène Jansson: Den Blå Stadens Målare*; Folke Lalander, Inga Zachau, and Ulf Linde, *Eugène Jansson*; Henri Loyrette, ed., *Eugène Jansson: Nocturnes suédois*; and Greger Eman, "Bröderna Jansson," in *Sympatiens hemlighetsfulla makt*, 208-245.

[11] August Strindberg, *Tjänstekvinnans Son I-II*, August Strindbergs *Samlade Verk*, vols. 20-21, 177.

[12] August Strindberg, "The Reward of Virtue," *Getting Married*, 52. Original in August Strindberg, "Dygdens Lön," Giftas I-II, August Strindbergs Samlade Verk, vol. 16, 31-34.

[13] For more on the celebrated blasphemy trial in 1884, see: Mary Sandbach, Introduction, August Strindberg, Getting Married, 14-17; Olof Lagerkrantz, *August Strindberg*, 137-139; Michael Meyer, *Strindberg: A Biography*, 129-141, 161-162; Michael Robinson, ed., *The Cambridge Companion to August Strindberg*, 7-9, 49, 60; Göran Söderström, *Strindberg: Ett Liv*, 140-143.

[14] In her introduction to *Getting Married*, Mary Sandbach writes that "in the main, the story is concerned with...the oppression of the lower classes...and the terrible effects of abstinence" (23). Sandbach explains that Strindberg's criticism of abstinence stemmed from the ideas of both George Drysdale, who "believed that you could not have a healthy mind unless you had a healthy body, and that body could not be healthy if it was starved of sex" (24), and Max Nordau, who "thought that physical love was the only natural and healthy love, and that people needed sex more than they needed food" (24).

[15] Havelock Ellis, "Autoerotism: A Psychological Study," *The Alienist and Neurologist* 19, 260-299. Paul Näcke, "Die sexuellen Perversitäten in der

Irrenanstalt," *Wiener klinische Rundschau* 27–30; also published in *Psychiatrische en neurologische bladen* 3, 122-149. Sigmund Freud, "The Sexual Aberrations" in *Three Essays on the Theory of Sexuality* (1905), "Leonardo da Vinci and a Memory of His Childhood" (1910), "On Narcissism: An Introduction" (1914), *The Standard Edition of the Complete Psychological Works of Sigmund Freud*, ed. and trans. James Strachey et al., vols. 7, 11, 14.

[16] For more on the first appearance of the words "homosexual" and "homosexuality" (in correspondence between the Austro-Hungarian scholar Karl-Maria Kertbeny and the German activist Karl Heinrich Ulrichs) in 1869, and on this vast body of work in sexology, psychology, and criminology on sexual inversion, see: David Halperin, *One Hundred Years of Homosexuality and Other Essays on Greek Love*; Rosario (1997); and Martin (2011).

[17] Freud, "The Sexual Aberrations" (1905), *The Standard Edition*, vol. 7, 136.

[18] Freud, "Leonardo da Vinci and a Memory of His Childhood" (1910), *The Standard Edition*, vol. 11, 100.

[19] Freud, "On Narcissism: An Introduction" (1914), *The Standard Edition*, vol. 14, 73.

The Ultimate Father and Daughter: Agamemnon, Electra and Their Legacy

Kathleen L. Komar

Given this volume's theme of fathers as both honored and challenged in western literature and culture, it seems fitting to close with an update on one crucial father figure, Agamemnon, and his loyal daughter, Electra, as they emerge in the 21st century, in particular, in cyberspace. This duo recalls many of the issues of patriarchy and gender conflicts that Ross Shideler so skillfully explores in his volume *Questioning the Father*.

The Beginnings of Patriarchy

Few fathers figure more prominently in the history of literature and culture than does Agamemnon. When he takes Klytemnestra as his bride, after killing her earlier husband and child, Agamemnon not only inherits her kingdom, but sets in motion the endgame of the curse of the House of Atreus. The battle between Agamemnon and Klytemnestra is the pivot on which the transition from an earlier, blood-based matriarchal system gives way to the law-based patriarchal tradition underpinning western culture. Agamemnon is indeed a father to be honored—and challenged. This essay will trace Agamemnon and his offspring (particularly his female offspring) into our own time and into a net he could not have anticipated when Klytemnestra threw her net over him in his bath in Mycenae. We will follow Agamemnon onto the Internet.

To begin at the end, Agamemnon is represented on the World Wide Web with an eponymous website, Agamemnon.com. While doing research for a book on late 20th century revisions of Klytemnestra,[1] I came upon a curious fact; the House of Atreus not only became big business on the American stage in the late 1990s, it also made inroads into cyberspace.[2] Myriad web sites were dedicated to various members of the House of Atreus—including: Electra.com, Iphigenia.com, and Orestes.com. Agamemnon.com was still available when I first checked in 1999. By June 2000 the site had become Agamemnon Film, owned (appropriately) by Charlton Heston and his son Fraser. And Agamemnon.org was an entertainment site for downloading music and games. (This website has since ceased to exist and the domain name is available for purchase as of December 2014.) Even Atreus.com appeared as a web-page design company (since migrated to a new website). And Atreus.org is a game design site that seems to specialize in training games for espionage. Atreushouse.com is a website for a bed and breakfast in Texas with an invitingly cozy white cottage on its home page. One can only imagine that anyone staying at Atreus House is blissfully unaware of the history of this classical family name. Guests must at least be hesitant to soak in the inviting antique tubs… In Germany, Atreus.de is an interim management site. And Orestes.de (and Orestes/Elektra) is a ticket sales site. Elektra.de is a site for creative lighting design.

But to return to our main character, Agamemnon.com is certainly a site celebratory of the father. Run by Charlton Heston's son Fraser Heston. Fraser points out that his career began as he played the infant Moses to his father's adult Moses in Cecil B. DeMille's "Ten Commandants" in 1956. Under the section featuring films produced by Agamemnon Film, Charlton Heston appears as the lead in many of the iconic dominant male parts of the epic western tradition— including: Ben Hur, Moses, Anthony (of Anthony and Cleopatra), the tough western rancher father in "Proud Men," Sherlock Holmes, and Long John Silver, among others. The site creates a lasting tribute to the elder Heston as "a man for all seasons" (in which he also stars) and a patriarch for all time.

In many ways, this is a fitting invocation of the classical Agamemnon's memory. To provide the briefest of classical contexts for Agamemnon's and Klytemnestra's story, this couple embodies the struggle between two cultural traditions and world orders, matriarchy and patriarchy. Agamemnon is the leader of the Greek forces in the Trojan war, willing to sacrifice his daughter, Iphigenia, in order to gain favorable winds to take his fleet of warriors to Troy. He is firmly embedded in the heroic, epic tradition that becomes a major part of the foundation of western, patriarchal culture. Klytemnestra represents the feminist cause par excellence. Hers is the story of the struggle of female blood right against male law.[3] It is the struggle of the female against the establishment of the patriarchal order. A woman whose name used as a common noun came to mean "adulteress" or "murderess," Klytemnestra has an even more clearly negative place in classical hearts than her sister Helen.[4] We know from Aeschylus's *Oresteia*, Sophocles' *Electra*, and Euripides' *Electra* that she kills her husband Agamemnon along with his captive Cassandra upon their return from the Trojan War. She is, in turn, killed by her son Orestes to avenge his father's death thus precipitating the trial of Orestes under Athena's judgeship in Aeschylus's *Eumenides*—the trial in which the rule of law and the fathers is given precedence over maternal blood rights. What remains in question is why Klytemnestra does what she does.

Stesichorus, who seems well disposed toward all of Leda's children, blames Aphrodite for making Tyndareus's daughters unfaithful in retribution for their father's forgetting to make sacrifices to her.[5] Explaining both Helen's and Klytemnestra's behavior as caused by the gods, Stesichorus alleviates their personal guilt. (The tendency to blame the gods for men's difficulties is rather common in Classical literature and is often used to alleviate man's own responsibility for an unpleasant situation.) We should note, however, that the original transgression is committed by the father, Tyndareus, who condemns his daughters to suffer for his oversight.

The more standard view of Klytemnestra as an adulterous murderess is rather surprising, given the totality of her history. Klytemnestra, unlike her sister Helen, was not wooed by all of Greece, but rather taken by Agamemnon from her first husband, Tantalus, whom Agamemnon killed along with Tantalus and

Klytemnestra's child.[6] Having lost her first child to Agamemnon, Klytemnestra must have been even more outraged when he also sacrificed Iphigenia to his military ambitions. Most classical reference handbooks ignore this early history and begin Klytemnestra's description with her marriage to Agamemnon, thus giving us an entirely different image of her motivations and neglecting Agamemnon's ruthlessly self-interested bid for power.[7]

Much is at stake in how one interprets the mother, Klytemnestra, and her killing of the father, Agamemnon. Is she a murdering adulteress as Homer's dead Agamemnon laments, and thus a usurper of the rightful place and power of the father? Is she an avenging mother visiting retribution on a filicidal father as Euripides' *Iphigenia in Aulis* would lead us to think? Is she a woman hungry for power and sexual satisfaction as both Sophocles' and Euripides' Electras argue, or one seduced by a cunning Aegisthus who wants to become the patriarch himself as Homer's Nestor suggests? And the most crucial question: Does mother right hold up against father right. Together Klytemnestra and Agamemnon embody this moment of cultural struggle and transition. And as we know from hindsight, Agamemnon and the patriarchal legal system of the west will prevail and will persist into our own times.

Perhaps the most striking feature of the classical Agamemnon and Klytemnestra's story is the destructive violence of their battle for individual women and for the family. The sacrifice of her daughter Iphigenia to the military aspirations of Agamemnon and his Greek companions provides the usual starting point for analyses of Klytemnestra's actions and motivations. But long before these events, Agamemnon abducts Klytemnestra and murders her first husband and child, thus founding his own fatherhood and patriarchal position on the blood of an earlier family. One can easily imagine why Klytemnestra turns to mariticide. This undercurrent of murder and revenge continues as Klytemnestra herself kills Cassandra and helps to murder Agamemnon upon his return from the Trojan War, thus moving from violence against women to violence by women.

Klytemnestra's violence is sparked by a maternal rage that clearly threatens the rising patriarchal dominance. She usurps male prerogatives of wielding power, ruling, and killing a man. The threat of Klytemnestra's maternal anger is so powerful that it must be suppressed in order for paternal civilization to endure. The Erinnys or "female furies" must become the Eumenides in order to establish the polis and the rule of law, which is based in patriarchal legal rules rather than matriarchal blood rights. As Luce Irigaray has pointed out, Orestes' murder of his mother, which precedes and supersedes the murder of the father in the Oedipus myth that Freud emphasizes, becomes a necessary founding gesture for Athens and by extension for the rule of law and thus patriarchal civilization itself.[8] Agamemnon is thus not only a patriarch but the patriarch upon whose tomb western civilization is founded. He is thus the ultimate father in a very real sense.

This battle between mother and father at the base of western civilization is continued into the children's generation as the dead father, Agamemnon, is avenged by both his male offspring, Orestes, and his female child Electra. After killing her husband, Klytemnestra treats her daughter Electra badly. Electra loudly bewails her fate and waits for the return of Orestes to seek her own vengeance for their father's death. She and Orestes plot to kill their mother, and Orestes carries out the deed. (See Eruipides' *Electra* [413 BC] and Sophocles' *Electra* [414? BC] for two different interpretations of these events.) Both Iphigenia, by accepting her sacrifice for the good of the Greeks, and Electra, by avenging her father and the patriarchal order at the cost of her mother's life, support the rising patriarchal system that their mother fought. In the Greek context, then, the children (both male and female) of the father Agamemnon help to solidify the patriarchy at the ultimate expense of mother.

Agamemnon's Female Offspring: Online Elektra

At this point, it might be helpful to shift our focus from Agamemnon himself to his female offspring and loyal daughter,

Elektra—to see whether the celebration of the father on the Hestons' Agamemnon.com carries over to other perspectives on the Internet. As the millennium came to a close, Electra moved from classical mythology and theater to the World Wide Web.[9] Of all of Klytemnestra's progeny, Electra seemed closest to the hearts of late 20th century women. The rebel daughter who stands up for (male) right and for her betrayed father, the daughter who breaks free of her mother's domination in order to mourn her father and find a life of her own seemed very attractive to young women in the late 1990s. [10] However, not many of these women were aware of Klytemnestra's story. If they knew the name at all, it was as the betraying and murderous wife, the destructive woman. The reaction of audiences to Elektra in Ruth Margraff's 1997 punk rock opera, *The Elektra Fugues*, (which I saw in the Culver City production in 1999) for example, was one of passionate sympathy—particularly among those women I spoke to who did not know more about Klytemnestra. These women were not troubled by the fact that Klytemnestra's own fight was a battle of Mother Rights versus the newly emerging patriarchy. They were free to admire Elektra's irrepressible determination and loyalty. This kind of admiration— along with the revival of Electra on Broadway in the 1990s[11]— apparently made Electra a recognizable and positive icon, whose name was sufficiently well-known to merit being used for a website, "Electra.com." Electra, alone among Klytemnestra's daughters, conquered the internet by having a virtual empire built in her name.[12]

Described in a *Time digital* article as a "hip women's site," Electra.com began (at least in the week when I first visited the site in March of 1999) quite unintentionally ironically with an 1950s-vintage drawing of a mother hugging her baby daughter next to the quotation, "Your Mom wanted the best for you, don't you deserve it?" with the name Electra in bold and highlighted beneath the quotation.[13]

The authors of this site were clearly not troubled by (or apparently aware of) the classical stories that attend Electra and her "Mom." The site was practically oriented, flanking the vision of a loving mom with an ad for online health insurance. The site did, however, capture some of the ancient Electra's intensity and focus. In a section entitled "Simplify Your Life," the site suggests that "Electra helps you <u>define what's important</u> and weed out the rest" (underlining in the original).[14] This ability was certainly one evidenced in the ancient Electra's life (which was obsessively focused on avenging her murdered father) and recalled by all the 1990s revisions of her story.

The section "<u>Electra Women</u>" (with a photo of Josephine Baker) aimed to provide young women with role models and with the courage to follow their dreams (or in the classical Electra's case, their nightmares). The site, on the first day I visited it, began:

> Maya Angelou wrote a poem entitled Phenomenal Woman that inspired women to realize just how fabulous they are in their everyday lives. As we celebrate **Women's History Month** we take a closer look at the courageous <u>Electra Women</u> who have made history. We hope that after reading their stories you will agree that they are nothing short of phenomenal. [all underlining, boldface, and punctuation in the original]

Electra clearly became a symbol for the woman of courageous determination, who overcomes all obstacles to achieve her goals. Electra, not Klytemnestra, came to be the central woman to appreciate and emulate as the last millennium ended. The daughter who supported the rise of the patriarchy in the classical story becomes the internet model for women of courage and historical importance.

While she does indeed present a strong and successful female character, the ancient Electra is a much more troubled figure than her late 20th century counterpart. The end of the last millennium managed to remove Electra's trauma-inducing mother, Klytemnestra, entirely in favor of a more unproblematically loving "mom." Electra becomes the image of the strong and accomplished woman; the fact that she works entirely in the service of the male order in the classical texts has disappeared in the website along with her desire to execute mom. In short, despite her interactive mode, this 1999 Electra has become rather one-dimensional. In many ways Electra's sister Chrysothemis might be a better figure for this website (provided any young woman today who was not a classics scholar would recognize her name). With all the advice on money, career and relationships, women's health and dating, which the Electra.com website offers, it would be easier to picture the good and dutiful daughter Chrysothemis exploring its frames than the raging Electra. This more domesticated and somewhat tamer Electra would have fit well into "Chick Lit" boom that was taking place at the same time, featuring characters such as Bridget Jones in the novel and film, *Bridget Jones's Diary*.[15]

Both Klytemnestra and her rebellious daughter Electra have been tamed and domesticated on Electra.com, as have the other forces at work in Greek tragedy. Fate and the manipulative gods have been replaced by astrological forecasts. "Are there invisible forces affecting your life?" the website asks. Yes, but Apollo, Athena and the curse of the House of Atreus have been replaced by our daily astrology reading. We can no longer claim, as the classical Orestes does after slaying Klytemnestra, that a god made us do it. We live in a less divine but perhaps more trivially superstitious universe than the ancient Klytemnestra. This website implied that our fates concern small personal events such as dating, personal health and hygiene, finding a job; our personal actions do not often rise to the public and political power generated by the classical Klytemnestra or Electra. As the last millennium came to an end, women (at least as defined by this website) seem to have hunkered down or "cocooned" at home, more comfortable with Martha Stewart as a role model than Klytemnestra—or the ancient Electra. Although Electra's website talks about women who have acted in history and politics, it is geared to women who focus on home. Like her Furies, Klytemnestra is tamed here; she becomes again the peaceful keeper of the hearth, the good mate and mother. This is the *Eumenides* writ small—or rather, writ electronic.

Electra too has undergone a serious metamorphosis as the twentieth century closed. The classical figure who endlessly digs her father's grave and demands her mother's death has taken to listing jobs, "temping for a living," and reading horoscopes about dating. Electra does, however, gain one important feature in the late twentieth century; she replaces her much-loved sister Iphigenia. It is as though Klytemnestra's story has been rewound to a point before the loss of her daughter. The doting mother again holds her loved daughter and "wants the best for her." The daughter, however, has changed from Iphigenia to Electra. Like her sister Iphigenia, who, at least in Euripides' version, comes to accept her fate as sacrifice to the war and male aspirations, Electra too supports her father and the male power structure. Like Iphigenia's death, Electra's success in killing her mother helps reaffirm the patriarchy. Patriarchal violence disrupts female-female relationships, and thus dismantles a matriarchal order which might challenge it, thereby protecting itself. But if Electra could be taken back to a time before Klytemnestra's loss and rage and installed as the cherished child, Electra's strong will and spirit could be nurtured by female love. Electra would then become the daughter she may have wanted to be, and Klytemnestra would become a mother she could love in return.

The implication here is that a viable family unit has been reestablished without the battle to the death between Mother Right and father's law. Interestingly, however, the Electra.com website did not mention the father (Agamemnon or any other father) at all. He

has been narratively displaced and replaced by a loyalty to the
mother. This move interestingly parallels one made in the one
eponymous 21st Century film, *Elektra*, from 2005 and starring
Jennifer Garner as a martial arts avenger not of her murdered
father, but of her murdered mother.

In fact, the whole Electra.com world became a female domain.
Men are mentioned only as potential dates or mates. One article is
even entitled "Token Male: A man's point of view in a woman's
world." But this women's world has contracted drastically from that
in which the ancient Klytemnestra and Electra operated.
Electra.com created a world geared to female "18-to-34-year-olds,"
who will find the perfect mate, attract him with the perfect body
(having attained it by knowing the really low-fat foods), and raise
happy families while holding down a not-too-high-pressure job and
investing for retirement. Issues of power, politics, struggles for
dominance, and most crucially, the conflict between home and
public arena are all airbrushed out of this reassuring picture. If fate
exists, it can be read in an astrological chart. In this world, female
children are not sacrificed for war nor suppressed by their mothers.
Mom has never touched a *labrys* nor would she think of neglecting
one child for another. Electra has moved to a reassuring, safe
fantasyland and taken her mother, Klytemnestra, with her. There is
no need to murder the father; he is simply ignored.

Strangely enough, Electra.com was part of a new media empire
aimed at a female audience and meant to announce a new woman
for the new millennium. Tracing Electra.com back to its mother
organization by links on its screens, I discovered a group called
(oxygen)media, inc. headed by Gerry Laybourne.[16] This group, as its
manifesto asserted in 1999, was out to create a new vision of media
for the millennium. It declared its audience to be "women of the
Millennium" and their children. These groups were identified as
"choked by stale content" of television and the internet and seeking
a breath of new air—enter (Oxygen)media, inc. Oxygen originally
had a variety of websites for healthy living (thrive.com) and women
(electra.com and momsonline.com); it was associated with the Walt

Disney Company, America Online, Carsey-Werner-Mandabach (an independent production company responsible for television shows such as "Roseanne," "Cybill," and "Grace Under Fire"), and finally Oprah Winfrey and her HARPO Entertainment Group.

Surprisingly well connected, then, (oxygen)media, inc. was the vision of its director, Gerry Laybourne, who was featured prominently on the oxygen.com website. Laybourne was the self-declared arbiter of what women wanted in 1999 and in the new millennium. Given her ability to produce high-quality programming for children on the Nickelodeon channel, she was obviously an important voice in media of the day. She was competing quite successfully in a male-dominated media world. Some of what she had to say was interesting; some of it gave one pause. Her stress on the economic capabilities of women provided useful data. (In her website page entitled "The Facts," which presented data on women, Laybourne pointed out, for example, that "American women are, in effect, the largest 'national' economy on earth.") Laybourne sees the leadership style of the 21st century being described by words "more typically feminine," such as: collaborative, flexible, celebratory, encouraging, personal, rewarding, open, "we"-oriented. This assertion is somewhat difficult to accept. How do Klytemnestra and her late 20th century offspring fit into the open, collaborative, encouraging, vision that Laybourne sees for the 21st century? While I may agree that such a leadership style is desirable, I cannot see it as "more typically feminine." This seems to be a "feminism" that wants the world to be less complicated than the battle to the death between the ancient mother and daughter.

(oxygen)media.com created a feel-better-about-yourself, self-help guide to living for a female audience. It provided some uplifting (and some silly) information for women. But while it did include some economic issues, it tended to focus on women as consumers of media ("spending 8.8 hours per day with some form of media" according to Laybourne's "Fact Sheet") or as wives and mothers. It seemed mostly unconcerned with politics or issues of power in a larger social arena than that of personal relationships.

With this group as a mother organization, it is not surprising that Electra.com was filled with articles on "Home How-To's," "Lowfat life," and "The Dating Diva." As the millennium drew to a close, the world of the classical Klytemnestra and Electra contracted back into the home. The Furies are tamed by helpful psychiatric hints, women learn to be well-adjusted wives and mothers who can hold down a job and tend the family simultaneously. This site may declare women to be dominant, but they are not very interested in overthrowing the father or the patriarchy. The shrill, critical, female voices of feminist writers of the 1970s and 1980s became cheerier and more optimistic in the late 1990s—largely by constricting women's field of vision.

Electra Rewired

However, Electra.com could be interpreted as shifting the model in a new direction rather than as simply reverting to a pre-feminist or moving to a post-feminist position. This Electra could be seen as realigning herself with her mother and leaving dad out of the picture entirely. This Electra has truly buried her father—but then returned to her mother. Klytemnestra has been reconceived as the loving mother she once was. Electra and Iphigenia merge, mother remains joyfully alive, and father is conclusively buried. The ultimate patriarch, Agamemnon, is nowhere to be seen, thus Electra.com finally displaces the father in favor of a woman-centered society. Electra is reinscribed into a female world with women (like Gerry Laybourne) in power and in control of the media.

Electra.com and the shift in thinking she represents may not be the feminism of the 1960s, 70s or 80s, but I would not call it "post-feminist" either. It seems rather to be a post-modern feminism. Using bits and pieces of earlier culture but reassembling the shards without too much regard for preserving any originary moment, this new slant on feminism seems to toy with the cultural and gender traditions that once held women captive. And Agamemnon has no part in it. He may be preserved by Charlton Heston and his son, but in a site designed by women, the father has been written out.

This 1990's revision of Electra seems to imply that women must move beyond the ancient myths to create a new gender plot. The website does not look back more than fleetingly to the Greek cultural materials. It is not seeking origin, but rather using the Greek texts and myths as shards of a cultural tradition to be reshuffled into a new post-modern arrangement. By the time we get to the online incarnations of the women of the House of Atreus, their story is no longer simply being revised; it is being atomized and reassembled with a strong admixture of very popular culture. The leveling effect that puts Klytemnestra in the company of Electra.com and Oxygen.com is quite striking.

This revision of Electra does not take the concept of a founding moment so seriously. In the 1990s, women feel uninhibited in rewriting Western history into a simultaneous collage of radically different possibilities. Electra.com can love Mom and eliminate the male visually and psychologically. 1990's Internet sites take an ironic side-glance at the founding myths, they are no longer determined by them. This may be due in part to the fragmentation of those earlier myths and our lack of memory of them. But this new approach also represents a challenge to those cultural foundations.

As the last century and the millennium ended, Iphigenia, Electra and Orestes made us pause to reconsider their modern fates enwrapped in a new "net." The internet takes Agamemnon and his children into entirely new cultural territory in which not just the House of Atreus but the concepts of "high culture" and "founding moments" themselves are dialogized, atomized and recast in a venue in which pop icons merge with their classical counterparts. We embarked upon a new, more iconoclastic sense of "culture" and "authority" as webmistresses replace more traditional female authors.

The interaction of ancient founding myths and absolutely contemporary technology does indicate, however, that culture continues to operate in an evolutionary mode—even if a radical one. While new cyber games appear, "high culture" infiltrates the web matrix to keep alive the narrative explorations of our most crucial cultural tensions. The political and cultural power struggle between men and women, fathers and mothers, becomes much more complex in cyberspace where gender is harder to detect. Nonetheless the ethical questions concerning the founding moments of western culture as embodied in Klytemnestra's mariticide, Agamemnon's slaughter, and Electra's and Orestes' matricide persist—even if atomized and dialogized—as we venture onto the internet superhighway.

A second type of cultural incorporation in cyberspace is also embodied in Electra.com. In this case only an echo of any ancient story remains—and that a faint one. Electra has metamorphosed into a later self, her ancient self is no longer recognizable except as the powerfully focused and ambitious young woman who succeeds in enacting her will despite all obstacles. Unlike her mother, Klytemnestra, whose story reaches the Web almost in its entirety, Electra becomes a vaguely positive invocation of the strong female with the details of her drama lost to view.[17] Her homophonic relationship to electricity—and their etymological resonances of meteoric qualities and the production of energy by friction—help Electra to gain footing in a new cultural arena that remains largely unaware of her heritage. This lack of genealogy may make Electra.com more available for forging new female selves not staked to a traumatic past. And it helps to liberate her from Agamemnon and the dominance of the patriarchal figure.

Agamemnon.com, on the other hand, reinscribes the patriarchal genealogy and moves it forward from Moses and Ben Hur to Charlton Heston. Heston is, perhaps, an appropriate reembodiment of Agamemnon—a patriarch and dominant personality whose power persists only in the patriarchal narrative itself, passed from father to son to male offspring across the millennia. Even in cyberspace, Heston is an actor whose time upon the stage has passed and who is now remembered as a cultural shadow of other patriarchal figures.

Postscript

One more note must be added in concluding this discussion: both Electra.com and Iphigenia.com have been swallowed by larger websites in the last few years. Electra.com first moved under Oprah.com, Oprah Winfrey's website that supplies many of the same kinds of articles and information about personal fulfillment, fitness and lifestyle that Electra.com used to provide. I can only surmise that Oprah provides a much more recognizable role model than Electra used to. Indeed, if Electra has metamorphosed into Oprah, we find her reembodied in a woman of considerable power, wealth and control, who focuses on women and their lives but has reintroduced a male voice in the form of a popular psychologist, Dr. Phil.[18] Perhaps we are witnessing a reintegration of the male and female in a newly conceived world where women seem quite able to hold the kingdom of television or the internet. Oprah, who herself had to overcome an abusive father, revises the picture by introducing a new male authority who works for and with women. Perhaps the post-modern mélange of cultural shards has resolved into a 21st century rebuilding of the kingdom of women that can integrate men without being dominated by them and that dwarfs the celebration of the father in Agamemnon.com.[19]

While this metamorphosis may present a note of optimism regarding the roles and power of women, it also displaces the classical female names and figures totally. By April 2002, no traces of Electra.com remained.[20] Agamemnon.com, however, stubbornly persists.

Notes

[1] See my volume *Reclaiming Klytemnestra: Revenge or Reconciliation*. The study focuses on the battle between Mother Right and the newly arising patriarchal law as depicted in Aeschylus's *Oresteia* and replayed by a number of contemporary women writers in the 1980s.

[2] Frank McGuinness's adaptation of Sophocles' *Electra* under the direction of David Leveaux ran quite successfully on Broadway and was nominated for several Tony Awards. The play, which debuted at the Ethel Barrymore Theater on West 47th Street in New York in December of 1998 and was to have run until January 17, 1999, was extended for several months due to overwhelming demand for tickets. In the 1990s, the House of Atreus was reviving in several areas of the country and in varied artistic media. Garrett Fisher's opera *Agamemnon*, which uses Taiko drummers as well as masks, played in Seattle's Nippon Kan Theater in June of 1998.[2] Euripides' *Orestes* was revived in April and May of 1998 at the Franklin College Theater in Indiana. Playwright Ellen McLaughlin staged *Iphigenia and Other Daughters* at New York's Classic Stage Company in 1995, and Ruth Margraff presented an opera, *The Elektra Fugues* in New York's HERE Theater in 1997, which was later done as a play in Culver City, California in 1999. *The Greeks*, an adaptation by Kenneth Cavander based on Euripides, Aeschylus and Sophocles and commissioned by the Royal Shakespeare in 1980, ran in Los Angeles in a six-hour production in September, 1999.

[3] Aeschylus's *Oresteia* (and particularly the "Eumenides") records the shift in western civilization away from privileging kinship or "blood" relationships (which favor a matriarchal order, since the blood relationship between mothers and children is indisputable) over non-kin relationships or duties prescribed by culture or honor. The question in the "Eumenides" is whether Orestes should be punished by the (female) Erinyes for the murder of his mother (a "blood" murder) or whether his duty to avenge his father (and the patriarchal claim to dominion) outweighs the blood rights of his mother. In the end of Aeschylus's version, the rights of the father (and claims of law) outweigh those of the mother (and claims of blood). The shift from matriarchy to patriarchy and

from blood rights to law becomes institutionalized in the law court of Athens, which is founded to decide Orestes' case and which acquits him.

[4] Charles Martin Robertson and Herbert Jenning Rose, entry on Clytaemnestra in *The Oxford Classical Dictionary*, pp 256-7). "Her name occasionally occurs as a common noun meaning 'adulteress' (as Quintilian, Inst. 8. 6. 53), or 'murderess' (see Horace, Sat. 1. 1. 100, where 'fortissima Tryndaridarum' stands for Clytaemnestra)."

[5] Richmond Lattimore translator, *Greek Lyrics*, p. 23. Taken from Stesichorus' "Helen and Klytaimnestra."

[6] Richmond Lattimore translator, *Greek Lyrics*, p. 23. Taken from Stesichorus' "Helen and Klytaimnestra."

[7] Both *The Oxford Classical Dictionary* and Seyffert's *Dictionary of Classical Antiquities* identify Clytemnestra primarily as the daughter of Tyndareus and the wife of Agamemnon—whom she slew. Only Edward Tripp's description in *The Meridian Handbook of Classical Mythology*, pp. 167-68, more sympathetically takes into account Clytemnestra's early history and Agamemnon's double murder.

[8] See Luce Irigaray, *Le corps-à-corps avec la mère*, 15 ff.

[9] One wonders if the aural proximity of Electra's name to "electric" or "electronic" contributes to its choice as a title for Electra.com. I attempted several times to contact both Gerry Laybourne and the Webmaster for Electra.com to get more information on the choice of name for the site, but I got no response.

[10] Playwright Ellen McLaughlin staged *Iphigenia and Other Daughters* at New York's Classic Stage Company in 1995, and Ruth Margraff presented an opera, *The Elektra Fugues* in New York's HERE Theater in 1997, which was later done as a play in Culver City, California in 1999.

[11] The House of Atreus became big business in the United States in the late 1990s. After early development at the Donmar Warehouse in London and a 1998 run at the McCarter Theater in Princeton, Frank McGuinness's adaptation of Sophocles' *Electra* under the direction of David Leveaux ran quite successfully on Broadway and was nominated for several Tony Awards (including a nomination for Zoe Wannamaker as Electra). The two main female roles, Electra (played by Wannamaker), and Clytemnestra (played by Claire Bloom), impressed audiences with the power and timeliness of the ancient tale. At Princeton, Leveaux used footage of the carnage in Sarajevo and Bosnia to underscore this point. The play, which debuted at the Ethel Barrymore Theater on West 47th Street in New York in December of 1998 and was to have run until Jan 17, 1999, was extended for several months due to overwhelming demand for tickets. And all this after several years of musicals dominating Broadway!

[12] Iphigenia.com was a single poem in 1999. The site is now empty.

[13] Anita Hamilton, "Geraldine Laybourne Brings Women a Breath of Fresh Air," in *Time digital*, March 1999, 23-24. *Time digital* is actually a printed magazine with an accompanying website (www.timedigital.com), distributed by *Time Magazine* and featuring technical and internet materials. Its subtitle is "Your Guide to Personal Technology."

[14] All of my quotations here are taken from the Electra.com website of March 20, 1999.

[15] *Bridget Jones's Diary* was written by Helen Fielding in 1996 and published by Picador in London. It was later made into a film (2001) and a musical in (2009). It has remained widely popular and spawned a sequel and a number of related texts by other female writers.

[16] Gerry Laybourne is "A legend in the cable industry for taking the fledgling network Nickelodeon from a blip on the TV ratings chart in 1980 to the top channel for kids when she left in 1996" (*Time digital*, 23). She also served as president of ABC/Disney Cable Networks for two years. Oxygen Media is "a new TV channel with related websites that will cater to women" (*Time digital*, 23). Tracing this new women's media

empire to 2002, we find that Oxygen was not the overwhelming success Laybourne expected. When compared with two other "women's networks (WE and Lifetime), Laybourne's Oxygen comes in a distant third in terms of viewers. According to Michelle Orecklin's article "What Women Watch," "Oxygen on average is watched in only 52,000 households in prime time, WE in 110,000. Lifetime averages 1.9 million homes" (*Time Magazine*, May 13, 2002, p. 65). By the time of Orecklin's article, Oxygen was forced to lay off many of its website employees, merge sites and concentrate more on television.

17 See my analysis of "The Trial of Clytemnestra" at the website http://members.tripod.com/NWO_2/index.html   in   *Reclaiming Klytemnestra*.

18 Dr. Phil is Dr. Phil McGraw, with a degree from North Texas State (according to Oprah's website under "About Dr. Phil McGraw."). Dr. Phil is a consultant to corporations on "life strategies" and provides advice to Oprah's viewers and web visitors on how to conduct one's life or how to reform bad habits in order to reach happiness. He eventually got his own television show that became a smash hit by 2003. His guests and "patients" (as well as his audience) are overwhelmingly women.

19 Oxygen.com does continue to exist. Its stated purpose (as displayed on its website on April 13, 2015) is as follows: "Oxygen Media is a multiplatform entertainment brand that targets young, multicultural women. The network's relevant and engaging content reflects how real women with real stories see the world – vibrant, optimistic and bold. Oxygen is the destination where women can come together across multiple platforms to have fun and encourage each other through their individual and collective journeys. The growing network's unscripted original programming includes 'Sisterhood of Hip Hop,' 'The Prancing Elites Project,' 'Funny Girls' and the popular 'Preachers' franchise."

20 Typing in her web address merely brings up a notice that this site is not reachable. We no longer are led to Oprah through Electra; her name becomes a dead end. I did still in April 2002 locate some sites related to Electra—including a rock band named "Writhing Electra," which can be reached at www.writhingelectra.com and has a soulful female lead singer

backed (appropriately) by three male colleagues. While lyrics such as "Standin' and Cryin'" do invoke some memories of Electra, they are very faint ones indeed. I also found a Scottish security company (www.electra-com.uk.com) and a Czech Internet café (www.electra.cz), which seem interested primarily in the homophonic connection of Electra. In short, Electra seems to have disappeared entirely by mid 2002. The media run of the House of Atreus may have subsided by this date. We can only wonder if the end of the 21st century might see a rebirth of the famous family and a reemergence of Klytemnestra and her daughters—or perhaps of the father, Agamemnon.

Appendix: Screen shot of Electra.com

Epilog

The Longing of the Seasoned Man
(A Shaggy Dog Story aka A Tribute to Ross)

Mary Kay Norseng

Ross bookended my own career at UCLA. He came four years before my arrival in 1973, and he remains six years and counting after my retirement in 2008. (To Ross "retirement" does not really mean retirement.) During my first year as a member of the Scandinavian faculty I learned that Ross wore many hats, all with panache: the Scandinavian scholar, the Comparative Literature scholar, the colleague, the teacher, the administrator, the translator and the poet. I engaged with them all in the offices and corridors of Royce Hall. All but one. The poet worked alone and at night, sitting in his apartment in Westwood looking out at life (the frat house across the street) and death (the Veterans' Cemetery in the distance). Rumor had it that a sip of cognac and a cigarette accompanied his midnight ritual. One of the poems from those early years was "The Audience":

> Language almost says itself.
> I can hear it sometimes
> speaking clearly and succinctly
> to an audience that I
> do not quite understand.
> It speaks to more than my ears
> yet if I try to understand precisely
> to whom it addresses itself,
> as if I stood up in the audience
> and said, "That is interesting, but..."
> I never get beyond standing up.
> It stops speaking and I am left
> alone in an empty auditorium.

I have stood for hours
looking at the rows of vacant seats,
the curtains drawn back on the stage,
the balcony, dark and a little ominous,
pondering the question of speaker
and listener. When I listen long enough
the audience starts filing in,
the seats fill and the room goes dark.
Then language appears and words
are sufficient, seem adequate to us all.
But if I glance to the left or right
and see the faces, male and female,
young, old, beautiful, ugly, etcetera,
all looking like me and listening
to a voice, I start sweating
and want to get out of there,
or to find out how it knows
what it knows, how it tells us
what we felt years ago,
what happened to us in high school,
why we are so curious at middle age
to know if anything we have done
or said will be of importance?

There are only a few older people
who sit quietly listening to what it says
as if they have heard it before,
its pain, its titillation and frustration.
Is it to them that it speaks,
and if so, why don't they answer
instead of just sitting there listening
as if this voice was their only child?

"The Audience" was published in *Poetry Magazine* in 1975 (36-
37). Thirty-nine years later we, Ross's colleagues, have come
together to address his poet's question: how will he know if "[he

has] done anything or said anything that will be of importance?" Let us count the ways.

"A man's work is nothing but this slow trek to rediscover, through the detours of art, those two or three great and simple images in whose presence his heart first opened." I recently came across this quotation by Albert Camus. Provoked by the idea of my own personal set of heart-opening images, and at the same time mulling over topics for my contribution to Ross's retirement celebration, I thought of two images that have become such part and parcel of my everyday emotional memory weave that I barely realize I'm even thinking about them. They come like little puffs of thought and feeling. Both stem from my first seven years at UCLA and my first seven years of working with Ross. Both are short, collapsed scenarios about living. I dare say they are not the elemental images that Camus had in mind, but my heart does open to them.

The first is a lesson I learned from a man in a canning factory, peas, corn, tomatoes, I can't remember. But there was this man, an older man, who had worked a long time in the canning factory, and he would say, "life is like a ladder, and when the sun shines, you climb, and you climb, and you just keep on climbin'; and when the rain comes, and the winds start blowin' and the storm rages, you just hold on, you hold on tight, you just hold on, and then when the sun shines again, you climb and you climb and you keep on climbin'." I loved this story and I loved the way he told it, because I could feel the hot sun and I could feel the lashing rains, and I loved to tell it myself, and I told it over and over again, and it got more and more dramatic with each telling, and one night at a party I told it, and Ross was there, and as I got to the last "you just keep on climbin'," Ross yelled out, "That's MY story!" Embarrassed! Shocked! If the ladder were real I would have fallen off. How could I have fooled myself into thinking it was my story, I who had never worked in a canning factory? I apparently wanted that story so bad that I internalized it whole and never looked back. Ross's reaction? He just laughed his generous laugh and essentially gave me the story, and I have, indeed, made it mine. A young girl climbs and holds tight and climbs again, long dark hair blown by the wind, lashed by the rain, dried by the sun, a young girl climbing and holding tight and climbing again. I love that girl. She opens my heart every time. Thanks for the story, Ross! It's our story now.

Thinking of my girl climbing toward the sky made me think of a poem I had read back in the late 1970s, but this was of a young boy looking upward. Ross published "What My Father Knows," in *Paris Review* in 1978 (72: 10):

> My father raised me to know
> that I am not different
> from anyone else. This knowledge
> makes me respond to you all
> with doubt.
>
> If you dreamed
> as an eight year old of shoveling coal into a furnace
> and the furnace exploded
> blowing you sky high,
> and you saw from up there,
> while hanging to a stove pipe
> the entire city, then
> came down slowly
> to the basement again,
> why don't you wish
> to be a bird as I do?
>
> And assuming
> that you discovered around fourteen
> that your parents were nice
> but not your own
> and you watched every night
> for a starship to arrive,
> why aren't you aware of how alien
> we all are to this planet?

Perhaps most confusing
is that I know you have spent
as many days and nights
as I have fearing death
and dreaming of a private escape
or of a discovery to save everyone,
yet still you seem to forget
what heroes and heroines we are
to get up every morning,
to go to bed every night.

What opens this boy's heart? Flight, birds, explosions, the night sky, the longing for another world where belonging is a given? I know that in the early 1950s a young Ross growing up in Oakland waited at his bedroom window to be taken up in a starship by his authentic kin.

The boy's longing for the beyond leads me to the second of those heart-opening images that took root in the 1970s. It is the horizontal cousin to the ladder's vertical climb, the moon to the ladder's sun, and it too brings me joy, but of another kind, more melancholy, more bittersweet. It comes from a letter the Norwegian poet, Sigbjørn Obstfelder, wrote to a friend in the 1890s. Obstfelder, whose most famous poem ends with the words, "I've come to the wrong planet," was the poet par excellence of alienation in Scandinavian *fin de siècle* literature. He beat Ross to the "wrong planet" line by about eighty-five years. Ross, steeped in the poetry of the Symbolists, Baudelaire, Mallarmé and Rimbaud, was a particularly helpful mentor during the writing of my book on Obstfelder, and thus Ross is connected, though more tangentially, to this memory as well. Obstfelder was the master of the prose poem, and though the following is a letter fragment, it could just as easily be called a poem in prose:

I have been sad. I have surely said it before: It
seems as if life rows away from me....I walk in
the dark. I pick a white anemone. I hold it in my
hand, tear it apart. Why does it exist? And I
yearn. From the snow I yearn for the first white
flower of the field. But when the first white
flower of the field has come with her sisters a
new longing springs forth, and I yearn for the
trees' dry branches to leaf and bud. And when all
the crowns stand fragrant and green, then I look
from the green of the trees down toward the
earth and ask: --For what am I yearning? For the
white, for the white of the chokecherries' bloom.
And now the chokecherries' bloom has come
too. And always, always I go there...asking: Are
you yearning, Sigbjørn, for what are you
yearning?"(1893)[1]

Obstfelder's longing is common to most of us. We see a maple
in the spring with its young green leaves, and we image how
beautiful it will be when it is on fire in the fall. For Obstfelder the
white of winter ignites a yearning for the white of spring, and the
white of spring for the white of summer. In the original Norwegian
the word for Obstfelder's "yearning" is lengsel, the romantic's
longing for the pure, the whole, the perfect, the beautiful, the
unattainable, the inexpressible. I seldom give Obstfelder a thought
these days, but this particular image comes to me often, drawn as I
have always been to the poetry of longing for which beauty is the
prompt. There are many names for it, this melancholy shot through
with joy: The yearning for the "blue flower." "Sehnsucht." C.S. Lewis
called it "Joy."

   "All joy emphasizes our pilgrim status; always reminds,
beckons, awakens desire. Our best havings are wantings" (C.S.
Lewis, letter, 1955). I am reminded of Ross's boy and Obstfelder's
man of the seasons. In his short memoir, Surprised by Joy (1955),
Lewis traces the root structure of his religious re-conversion. He

writes eloquently about what he calls "an unsatisfied desire which is itself more desirable than any other satisfaction. I call it Joy...." One of the first times he was consciously awakened by Joy was as a young boy reading an English translation of the Swedish poem "Drapa" or "Death," written by the early 19th century Romantic poet Esaias Tegner about the death of the God Balder, the god of light and purity whose own death signals the death of the Nordic gods. The line that opened the young Lewis's heart was, "I heard a voice that cried, / Balder the beautiful / Is dead, is dead----." Lewis goes on to say:

I knew nothing about Balder but instantly I was uplifted into huge regions of northern sky, I desired with almost sickening intensity something never to be described (except that it is cold, spacious, severe, pale and remote) and then, as in the other examples, found myself at the very same moment already falling out of that desire and wishing I were back in it. [2]

Lewis insisted that his joy "must have the stab, the pang, the inconsolable longing" he had felt reading Tegner's poem. Those of us like Ross and I who have spent our adult lives studying Scandinavian literature, know that its poetry runneth over with stabs and pangs of the most beautiful, most inconsolable sort of longing. Ross wrote his dissertation, published as *Voices Under the Ground* (University of California Press, 1973), about one of the great Swedish poets of mystic longing, Gunnar Ekelöf:

What I mean
what I want
is something else
always something else—

Man's external conditions
Now, here, only this, the fact
Man's internal conditions:
Whenever, only not now
wherever, only not here

whatever, only not this—

(From the poem "The Gymnosophist," translated by Ross in *Voices Under the Ground*, 144-45)

When the Swedish poet Tomas Tranströmer was awarded the Nobel Prize in 2013 Ross was interviewed by UCLA television as the resident scholar of Swedish poetry. He said of Tranströmer's work, "the concrete is hallowed by an implied metaphysical resonance." I offer one short poem about the longing for home. Unlike Ekelöf's gymnosophist, who lives in the abstract, Tranströmer's traveler feels his intense yearning flowing, pulsing, pounding in both body and soul:

> A telephone call flowed out into the night, and it gleamed
> here and there in fields, and at the outskirts of cities.
> Afterward I slept restlessly in the hotel bed.
> I resembled the compass needle the orienteer runner
> carries as he runs with heart pounding.

("Calling Home," translated by Robert Bly in *The Half Finished Heaven: The Best Poems of Tomas Transtromer*, Graywolf Press, 2001)

Ross said in the interview that Tomas Tranströmer was his "ideal." Not bad!

Around the time I was mulling over the sentiments of Camus and Obstfelder and Lewis and Ekelöf and Tranströmer and poetry and longing and, of course, Ross, a poem came to me via e-mail. I think Ross would call this a "demonstration." It spoke of life and longing and melancholy shot through with joy, of a successful man, a seasoned man, like our man of the hour. It came from Ricardo Sternberg, the Brazilian/Canadian poet recently referred to as "the best poet writing in Canada today." Ricardo, a contributor to this volume of essays, was himself a student of Ross's in the 1970s. Ross and Stephen Yenser, Professor of English at UCLA, wrote the recommendations that sent Ricardo to Harvard where we could say his life as a poet began. With Ricardo's permission I will close with his poem "A Prince's Soliloquy," published early in 2014 in his new collection, *Some Dance* (McGill-Queens University Press):

> Truth be told,
> I wish she would
> unkiss me.
>
> turn me back
> into the frog I was
> and happy being.
>
> Give me back nights
> I dared the moon,
> fat and round,
>
> to step down
> and skinny-dip
> until dawn.
>
> My velvet britches?
> That silver crown?
> Nothing here even close
>
> to those moments
> when she dropped her cloak,
> tested the water
>
> with her toes,
> then slipped in and silvered
> my dark pond. (70-71)

The frog has played the prince and played him well. He has worn his velvet britches and his silver crown with style. But he yearns for those frisky and free, sensuous and sensual nights of yore. Is his dark pond still there? Can he shed his fancy clothes? Will he once again play in the moonlight? Oh, let it be so.

Ross: You have worn your suits and ties with style, and you have played your parts well: teacher, scholar, translator, colleague, dean and chair. You have earned your silver pond. The water is nice and warm. Slip back in and dare the moon. You've got some poems to write.

Notes

[1] Sigbjørn Obstfelder: Letter to Ada Eckhoff, July 1, 1893, in *Brev fra Sigbjørn Obstfelder*, ed. Arne Hannevik, Oslo, 1966, p. 82. Translation, MK Norseng, *Sigbjørn Obstfelder*, Boston, 1982, p. 4.

[2] C.S. Lewis: *Surprised by Joy: The Shape of My Early Life*, C. S. Lewis, New York, 1955, p. 17.

References

Agamben, Giorgio. 2000. *Means Without End: Notes on Politics.* Translated by Vincenzo Binetti and Cesare Casarino. Theory Out of Bounds 20. Minneapolis: Univ of Minnesota Press.

Agrelio, Nicolao P. 1738. *Institutiones arithmeticae. Eller kort vnderwisning, om d ...reglor...som i dagelig räkning mäst brukelige äro:...men nu förökt med... vnderrättelse om wexel-räkningar och italienska bokhålleriet.* Stockholm: Horrn.

Alighieri, Dante. 1319. "The Epistle to Can Grande." http://bit.ly/1Tc6Aia

Amerikanska humorister: Bilder och dikter af Artemus Ward, Charles Dudley Warner, Mark Twain, Bret Harte, the Danbury Newsman, T. B. Aldrich. 1878. Translated by A[ugust] S[trindberg]. Vol. 2. Ny följd. Stockholm: Jos. Seligmann and C:IS förlag.

Andersen, Hans Christian. 2004. *De to Baronesser.* Romaner II, vol. 5. Edited by Klaus P. Mortensen. Copenhagen: Gyldendal.

Andersen, Hans Christian. 2004. *Lykke-Peer.* Romaner III, vol. 6. Edited by Klaus P. Mortensen. Copenhagen: Gyldendal.

Auden, W. H. 1961. Introduction to *The Complete Poems of Cavafy.* Translated by Rae Dalven. Pp. 7-15. New York: Harvest.

Auerbach, Erich. 1984. *Scenes from the Drama of European Literature.* Theory and History of Literature 9. Minneapolis: Univ of Minnesota Press.

Auerbach, Erich. 2014. "Figura." Chap. 7 in *Time, History, and Literature: Selected Essays of Erich Auerbach.* Edited by James I. Porter. Translated by Jane O. Newman. Pp. 80-104. Princeton: Princeton Univ Press.

Baelter, Sven. 1762. *Historiska anmärkningar om kyrcko-ceremonierna...efter reformationen til närwarande tid.* Stockholm: Peter Hesselberg.

Bellman, Carl Michael. 1921-2003. *Carl Michael Bellmans skrifter.* Standardupplaga. 20 vols. Stockholm: Bellmanssällskapet.

Bellman, Carl Michael. 1947. *Carl Michael Bellmans levernesbeskrivning.* Edited by Olof Byström. Stockholm: Bellmanssällskapet. With a facsimile of the original manuscript.

Bennich-Björkman, Bo. 1970. *Författaren i ämbetet: Studier i funktion och organisation av författarämbeten vid svenska hovet och kansliet 1550-1850.* Studia litterarum Upsaliensia 5. Uppsala: Appelberg.

Binzer, Ina von. 1956. *Alegrias e tristezas de uma educadora alemã no Brasil.* Translated by Alice Rossi and Luisita da Gama Cerqueira de Carvalho. São Paulo: Anhembi.

Binzer, Ina von. 1980. *Os meus romanos: Alegrias e tristezas de uma educadora alemã no Brasil.* Translated by Alice Rossi and Luisita da Gama

Cerqueira. Coleção Literatura teoria e literária 39. São Paulo: Paz e Terra.

Bishop, Elizabeth. 1962. *Brazil.* Life World Library. New York: Time Inc.

Björkman, Axel. 1892. *Bellmansforskning.* Stockholm: Samson & Wallin.

Borgström, Eva. 2004. "Emancipation och perversion: Strindberg och den besvärliga (homo)sexualiteten." *Res Publica,* no. 62-63: 216-44.

Borgström, Eva. 2008. *Kärlekshistoria: Begär mellan kvinnor i 1800-talets litteratur.* Göteborg: Kabusa böcker.

Borgström, Eva. 2010. "'Jag hatar henne eftersom jag älskar henne': En dåres försvarstal." In *Om Strindberg.* Edited by Lena Einhorn. Pp. 128-39. Stockholm: Norsted.

Bratkowski, Piotr. 2014. "Normalność 2.0." *Newsweek,* January 20-26, 37.

Burton, Richard Francis. 1969. *Explorations of the highlands of the Brazil: with a full account of the gold and diamond mines, also canoing down 1500 miles of the great river São Francisco, from Sabará to the sea.* New York: Greenwood Press. Reprint of the 1869 edition.

Byström, Olof. 1944. "Carl Bondes vänkrets." *Bellmansstudier* 10. Pp. 83-104. Stockholm: Bellmanssällskapet.

Carlsson, Ingemar. 2013. "Inledning—Dalins och Bellmans första möte." In *Ämneswennen och hofskalden: Om sambandet mellan Olof von Dalin och Carl Michael Bellman.* By James Massengale. Pp. 9-21. Varberg: CAL-förlaget; Falkenberg: Olof von Dalinsällskapet.

Carlsson, Sten. 1949. *Ståndssamhälle och ståndspersoner 1700-1865: Studier rörande det svenska ståndssamhällets upplösning.* Lund: Gleerup. 2nd rev. ed. 1973.

Cavafy, C. P. 1963. *Peza* [Prose Works]. Athens: Fexis.

Cavafy, C. P. 2009. *Collected Poems.* Translated by Daniel Mendelsohn. New York: Knopf.

Ekman, Stefan. 2004. *"I skuggan af Din Graf, jag på min Lyra slår":* Carl Michael Bellmans dikter över döda i relation till dikttypens svenska tradition och funktion i nyhetspressen under senare delen av 1700-talet. Stockholm: Proprius.

Ellis, Havelock. 1898. "Autoerotism: A Psychological Study." *The Alienist and Neurologist* 19 (April): 260-99.

Eman, Greger. 1999. "1907: Det homosexuella genombrottet." In *Sympatiens hemlighetsfulla makt: Stockholms homosexuella 1860-1960.* Edited by Göran Söderström. Pp. 149-64. Stockholmsmonografier 78:2. Stockholm: Stockholmia förlag.

Eman, Greger. 1999. "Bröderna Jansson." In *Sympatiens hemlighetsfulla makt: Stockholms homosexuella 1860-1960.* Edited by Göran Söderström. Pp. 208-45. Stockholmsmonografier 78:2. Stockholm: Stockholmia förlag.

Fielding, Helen. 1996. *Bridget Jones's Diary: A Novel.* London: Picador.

Forster, E. M. 1951. "The Complete Poems of C. P. Cavafy." In *Two Cheers for Democracy.* London: Edward Arnold Publishers.

Forster, E. M. 1962. *Pharos and Pharillon.* New York: Knopf.

Foucault, Michel. 1977. "What Is an Author?" In *Language, Counter-Memory, Practice: Selected Essays and Interviews.* Edited by Donald F. Bouchard. Translated by Donald F. Bouchard and Sherry Simon. Pp. 113-38. Ithaca, NY: Cornell Univ Press.

Franke, Eva Akinvall. 2004. *Eko av Glas: Läsningar genom ett sekel av Hjalmar Söderbergs verk Doktor Glas; En receptionsestetiskt orienterad studie.* MA thesis. Univ of Borås, Sweden. Accessed April 2, 2014. http://hdl.handle.net/2320/1143

Freud, Sigmund. 1953-1974. "Leonardo da Vinci and a Memory of his Childhood." In *The Standard Edition of the Complete Psychological Works of Sigmund Freud* 11. Edited and translated by James Strachey et al. London: Hogarth Press.

Freud, Sigmund. 1953-1974. "On Narcissism: An Introduction." In *The Standard Edition of the Complete Psychological Works of Sigmund Freud* 14. Edited and translated by James Strachey et al. Pp. 73-102. London: Hogarth Press.

Freud, Sigmund. 1953-1974. "The Sexual Aberrations." In "Three Essays on the Theory of Sexuality" (1905) in *The Standard Edition of the Complete Psychological Works of Sigmund Freud* 7. Edited and translated by James Strachey et al. Pp. 16-136. London: Hogarth Press.

Gauffin, Axel. 1930. "När Bellman förhördes i multiplikationstabellen." In *Bellmansstudier* 4. Pp. 35-51. Stockholm: Bellmanssällskapet.

Geddes, Tom. 1975. *Hj. Söderberg: Doktor Glas.* Studies in Swedish Literature 3. Hull, UK: Hull Univ, Department of Scandinavian Studies.

Graham, Maria. 1990. *Diário de uma viagem ao Brasil* [Journal of a Voyage to Brazil]. Translated by Américo Jacobina Lacombe. Coleção Reconquista do Brasil 2a sér., vol. 157. Belo Horizonte: Editora Itatiaia; [São Paulo]: Editora da Universidade de São Paulo.

Gribben, Alan. 1984. "Autobiography as Property: Mark Twain and His Legend." In *The Mythologizing of Mark Twain.* Edited by Sara deSaussure Davis and Philip D. Beidler. Pp. 39-35. [Tuscaloosa, AL]: Univ of Alabama Press.

Grojnowski, Daniel, ed. 2007. *Confessions d'un inverti-né: Suivies de Confidences et aveux d'un Parisien.* By Arthur W. Preface by Émile Zola. Paris: José Corti.

Halperin, David. 1990. *One Hundred Years of Homosexuality and Other Essays on Greek Love.* New York: Routledge.

Hamilton, Anita. 1999. "Geraldine Laybourne Brings Women a Breath of Fresh Air." *Time Digital*. Your Guide to Personal Technology. March, 23-24.

Hemingway, Ernest. 2002. *Green Hills of Africa*. New York: Simon and Schuster.

Hillbom, Gunnar. 1991. *Kring källorna till Fredmans epistlar*. Filologiskt arkiv 36. Stockholm: Almqvist & Wiksell.

Holmbäck, Bure. 1988. *Hjalmar Söderberg: Ett författarliv*. Hjalmar Söderberg sällskapets skriftserie 6. [Stockholm]: Bonnier.

Holmbäck, Bure, Björn Sahlin, Lars Sjöstrand, and Nils O. Sjöstrand. 2003. *Viljans frihet och mordets frestelse: Iakttagelser angående Doktor Glas*. Söderbergsällskapets skriftserie 14. Stockholm: Proprius förlag.

Howells, William Dean. 1910. *My Mark Twain: Reminiscences and Criticisms*. New York: Harper.

Irigaray, Luce. 1981. *Le corps-à-corps avec la mère*. Conférence et entretiens. Montréal: Les Éditions de la pleine lune.

Jameson, Fredric. 1981. *The Political Unconscious: Narrative as a Socially Symbolic Act*. Ithaca, NY: Cornell Univ Press.

Jamieson, Theresa. 2009. "'The Shadow Who Wished to Become a Man': *Doctor Glas* in the Twenty-First Century." *Neo-Victorian Studies* 2, no. 2 (Winter 2009/2010): 212-36.

Janicka, Elżbieta. 2011. *Festung Warschau*. Warszawa: Wydawnictwo Krytyki Politycznej.

Jeffreys, Peter, ed. 2009. *The Forster-Cavafy Letters: Friends at a Slight Angle*. Cairo: The American Univ in Cairo Press.

Johannesson, Kurt. 1977. "Bellman och ceremonierna." In *Tio forskare om Bellman*. Edited by Horace Engdahl. Pp. 96-113. Filologiskt arkiv 20. Stockholm: Almquist & Wiksell.

Kierkegaard, Søren. 1990. "Andersen as a Novelist." In "From the Papers of One Still Living" in *Early Polemical Writings*. Edited and translated by Julia Watkin. Pp. 61-102. Kierkegaard's Writings 1. New Jersey: Princeton Univ Press.

Kierkegaard, Søren. 1997. "Om Andersen som Romandigter." In *Af en endnu Levendes Papirer* [From the Papers of One Still Living]. Edited by Niels Jørgen Cappelørn, Joakim Garff, Johnny Kondrup, Alastair McKinnon, and Finn Hauberg Mortensen. Pp. 15-57. Søren Kierkegaards skrifter 1. Copenhagen: Gads forlag.

Komar, Kathleen L. 2003. *Reclaiming Klytemnestra: Revenge or Reconciliation*. Urbana-Champaign,: Univ of Illinois Press.

Lagerkrantz, Olof. 1984. *August Strindberg*. Translated by Anselm Hollo. New York: Farrar, Straus, Giroux.

Lalander, Folke, Inga Zachau, and Ulf Linde. 1998. *Eugène Jansson: 1862-1915*. Liljevalchs katalog 438. Stockholm: Liljevalchs konsthall.

Lattimore, Richmond, trans. 1949. *Greek Lyrics*. 2nd ed. Chicago: Univ of Chicago Press.

Lewis, C. S. 1955. *Surprised by Joy: The Shape of My Early Life*. Harvest Book 102. New York: Harcourt, Brace & World.

Levertin, Oscar. 1908. "August Strindberg." In *Svensk litteratur* 1. Pp. 5-74. Samlade skrifter 13. Stockholm: Bonnier.

Linde, Ebbe. 1978. "Hjalmar Söderberg." In *Författarnas litteraturhistoria* 2. Edited by Lars Ardelius and Gunnar Rydström. Pp. 252-63. Stockholm: Författarförlaget. Originally published in 1936 in *Göteborgs Handels- och Sjöfartstidning*.

Lönngren, Ann-Sofie. 2012. "Triangular, Homosocial, Lesbian: A Queer Approach to Desire in August Strindberg's Novel *A Madman's Manifesto*." *Contagion*, vol. 19: 205-29.

Lost Bodies. Performance of Cavafy's "The Regiment of Pleasure." http://bit.ly/1TdedVG

Loyrette, Henri, Inga Zachau, Hans Henrik Brummer, and Ulf Linde. 1999. *Eugène Jansson 1862-1915: Nocturnes suédois*. Paris: Réunion des Musées Nationaux / Musée d'Orsay.

Machado de Assis. 1968. *Dom Casmurro: Romance*. Rio de Janeiro: Record.

Mann, Thomas. 1960. *Reden und Aufsätze* 2. Gesammelte Werke 10. Frankfurt am Main: S. Fischer.

Margaronis, Maria. 2009. "Mixing History and Desire: The Poetry of C.P. Cavafy." *The Nation*, August 3. http://bit.ly/23Jiz9R

Martin, Brian Joseph. 2011. *Napoleonic Friendship: Military Fraternity, Intimacy, and Sexuality in Nineteenth-Century France*. Becoming Modern— New Nineteenth-Century Studies. Durham: Univ of New Hampshire Press.

Massengale, James. 2013. *Ämneswennen och hofskalden: Om sambandet mellan Olof von Dalin och Carl Michael Bellman*. Varberg: CAL-förlaget; Falkenberg: Olof von Dalinsällskapet.

Medhurst, Andy. 1997. "Camp." In *Lesbian and Gay Studies: A Critical Introduction*. Edited by Andy Medhurst and Sally R. Munt. P. 276. London: Cassell.

Meir A. Goldschmidt. 1857. "Anmeldelse af 'At være eller ikke være.'" *Nord og Syd*, vol. 3: 97-108. Accessed April 2, 2014. http://bit.ly/24QrprY

Meir A. Goldschmidt. 1849. "Anmeldelse af 'De To Baronesser.'" *Nord og Syd*, vol. 5: 72-92. First Quarter. Accessed April 2, 2014. http://bit.ly/24QpIeb

Mendelsohn, Daniel. 2009. Introduction to *Collected Poems*. By C. P. Cavafy. Translated by Daniel Mendelsohn. Pp. xv-lx. New York: Knopf.

Meyer, Michael. 1987. *Strindberg: A Biography*. Oxford Lives. Oxford: Oxford Univ Press.

Møller Jensen, Elisabeth. "About the Print Work." Prefaces to *The History of Nordic Women's Literature*. Accessed April 4, 2014. http://bit.ly/1UUEbQc

Møller Jensen, Elisabeth. "Om bogværket." Prefaces to *The History of Nordic Women's Literature*. Accessed April 4, 2014. http://bit.ly/1Wrfj45

Näcke, Paul. 1899. "Die sexuellen Perversitäten in der Irrenanstalt." *Wiener klinische Rundschau*, no. 27–30.

Newman, Jane O. 2014. "Translator's Note." In *Selected Essays of Erich Auerbach: Time, History, and Literature*. Edited by James I. Porter. P. xlviii. Princeton: Princeton Univ Press.

Obstfelder, Sigbjørn. 1966. Letter to Ada Eckhoff, July 1, 1893. In *Brev fra Sigbjørn Obstfelder*. Edited by Arne Hannevik. P. 82. Oslo: Gyldendal. Translation by M. K. Norseng. 1982. *Sigbjørn Obstfelder*. Boston: Twayne. P. 4.

Oxygen LLC Media. [2015]. "Oxygen." ["About Us."] Accessed April 13, 2015. http://bit.ly/1UUESZy

Page, P. K. 1987. *Brazilian Journal*. Toronto: Lester & Orpen Dennys.

Pereira, Paulo Roberto, ed. 1999. Introduction to *Os três únicos testemunhos do descobrimento do Brasil*. Rio de Janeiro: Lacerda Editores.

Pyzik, Agata. 2014. "Poland Is Having a Sexual Revolution in Reverse." *The Guardian*, February 11. Accessed January 15, 2015. http://bit.ly/1RUZE9b

Rivers, Christopher. 2001. "Improbable Prescience: Émile Zola and the Origins of Homosexuality." *Excavatio* 14 (1-2): 49-62.

Robinson, Michael, ed. 2009. *The Cambridge Companion to August Strindberg*. Cambridge Companions to Authors. Cambridge: Cambridge Univ Press.

Roilos, Panagiotis. 2009. *C. P. Cavafy: The Economics of Metonymy*. Traditions. Urbana-Champaign: Univ of Illinois Press.

Rosario, Vernon. 1997. *The Erotic Imagination: French Histories of Perversity*. Ideologies of Desire. New York: Oxford Univ Press.

Rosen, Karl. 1993. "Émile Zola and Homosexuality." *Excavatio* 2 (Autumn): 111-15.

Roy, Matthew. 2001. "August Strindberg." In *Who's Who in Gay and Lesbian History: From Antiquity to World War II*. Vol. 1. Edited by

Robert Aldrich and Gary Wotherspoon. P. 504. New York: Routledge.

Roy, Matthew. 2001. *August Strindberg's Perversions: On the Science, Sin, and Scandal of Homosexuality in August Strindberg's Works*. PhD diss., Univ of Washington.

Sandbach, Mary. 1972. Notes to *Getting Married*. By August Strindberg. Translated by Mary Sandbach. New York: Viking Press.

Sanders, Karin. 2014. "Anxious Authors and Uncanny Shadows: Hans Christian Andersen in Dialogue with Søren Kierkegaard." In *More Than Just Fairy Tales: New Approaches to the Stories of Hans Christian Andersen*. Edited by Julie K. Allen. Pp. 47-56. San Diego: Cognella Academic Publishing.

Schoolfield, George C. 2003. *A Baedeker of Decadence: Charting a Literary Fashion 1884-1927*. New Haven: Yale Univ Press.

Seferis, George. 1984. *Dokimes* I. Athens: Ikaros.

Sennefelt, Karin. 2006. "Frihetstidens politiska kultur." In *Frihetstiden*. Edited by Jakob Christensson. Pp. 17-49. Signums svenska kulturhistoria 4. Lund: Signum.

Shideler, Ross. 1973. *Voices under the Ground: Themes and Images in the Early Poetry of Gunnar Ekelöf*. Univ of California Publications in Modern Philology 104. Berkeley: Univ of California Press.

Shideler, Ross. 1975. "The Audience." *Poetry*, October, 36-37.

Shideler, Ross. 1978. "What My Father Knows." *The Paris Review* 72: 10.

Shideler, Ross. 1984. *Per Olov Enquist: A Critical Study*. Contributions to the Study of World Literature 5. Westport: Greenwood Press.

Shideler, Ross. 1999. *Questioning the Father: From Darwin to Zola, Ibsen, Strindberg, and Hardy*. Stanford: Stanford Univ Press.

Shideler, Ross, trans. 1977. *The Night of the Tribades: A Play from 1889*. By Per Olov Enquist. A Mermaid Drama Book. New York: Hill and Wang.

Shideler, Ross, trans. 1990. *The Hour of the Lynx: A Play*. By Per Olov Enquist. London: Forest Books.

Shmoop Univ. 2015. "Fredric Jameson's Comrades and Rivals." http://bit.ly/1NrdYa8

Sierakowski, Sławomir. 2014. "The Polish Church's Gender Problem." *New York Times*, January 26. Accessed January 17, 2015. http://nyti.ms/1OoDKXH

Simonsson, Ingmar. 1995. *Bellmans värld*. Stockholm: Astrate.

Söderberg, Hjalmar. 1967. *Doktor Glas*. Stockholm: Aldus / Bonnier.

Söderberg, Hjalmar. 1998. *Doctor Glas*. Translated by Rochelle Wright. Wisconsin Introductions to Scandinavia II, 8. Madison, WI: Department of Scandinavian Studies, Univ of Madison-Wisconsin.

Söderström, Göran, ed. 1999. *Sympatiens hemlighetsfulla makt: Stockholms homosexuella 1860-1960*. Stockholmsmonografier 78:2. Stockholm: Stockholmia förlag.

Söderström, Göran. 2002. "Strindberg och homosexualiteten: En biografisk studie." *Lambda Nordica* 1: 22-44.

Söderström, Göran. 2013. *Strindberg: Ett liv*. [Stockholm]: Lind & Co.

Spillers, Hortense. 2000. "Mama's Baby, Papa's Maybe: An American Grammar Book." In *African-American Literary Theory: A Reader*. Edited by Winston Napier. Pp. 257-279. New York: New York Univ Press.

Stålmarck, Torkel. 2000. *Bellman i verkligheten: Familjeliv, sällskapsliv, konstnärsliv*. Stockholm: Norstedt.

Stenport, Anna Westerstahl. 2010. *Locating August Strindberg's Prose: Modernism, Transnationalism, and Setting*. Toronto: Toronto Univ Press.

Sternberg, Ricardo. 2014. "A Prince's Soliloquy." In *Some Dance*. Pp. 70-71. Hugh MacLennan Poetry Series. Montreal: McGill-Queens Univ Press.

Strindberg, August. [1948]-2001. *August Strindbergs Brev*. Edited by Torsten Eklund. 22 vols. Strindbergssällskapets skrifter. Stockholm: Bonnier.

Strindberg, August. 1958. "De Perversa." In *Vivisektioner II*. Translated by Tage Aurell. Pp. 152-157. Strindbergssällskapets skrifter. Stockholm: Bonnier.

Strindberg, August. 1961. "Mannaår och ålderdom." In *August Strindberg*. Vol. 2. Edited by Stellan Ahlström and Torsten Eklund. Ögonvittnen. Stockholm: Wahlström & Widstrand.

Strindberg, August. 1972. "The Reward of Virtue." In *Getting Married*. Translated by Mary Sandbach. P. 52. New York: Viking Press.

Strindberg, August. 1979. *Giftas: Äktenskapshistorier I-II*. Förf:s mästerverk i urval. Stockholm: Bonnier.

Strindberg, August. 1982. "Dygdens Lön." In *Giftas I-II*. Edited by Ulf Boëthius. Pp. 31-34. August Strindbergs samlade verk nationalupplaga 16. Stockholm: Norstedt; Uppsala: Almqvist & Wiksell.

Strindberg, August. 1984. *Fadren: Fröken Julie; Fordringsägare*. Edited by Gunnar Ollén. August Strindbergs samlade verk nationalupplaga 27. Stockholm: Norstedt; Uppsala: Almqvist & Wiksell.

Strindberg, August. 1989. *Tjänstekvinnans Son I-II*. Edited by Hans Lindström. August Strindbergs samlade verk nationalupplaga 20-21. Stockholm: Norstedt; Uppsala: Almqvist & Wiksell.

Strindberg, August. 1992. *Strindberg's Letters*. Vol. 1. Translated and edited by Michael Robinson. Chicago: Univ of Chicago Press.

Strindberg, August. 1999. *En dåres försvarstal: Roman* [Le plaidoyer d'un fou: Roman]. Edited by Göran Rossholm. French text by Gunnel Engwall. Translated by Hans Levander. August Strindbergs samlade verk nationalupplaga 25. Stockholm: Norstedt; Uppsala: Almqvist & Wiksell.

Thorén, Sven. 1986. *I Zions tempel: Carl Michael Bellmans andliga diktning*. Skrifter utgivna av Litteraturvetenskapliga institutionen vid Göteborgs universitet 16. Göteborg: Litteraturvetenskapliga institutionen vid Göteborgs universitet; Källered: Kompendietryckeriet.

Törnqvist, Egil. 1988. "Mordet på Pastor Gregorius: Ett bidrag till tolkningen av *Doktor Glas*." *Tijdschrift voor Skandinavistiek* 9 (1-2): 144-55.

Tranströmer, Tomas. 2001. "Calling Home." In *The Half-Finished Heaven: The Best Poems of Tomas Tranströmer*. Translated by Robert Bly. P. 65. Saint Paul, MN: Graywolf Press.

Tripp, Edward. 1970. *The Meridian Handbook of Classical Mythology*. A Meridian Book. [New York]: New American Library. Originally published as *Crowell's Handbook of Classical Mythology*.

Twain, Mark. 1894. *The Tragedy of Pudd'nhead Wilson, and the Comedy, Those Extraordinary Twins*. Hartford: American Publishing Company.

Twain, Mark. 1910. *Mark Twain's Speeches*. New York: Harper.

Varnedoe, Kirk. 1982. *Northern Light: Realism and Symbolism in Scandinavian Painting, 1880-1910*. Brooklyn: Brooklyn Museum.Varnedoe, Kirk. 1988. *Northern Light: Nordic Art at the Turn of the Century*. New Haven: Yale Univ Press.

Venturino, Stephen. Notes on "Jameson *The Political Unconscious*." A Professor, In Theory. Reading Academic Books and Articles So You Don't Have To. http://bit.ly/1OjTFf2

Weibull, Lauritz. 1895. "Bellman såsom skald bedömd af sin samtid." In *Samlaren*. Pp. 79-130.

Witkowski, Michał. 2010. *Lovetown*. Translated by William Martin. London: Portobello Books.

Wollin, Nils. 1920. *Eugène Janssons måleri: Försök till gruppering och analys*. Sveriges allmänna konstförenings publikation 28. Stockholm: Sveriges allmänna konstförening.

Zachau, Inga. 1997. *Eugène Jansson: Den blå stadens målare*. Böcker om konst. Lund: Signum.

Zola, Émile. 1896. Preface to "Le Roman d'un inverti-né" in *Perversions et perversité sexuelles, tares et poisons, une enquête médicale sur l'inversion, notes et documents, le roman d'un inverti-né, le procès Wilde, la guérison et la prophylaxie de l'inversion*. By Georges Saint-Paul [Dr Laupts]. Collection jésuite des Fontaines. Paris: Georges Carré.

Index

www.ingramcontent.com/pod-product-compliance
Lightning Source LLC
Chambersburg PA
CBHW030415100426
42812CB00028B/2971/J